Glade B Curtis is board certified by the American College of Obstetricians and Gynecologists. He is in private practice in obstetrics, gynaecology and infertility in Sandy, Utah.

One of Dr Curtis' goals as a doctor is to provide patients with many types of information about gynaecological and obstetric conditions they may have, problems they may encounter and procedures they may undergo. In pursuit of that goal, he has written several books especially for pregnant women, including *Your Pregnancy Week-by-Week* and *Your Pregnancy Questions and Answers*.

Dr Curtis is a graduate of the University of Utah and the University of Rochester School of Medicine and Dentistry, Rochester, New York. He was an intern, resident and chief resident in Obstetrics and Gynecology at the University of Rochester Strong Memorial Hospital. He lives in Sandy with his wife and their five children.

D F Hawkins is a Fellow of both the Royal College of Obstetricians and Gynaecologists and the American College of Obstetricians and Gynecologists. He is an honorary consulting obstetrician and gynaecologist at Hammersmith Hospital in London and Emeritus Professor of Obstetric Therapeutics in the University of London. He is the consulting editor of the *Journal of Obstetrics and Gynaecology* and author or editor of numerous books and papers.

by the same author
Your Pregnancy Week by Week
Your Pregnancy Questions and Answers

Your Pregnancy Over 30

Glade B Curtis, MD FACOG

Consultant Editor:
D F Hawkins, MD FRCOG

ELEMENT
Shaftesbury, Dorset . Boston, Massachusetts
Melbourne, Victoria

© Element Books Limited 1998
Text © Glade B Curtis and Judith Schuler 1996

First published in the USA in 1996 by Fisher Books

This revised edition first published in the UK in 1998 by
Element Books Limited
Shaftesbury, Dorset SP7 8BP

Published in Australia in 1998 by
Element Books and distributed
by Penguin Books Australia Limited
487 Maroondah Highway, Ringwood,
Victoria 3134

Text illustrations by David Fisher
Cover illustration Courtesy of Fisher Books
Cover design by Bridgewater Books
Page design by Roger Lightfoot
Typeset by Bournemouth Colour Press, Parkstone
Printed and bound in Great Britain by J. W. Arrowsmith, Bristol

British Library Cataloguing in Publication
data available

ISBN 1 86204 210 1

Note from the Publisher
This book is in no way intended to replace, countermand or conflict with
the advice given to you by your own doctor. The ultimate decision
concerning care should be made between you and your medical
practitioner.

Credit
The material on pages 21–6 and 292–305 is copyright the Health Education
Authority, London, and is reproduced with their permission.

Acknowledgements

It is a joy for me to be able to share the excitement and anticipation of a couple expecting a baby. I want to thank my patients and their families for allowing me to share this important time with them. A special thanks to all the 'older' pregnant women. I see in my practice who helped me with their insights. Their questions and comments helped me to pull together what I believe is valuable information for any woman over 30 who is expecting a baby.

My thanks to my wife, Debbie, and our family who have supported me in the pursuit of a profession that requires me to give a lot of time and energy to my patients. Their unfailing support, which is an inspiration to me, has continued during this and other projects. My thanks also to my parents for their endless love and support.

Judi Schuler's insight, persistence, commitment to excellence and accuracy continue to inspire and challenge me. I appreciate her drive and ability to 'pull things together' and keep me focused.

Contents

PART ONE

Congratulations, You're Pregnant!

CHAPTER 1

Positively Pregnant

Pregnancy is an exciting time. The new life you carry is a source of joy for you, your partner and your family.

More women every year are happy to find they are pregnant in their 30s or 40s. If you waited to start a family, you are not alone. Many couples choose to postpone having children until careers are on track or relationships are firmly established.

In the 1980s, births to women in the 30- to 44-year-old age range nearly doubled. First births to women in their 30s in 1990 accounted for about one quarter of all births to women in that age group. Researchers believe that by the year 2000, 1 in every 12 babies will be born to a mother aged 35 or older.

When an older woman has a baby, her partner is usually older, too. A growing number of births are to couples who divorced and remarried and are starting a family together. Some couples have experienced infertility and do not achieve a pregnancy until they have gone through major investigation and testing or even surgery.

Susan, a 38-year-old recently married woman with two children, had a new partner who had not fathered any children. Susan came to the office concerned about their chances of conceiving. I gave her some suggestions and laid out a plan for the next few months. An ecstatic Susan called me two weeks later. She was pregnant and was probably a few weeks along when we had discussed the possibility of infertility.

Your Health   ˎ

Today, many healthcare professionals gauge pregnancy risk by the pregnant woman's health status, not her age. Pre-existing medical conditions are the most significant indicator of a woman's well-being during pregnancy and the baby's health. A healthy 39-year-old is less likely to develop pregnancy problems than a woman in her 20s who suffers from diabetes, for example. A woman's fitness level has a greater effect on her pregnancy than her age.

Most women who become pregnant in their 30s and 40s are in good health. A woman in good physical condition who has been exercising regularly usually goes through pregnancy as easily as a woman 15 to 20 years younger. An exception: women in a first pregnancy after 40 are somewhat more likely to encounter complications than women the same age who have had children. Most healthy women will have a safe delivery.

Some health problems are age related – the risk of developing many conditions increases with age. High blood pressure and some forms of diabetes are age related. You may not know you have these conditions unless you see a doctor regularly. Either can complicate a pregnancy and should be brought under control before pregnancy, if possible.

Play it safe. If you haven't had a check-up recently, get one. If you are 35 or older and haven't had your breasts checked, get this done before pregnancy. Eat healthily and follow a regular exercise programme as you prepare for pregnancy.

Achieving Pregnancy When You're Older

Age affects fertility; fertility begins to decline slowly when a woman is 20, and declines faster after 35. Partners older than 35 may take twice as long to conceive a child as a younger couple (1¹/₂ to 2 years). A woman over 40 may take longer to conceive because ovulation is less frequent. The good news is that advances in fertility and reproductive technology have helped women to conceive who might never have conceived before.

Older women may find it somewhat harder to conceive, because of the declining number and quality of eggs in the ovaries. Your doctor can learn more about your ovulatory cycle by administering a test called the *clomiphene challenge*.

Other factors can affect fertility. Large amounts of coffee can affect a woman's ability to conceive. One study suggested that drinking even one alcoholic beverage a day can lower a woman's chances of getting pregnant.

Some older couples turn to assisted reproductive technology to achieve pregnancy. This includes *in vitro* fertilization and gamete intrafallopian transfer (GIFT), or a donor egg may be paired to the partner's sperm. Success relates to the woman's age. For women at 34, the success of *in vitro* fertilization is about 14 per cent per menstrual cycle. At 44, a woman can expect a 3 per cent success rate with one cycle of this procedure.

The Question of 'Higher Risk'

Some patients ask me why having a baby when a woman is in her 30s or 40s is considered as 'higher risk'. Medical professionals originally chose the age of 35 as the dividing line between normal risk and high risk because of risks associated with results of the amniocentesis test. (*See* pages 105–7 for a detailed explanation of the test.)

When amniocentesis was first developed, researchers found a 0.5 per cent risk of having a miscarriage after the test. They compared this risk to that of giving birth to a baby with a chromosome disorder, which increases with the mother's age. At 35, a woman has a 0.4 per cent chance of giving birth to a baby with a chromosome disorder. When the risk of having the test was equal to the risk of giving birth to a baby with problems, the test was advised. Thus 35 became the age at which healthcare professionals recommended testing.

The age of 35 is no longer meaningful because amniocentesis is much safer now. The estimated risk of a miscarriage after amniocentesis is about 0.3 per cent. Perhaps more important, two-thirds of all babies born with Down's syndrome (the most common reason for a woman to have the test) are born to women *under* 35.

Still, pregnancy in your 30s and 40s slightly increases the risk of some problems:

- birth of a baby with Down's syndrome
- likelihood of the caesarean section delivery
- problems with diabetes and high blood pressure
- a harder, longer labour

I have found that older pregnant women are often well informed about pregnancy. They are typically interested in what is happening to them and their developing babies and are willing to ask questions. They want to be part of the decision-making process in their healthcare.

They usually seek antenatal care early and often prepare for pregnancy before getting pregnant. For these reasons, many researchers now believe that the risk does not increase greatly just because a woman is older. Other factors also influence a woman's health risks during pregnancy.

How Your Healthcare Professional Treats You

Doctors often treat older women with more caution. Your doctor may recommend more clinic visits, more testing, genetic counselling and screening for problems associated with pregnancy in older women.

Labour and delivery options may be more limited; you might be discouraged from using a general practitioner unit because your age 'puts you at greater risk'. However, good antenatal care can significantly reduce obstetric complications associated with age. Most women can have healthy pregnancies and deliver healthy babies into their 40s.

Genetic Counselling

If you or your partner is older than 35, genetic counselling may be recommended, which can bring up many questions. An additional concern is the impact the baby's father's age can have on a pregnancy.

Genetic counselling brings together a couple and healthcare professionals who are trained to deal with problems associated with the occurrence or risk of occurrence of a genetic disorder. Through genetic counselling, information researchers have about human genetics is applied to a particular couple's situation. Healthcare providers interpret the information so couples or families can understand it and can make informed decisions about childbearing. For further information on genetic counselling, *see* pages 69 to 71 and 215 to 217.

Father's Age

When a pregnant woman is older, risks to both mother and child increase somewhat during pregnancy. At this time, we have no clear indication that a man's age can affect a pregnancy because when a mother is older, the father is often older, too. It can be difficult to determine whose age – the mother's or the father's – matters the most in pregnancy.

Some studies demonstrate that men aged 55 or older are more likely to father babies with Down's syndrome. These studies indicate that the risk is higher still when the mother is also older. We estimate that at the age of 40, a man's risk of fathering a child with Down's syndrome is about 1 per cent; that rate doubles at age 45 but is still only 2 per cent.

When both parents are over 40, genetic counselling may be recommended. The risk of chromosome abnormalities exceeds 5 per cent in this situation.

Some researchers now recommend that men father children before the age of 40. This is a conservative viewpoint and not everyone agrees with it. More data and research are needed before we can make definite statements about a father's age and its effect on pregnancy.

Common Pregnancy Problems

Problems that doctors see more often in older pregnant women include pregnancy-induced diabetes, high blood pressure and placental problems. (*See* Chapter 16 for further information about these potential problems.) Older women do have more miscarriages, more Caesarean sections and are at a slightly higher risk of giving birth to a baby with genetic or chromosome abnormalities. Most older pregnancy women have uncomplicated pregnancies and deliver healthy babies.

Beginning in their late 30s, women are likely to develop medical conditions associated with reproductive organs, such as uterine fibroids. After 40, a woman may feel the physical strains of pregnancy more readily. She may be more bothered by haemorrhoids, incontinence, varicose veins, muscle aches and pains, and back pain.

Two serious pregnancy risks increase for women in their 40s – miscarriage and birth of a child with Down's syndrome. Miscarriage ends about 40 per cent of pregnancies in women who become pregnant after 40. Miscarriages are discussed on pages 204 to 206; a discussion of Down's syndrome begins on page 217.

The national average for caesarean sections is close to 15 per cent. The rate rises slowly with age.

The risk of a pregnancy ending in stillbirth (the baby being dead upon delivery) has fallen for women of all ages in recent years. For a mother older than 35, the risk is about 7 in 1,000. The risk of some birth defects does not increase for older mothers. These include neural-tube defects (spina bifida), cleft palate and club foot.

As a pregnant woman in your 30s or 40s, you can expect pregnancy to be an exciting time for you and your partner. You may feel the physical and emotional effects of being pregnant a little more than a woman in her 20s, but you will find that there are many positive steps you can take to help ensure your pregnancy will go as smoothly as possible for you and your baby. This book can help you.

CHAPTER 2

First-time or Repeat Pregnancy?

When greeting a pregnant patient for the first time, I ask, 'Is this pregnancy good, bad, exciting or scary for you?' I get answers ranging from 'Yes' or 'No' to 'All of the above.' Being pregnant can be scary and wonderful at the same time. It is a time of learning and spiritual, intellectual and physical growth. It is also a time to be open about your concerns.

Your First Pregnancy after 30

During any pregnancy, you may experience fatigue and emotional mood swings. Your changing body takes some adjusting to. People will give you advice and share stories about their own pregnancies, labours and deliveries. You will receive a lot of attention, sometimes unwanted.

You cannot avoid some of these experiences. Knowing the facts about pregnancy can prepare you to accept or ignore advice. Knowing how the female body reacts to pregnancy can help you to understand the changes you will experience and help you make intelligent choices as the need arises. If you are willing to adapt and adjust your lifestyle for the sake of your health and that of your growing baby, you can do a lot to make your pregnancy a happy, fulfilling experience.

You will Receive a Lot of Attention

A positive (or negative) side to a first pregnancy is the attention you receive. At times you may be irritated by people who ask you how you feel and what you are experiencing.

> Debbie was tired of wisecracks from co-workers about her pregnancy. She turned it back on them by asking them the same questions. When asked about her weight gain, she might reply with a grin, 'My doctor says I'm doing great with my weight gain. What has your doctor said about yours?' Her friends took it in good humour and got the message.

Allow people to help you and to do things for you. Some patients have told me that they really did not appreciate how much others were willing to do for them during their first pregnancy until they became pregnant again. Helpful attention is a luxury not always available in subsequent pregnancies, so take advantage of it!

Sharing the News

You may feel a little awkward telling family members, friends and co-workers that you are pregnant. Some people thoughtlessly offer their advice or opinions on 'being an older mother'.

If others are critical or do not have your best interests in mind, ignore them! Focus your attention on staying healthy and having a happy pregnancy. Your pregnancy is your business – you don't need the good opinion of anyone else to make it a positive experience for you.

When you announce to co-workers and supervisors that you are pregnant, be prepared for a range of reactions. Be clear that you have made the right decision. Assure co-workers that your pregnancy is just one aspect of your life (a very important aspect), and that you plan to continue your job as long as your are able.

Repeat Pregnancy

First-time pregnancy is unlike any other pregnancy you experience. Everything is new. In later pregnancies, things are different. Many women assume their second pregnancy will be just like their first. Often it isn't – your emotions in a repeat pregnancy may not be the same as a first pregnancy. You may feel more relaxed.

In a repeat pregnancy, you are often seen as a 'pregnant mother'. You may be reluctant to ask for extra attention, although you may need it more. A second pregnancy can be more stressful because of the extra demands on your time and energy. You must attend to your family's well-being, take care of yourself and perhaps a career as well. You may wonder where you will find the energy to satisfy everyone else's needs. Physical discomforts may bother you a bit more.

On the plus side, women usually have a shorter labour with their second child, often only about half as long as with a first baby. Pain does not lessen, but because labour is usually shorter and you know more of what to expect, it may be easier to handle.

Physical Changes

With a repeat pregnancy, you may 'show' sooner because your muscles and skin are more stretched. Some women think they are further along than they really are because they look pregnant sooner than they did the first time.

You may experience backaches more frequently because the ligaments that hold the uterus in place were stretched with your first pregnancy. You may carry your second pregnancy lower, which adds pressure to your back and sometimes to your bladder.

Be careful when lifting, especially young children. Bending over to pick up a toddler can cause back pain. To help with backache, practise the exercises you learn in childbirth education classes. A hot water bottle or a light maternity girdle also helps relieve backache.

Some Challenges with This Pregnancy

Because of demands on your time and energy, fatigue may be one of your greatest problems. It is a pregnant mother's most common complaint.

Rest is essential to your health and to your baby's. Seize every opportunity to rest or nap. Nap when your child does, or put up your feet. Don't take on more tasks or new roles. Don't volunteer for a big project at work or anywhere else. Learn to say 'No'. You'll feel better!

Moderate exercise can help to boost your energy level and may eliminate or alleviate some discomforts. Consider choosing an activity you can do with your child. Check with your doctor before you start an exercise programme. Exercise is discussed in depth in Chapter 13.

Stress can also be a problem. To alleviate feelings of stress, exercise, eat healthy, nutritious meals and get as much rest as possible. Take time for yourself. Don't let mood swings control you. If you feel one coming on, remember that it won't last for ever.

Some women find a pregnancy support group is an excellent way to deal with difficulties they may experience in a second pregnancy. Check with your doctor for further information. You and your partner might want to take a childbirth refresher course.

Involving Your Children

Being pregnant when you already have children is different from a first pregnancy. You will probably feel anxious about how the new baby will affect your older children and your relationships with them.

Explain in simple terms how pregnancy affects your body. Try to help your children understand any problems you may experience, such as morning sickness. If you are too tired to do some regular activities with your children, let them know that it is because of how you are feeling, not because of them. Reassure them over and over that as soon as you feel better, you will do as much as possible with them.

Let your children help to prepare for the new baby. Older children might help to choose the baby's name or decorate the nursery. A picture drawn by a big brother or sister adds colour to the baby's room and makes the older child feel very important.

Delay telling very young children about the baby until they can see for themselves that it is growing inside you. Even then, it may be better to wait until close to the baby's birth to tell a very young child (under 3). Time passes much more slowly for young children, and a few weeks can seem for ever! If possible, use a familiar reference point for the birth, such as Christmas or when school holidays start.

Ask your doctor or midwife if it is all right to bring one child with you to an antenatal visit, so the child can listen to the baby's heartbeat. Or take your child to the hospital nursery to see the new babies. Many hospitals offer preparation classes for siblings of an expected baby; choose one that is suited to your child's age.

> Abbie didn't know how much to tell her children about her pregnancy or how to explain things about it. She took Rob and Ian with her to the library to look for books in the children's section. She was amazed at how many excellent books were available, many with tasteful pictures and simple explanations. They took books home and spent time together going through them and talking about the new baby.

When your child asks questions, it is probably a good idea to keep answers simple. For example, if your young child wants to know how the baby eats while it is growing inside you, an explanation such as 'the baby gets its food from Mummy' will probably suffice. To your young child, your pregnancy is not very important.

You may need to provide older children with more information.

Answer their questions honestly, but even with older children, don't provide more information than they need. Most important, provide them with extra love and attention during this time, and plan time alone together with each of them after the baby is born.

Prepare Your Children for Your Absence

Let them know in advance who will be caring for them. If possible, include them in making this decision. While you are in hospital, it may be a good idea to have your children stay with someone they know and trust. If possible, allow your children to stay at home, where things are familiar. This is a time of great upheaval for your children – make it as easy as possible on them.

Making Changes in Your Child's Life

Encourage your child's independence from you. Let your partner take over part of your regular childcare duties so they can spend time together without you. It will help when you go to hospital or are busy after the baby is born.

If you must make changes in your child's routine, such as putting her in a new room or taking away her cot, do it before the baby comes. If the change occurs near the time of the baby's birth, the child may feel more displaced. Wait a while to give your older child's toys, clothes or bottles to the new baby, or it could cause resentment.

Don't try to make life easier on yourself by pushing toilet training or making your child give up the bottle. It can cause more problems than it resolves. Encourage your child towards independence in small steps at the appropriate time.

When You are Expecting More than One Baby

Older women are more likely to have twins. For older children, welcoming one baby into the family is hard enough. Making room for more than one baby can be that much more difficult. Make sure the older child has his own familiar place and keeps his own things. Reassure him of your love frequently, and give plenty of attention.

If you will need help after the babies are born, especially child care, have the helper start work before the birth. Your older children will get to know the care giver beforehand, and it provides a sense of continuity after the babies come home.

Encourage your older children to express their feelings about the forthcoming birth of the babies. Let them know that you understand why they might feel negative; help them to find positive ways to deal with their feelings.

Establish a regular, uninterrupted time with your older children before the babies are born and continue it after their birth. This might be story time in the evening or preparing for bed or bath time. These routines contribute to the child's sense of security. Tell your children that this time is important to you, and you will continue it after the babies are born. Then make every effort to do so.

CHAPTER 3

Your Career and Your Pregnancy

Working during pregnancy is an established concept today. More than half of all women work outside the home. Many women work until the day they deliver.

Whether you work throughout your pregnancy depends on your particular circumstances; it is a subject to discuss with your doctor. No matter what kind of job you do or whether you work full- or part-time, expect to modify some daily activities. If your profession is especially demanding, set priorities and establish guidelines with co-workers about how much you can work during pregnancy.

> Delfina never had much to do with the personnel officer at her workplace. At her husband's urging, she made an appointment with the woman to discuss her pregnancy. She found a friend and an advocate in Irene. With her help, Delfina made a lot of changes at work, including her work hours and breaks, so she could lie down. With these changes, she was able to work through her entire pregnancy.

If you are concerned about whether your workplace is a safe environment during your pregnancy, discuss the situation with your doctor. It may be difficult to know the specific risks of a particular job; the goal is to minimize any risks to you and your baby while enabling you to work. A normal, healthy woman with a normal job should be able to work throughout her pregnancy.

Work Precautions during Pregnancy

If you work during pregnancy, bear in mind a few precautions. You will probably have to slow down and lighten your duties. Expect to take things a little easier at work and at home – you may not be able to do some of the things you do when you are not pregnant. Ask for help when you need it.

> Kelly had an especially demanding job; some days she worked ten hours. She came to see me at the end of her sixth month looking terrible and hardly able to move. I told her that her pregnancy really had to come first, not her job. Her emphasis on work could have a negative effect on the health of her baby. She wouldn't last another week the way she was going, and I told her so.
>
> We decided that she would set some boundaries at work, and we devised a plan – eight-hour days that would decrease to four-hour days over the next three months. When she came in a month later, Kelly reported that things were much better at work. She had begun to train her temporary replacement. I told Kelly what I tell others about work and pregnancy – I wanted her to be able to work, but her pregnancy had to come first.

Making Changes

Your centre of gravity is changing, so you may have to change the way you do certain tasks – lifting, for example. Do most of your lifting with your legs. Bend your knees to lift; don't bend at the waist. As your abdomen grows larger, don't lift anything weighing more than 20 pounds.

Avoid activities that involve climbing and balance, especially during the third trimester. Talk to your supervisor about eliminating these activities. If you stand or sit all day at your job, you may have to make changes.

With a 'sit-down' job, get up and move around regularly to stimulate circulation. Sit in a chair that offers good support for your back and legs. Don't slouch or cross your legs while sitting.

Work Risks Associated with Pregnancy

If your job includes two or more of the following risks, talk with your doctor. He or she may want to monitor your pregnancy more closely.

Work-related pregnancy risks include:

- standing more than three hours a day
- work on an industrial machine, especially if it vibrates a lot or requires strenuous effort to operate
- strenuous physical tasks, such as lifting, pulling, pushing or heavy cleaning
- repetitive work, such as an assembly-line job
- environmental factors, such as high noise levels or extreme temperatures
- long work hours
- shift changes
- exposure to infectious diseases
- exposure to chemicals or toxic substances

> Aimee was a cashier at a large discount department store. Before pregnancy, her legs would ache after standing for an eight-hour shift. At her six-month visit, she was miserable. She had just finished a shift and couldn't get her shoes off because of the swelling. She needed to make some major changes.
>
> Aimee changed to a six-hour shift, with two breaks, during which she rested on her side on a couch for 30 minutes. She was able to sit on a stool while she worked. She found running shoes were very comfortable and maternity support hose helped a lot. Her boss was happy to work with her to make the changes possible.

Many women work at a computer or a visual display unit (VDU) and wonder if it can harm the baby. To date, we have no evidence that working at a computer terminal can harm a growing baby. However, if you work at a VDU, be aware of how long you sit and the way you sit, to keep good circulation in your legs. Get up and walk around frequently.

Some substances in the workplace can harm a developing fetus. If you think you may be exposed to hazardous substances, discuss it with your physician. Substances may also be brought into your home on your work clothes or those of someone else in your family. A discussion of hazardous environmental substances begins on page 59.

Job Stress and Fatigue

Some women experience stress on the job during pregnancy. Nearly every pregnant woman I know feels tired and fatigued at some time while she is pregnant.

To Relieve Stress

Some muscle exercises can help you to relieve stress; you can do them at home or on the job. I have a couple of favourites. The first one I recommend is to relax each muscle group in turn with a deep breath. Start with the feet and work up through the legs, hands, arms, torso, shoulders, neck and face. Continue for 10 to 20 minutes. (This exercise also works when you are lying in bed and are having trouble getting to sleep.)

The second exercise is also easy. Inhale slowly. Push your abdomen out as you breathe in. Count to four before exhaling. Let your shoulders and neck relax as you slowly exhale while counting to six. Repeat as often as needed.

Feeling Fatigued

Feeling fatigued can be a sign of pregnancy. For some women, the feeling lasts throughout their pregnancy. For others, stress on the job or at home can cause fatigue during the day or sleeping problems at night.

If possible, lie down during breaks or on your lunch hour. Even 10 or 15 minutes of rest can make you feel better.

Do some leg-stretching foot exercises several times each hour, whenever you can. Remove your shoes before doing the following exercise. Extend your legs in front, then point your toes and flex your feet. Repeat four or five times. This exercise helps circulation in your feet and may prevent some swelling in your legs. Stress and fatigue are discussed in depth beginning on page 34.

Travel during Pregnancy

Many women travel as part of their job. Travelling during pregnancy can be tiring and frustrating, but if your pregnancy is normal, you should be able to travel in the first and second trimesters without too much trouble. Consult your physician if you are considering travel in your third trimester.

The best time to travel, if you can choose, is during the second trimester. You will have more energy and you will feel better. Complications are less likely. In the first trimester, you may have morning sickness or feel very tired. In the third trimester, you may find it difficult to sit or to stand for long periods, and you may tire easily.

Travel Tips

The most important travel tip I can give you is *don't overdo it*. Pregnancy does impose some restrictions. If your company requires you to travel, limit the amount of time you are away from home.

If you experience nausea when travelling, carry crackers or some other bland snack food to nibble on. Prop up your feet when you sit for any length of time.

Discuss travel plans with your doctor. Most will tell you that it is safe to travel at certain times while you are pregnant, but each situation is different. Keep in mind the following general considerations about travelling during pregnancy:

- Avoid areas in which good medical care is not available or where changes in climate, food or altitude could cause problems.
- Don't plan a trip during your last month of pregnancy.
- If you have any problems, such as bleeding or cramping, don't travel.
- If you are uncomfortable or your hands or feet swell, sitting in a car or on a plane or walking a lot may make matters worse.
- Take a copy of your medical records when travelling.
- Keep your doctor's name and telephone number handy in case of an emergency.
- If your pregnancy is considered 'high risk', a trip during pregnancy is not a good idea.

Ways to Travel

Flying should not present a problem. Most airlines allow pre-boarding for passengers who need extra time. Take advantage of the offer. Try to book an aisle seat, so that you can stretch your legs and get up to walk more easily. Drink plenty of fluids, such as water and juice, because recirculated air in a plane is extremely dry.

Consider consulting with someone at the airline about your condition *before* you buy tickets. I have heard of some airlines refusing to carry a pregnant passenger without the written consent of her doctor.

If you haven't considered train travel recently, now might be the time to do so. Trains have wide aisles and roomy seats, and the ride is smooth. Moving around is easy.

Coach trips and sailing are probably not good choices. On a coach, leg room is limited and the ride is jarring, which could make you uncomfortable. If you are unused to it, the rolling motion of a ship or boat can be unsettling. Sea-sickness could add to pregnancy discomforts you may already have. If you do sail, most doctors believe that Dramamine (dimenhydrinate) is safe against sea-sickness, but a sea-sickness patch is *not* advised.

Car travel may be comfortable or uncomfortable, depending on how far along you are. Limit car travel to not more than five hours a day (sitting longer slows circulation). Stop at regular intervals to take short walks and use the toilet. When you sit in a car, tuck a pillow into the small of your back. Do 'ankle circles' while riding to increase circulation in your feet and legs. Always wear your seat belt.

Risks to Consider

If you travel, your discomfort level is likely to increase, especially if you are cooped up in a car or plane for hours. You may have trouble sleeping in a strange bed. If you travel during pregnancy and develop a complication while you're away from home, those who have been involved in your pregnancy and know your history will not be available to care for you.

Avoid travel during the last month of pregnancy. Labour could begin at any time, your water could break or other problems could occur. Your doctor knows what has happened during your pregnancy up to now and has a record of tests you've undergone – information that is important. If you check into a hospital to deliver in a strange city, some doctors will be unhappy because they don't know your medical history. It doesn't make sense to take any chances.

Many women want to know if their doctor can tell when they will go into labour so they can travel. Unfortunately, no one can predict when your labour will begin. Always discuss your travel plans with your doctor before you finalize them.

Health Insurance

If you have private health insurance, it may not cover private care for a pregnancy and delivery. This varies according to the health insurance company, and according to the policy you have. You must check with the insurance company. Some policies do not cover any costs related to pregnancy. Some major health insurers will only pay for evacuation of the uterus after a miscarriage or an emergency caesarean section. Some have policies which cover all complications of pregnancy and delivery, but policies which deal with the expenses of a normal pregnancy and delivery are hard to find.

Employment Rights

Since October 1994, as a working mother-to-be in the UK, you are entitled to maternity leave, protection against unfair dismissal for pregnancy-related reasons and protection against any risks to your health and safety in the workplace.

Every woman who is in work while she is pregnant is entitled to 14 weeks' maternity leave. When you return to work you will go back to the same job. This right applies to every employee who gives the required notice, with no requirement about the number of hours you work or length of time you have worked for the employer. Write to your employer at least 21 days before you start your maternity leave, telling him or her that you are pregnant and giving the expected date of childbirth. If circumstances (for example, illness) prevent you from giving 21 days' notice, you must write to your employer as soon as you can. You must also say the date you intend to start your maternity leave, but you only need to put this in writing if your employer requests it. If requested, you must also enclose a copy of your maternity certificate (form MAT B1; in Northern Ireland MB1) which your midwife or doctor can give you when you are about 24 weeks pregnant.

Antenatal Appointments

All pregnant women have the right to take time off work to attend antenatal appointments. This includes relaxation classes and parentcraft classes, including travelling time. You should not lose any pay for this. Your employer may wish to have a letter from your doctor or midwife saying that the classes are part of your antenatal care. You should let your employer know when you will need to attend antenatal appointments and he or she may ask for confirmation that you did attend.

If you are not paid or refused time off you can make a claim to an industrial tribunal within three months.

Maternity Leave

The earliest you can start your maternity leave is at 29 weeks pregnant, 11 weeks before the week your baby is due. It is up to you to decide when you want to stop work, and you can work right up until the week of childbirth if you so wish. The exception to this is if in the last six weeks of your pregnancy you have a pregnancy-related illness. If this happens, you may be required to start your maternity leave. During the 14 weeks of maternity leave you will receive all your contractual rights as if you were still at work. You will retain your holiday entitlement, pension rights and your company car, but you will only get maternity pay.

You do not have to give notice if you return to work at the end of your 14 weeks' maternity leave. If you want to return to work before that you must give your employer 7 days' notice in writing. Otherwise, your employer can send you away for 7 days or until the end of the 14 weeks, whichever is the sooner.

You are not allowed to work for two weeks after giving birth, so if your baby is born very late, and your 14 weeks' maternity leave runs out, it will be extended by two weeks from the date of birth of your baby. If you are ill at the end of your maternity leave and are unable to return to work, you should be able to get sick pay from your employer. If you give your employer a medical certificate before the end of your maternity leave, you will be protected against unfair dismissal for an additional 4 weeks.

If you think 14 weeks is not long enough for you and your baby, and you don't qualify for 'extended maternity absence', you can discuss this with your trade union or take independent advice. You may be able to use the sex discrimination laws to establish a right to a longer period of leave.

Extended Maternity Absence

If you have worked for the same employer for two years by the time you are 28 weeks pregnant, the end of the 12th week before the baby is due, and carry on working until at least the end of that week; and your employer employs more than five people, you may qualify for Extended Maternity Absence. This runs for 29 weeks from the beginning of the week in which your baby is actually born. You must give your employer written notice at least 21 days before you start your maternity leave, stating that you are pregnant, the expected date of childbirth and that you intend to return to work after the birth. If you cannot give 21 days' notice – for example, owing to illness – you must tell your employer as soon as you reasonably can. If requested, you must tell your employer the date you intend to start your maternity leave and enclose a copy of your maternity certificate.

Your employer may write to you at any time after 11 weeks from the start of your maternity leave asking you to confirm that you are going back to work and you must reply within 14 days if you wish to return. At least 21 days before you intend to return, you must write to your employer giving notice of the exact date of return – the 'Notified Date of Return'.

You can delay your return to work beyond 29 weeks after the birth if you are ill, when you must send a medical certificate. Your employer can delay your return for up to four weeks but he must tell you the reason and give you a new date for return. Interruption of work – for example, due to a strike – allows you to delay your return until work starts again. Your employer may allow you to delay your return to work after the 29 weeks by written agreement.

Dismissal because of Pregnancy and Maternity Leave

It is against the law for your employer to dismiss you or select you for redundancy for any reason connected with pregnancy, childbirth or maternity leave. It does not matter how long you have worked for the company or how many hours a week you work.

If you are dismissed during pregnancy or maternity leave, your employer must give you a written statement of the reasons. If you believe that the reason is related to your pregnancy, you need advice from your trade union, a Citizen's Advice Bureau or a solicitor. Your claim must be submitted to an industrial tribunal within three months of the dismissal. You can also claim that you have been discriminated against because you are a women if you are dismissed, demoted or have your working hours reduced.

Health and Safety Rights

If you are pregnant or have given birth within the last six months and are breast-feeding, your employer must make sure that the kind of work you are doing and the working conditions do not put your health or that of your baby at risk, but you must have notified the employer of your condition in writing. He or she is required to carry out a risk assessment in your workplace to implement any obligations in Health and Safety regulations.

If there is a risk, your employer must change your working conditions or hours. If this is not possible, he or she must offer you a suitable alternative job. If this is also not possible, he or she must suspend you on full pay, but you must not take up alternative employment.

Maternity Benefits and Pay

Prescriptions and dental treatment are free during pregnancy.

One-parent Benefit

This is a tax-free benefit of £6.30 per week for single parents living alone.

Income Support, Family Credit, Housing Benefit and Council Tax Benefit

Income Support is paid weekly to anyone who does not have enough money to live on. Rates vary according to circumstances. You should make a claim on form A1 from Social Security or unemployment offices.

Family Credit is a tax-free benefit paid to working families on low pay who have children.

Housing Benefit is to help you to pay your rent or mortgage if you are on Income Support or have a low income.

Council Tax Benefit is a reduction in Council Tax if you get Income Support or your income is low.

Milk and vitamins can be obtained free of charge if you have Income Support. Maternity Payments of up to £100 may be made to help you to buy things for your baby if you are on Income Support, Family Credit or a low income.

Statutory Maternity Pay

This is a weekly payment for a maximum of 18 weeks starting when you leave work, even if you do not plan to go back to work. In order to receive it you must have worked for the same employer for at least 26 weeks by the time you are 25 weeks pregnant and still be in your job by this time, and you must be earning £59 a week or more on average. It is up to you to decide when you want to start your maternity pay, the earliest being at 29 weeks pregnant. (If your baby is stillborn after 24 weeks, you can now receive statutory maternity pay.) You must decide when you want to stop work – you can work right up until the week your baby is due if you want to – and then start receiving maternity pay. The exception is if you have a pregnancy-related illness after 34 weeks, when your maternity leave and maternity pay will start. If your illness is not pregnancy-related, you can claim Statutory Sick Pay until your maternity benefits start.

For the first six weeks of maternity pay you receive 90 per cent of your average pay. After that you get the basic rate of £54.55 a week for up to 12 weeks. Your employer will deduct the necessary National Insurance contributions and tax.

To apply for maternity pay you must write to your employer at least three weeks before you stop work. You must send him or her a copy of your maternity certificate.

Maternity Allowance

If you are not eligible for Statutory Maternity Pay but have worked and paid full rate National Insurance contributions for at least 26 of the 66 weeks before the baby is due, you are eligible for a weekly maternity allowance. You can get this if you are self-employed, if you gave up work or if you changed jobs during your pregnancy. It is paid for up to 18 weeks, starting at any time after you are 29 weeks pregnant. The lower rate of £47.35 a week is paid to women who are either self-employed or unemployed during a qualifying week, 15 weeks before the childbirth is expected. A higher rate of £54.55 a week is paid to women who are employed in the qualifying week.

To claim Maternity Allowance, you will need to fill in form MA1 from your antenatal clinic or Social Security office (in Northern Ireland, your Incapacity Benefits Branch), and send it to the Social Security office as soon as you can after you are 26 weeks pregnant.

If you have not paid 26 weeks of National Insurance contributions by the time you are 26 weeks pregnant, you may decide to work later in the pregnancy and send the MA1 form off as soon as you have made the 26 contributions.

Incapacity Benefit

If you are unable to get Statutory Maternity Pay or Maternity Allowance but have worked and paid National Insurance contributions in the last three years, you may be able to receive this benefit (£46.15 a week). If you are not entitled to Maternity Allowance, your Social Security office should check to see if you can obtain any Incapacity Benefit when you send them your form MA1. They will also need a copy of the maternity certificate, MAT B1.

Child Benefit

Every mother gets a tax-free benefit weekly for each child, payable from birth. It is £10.80 a week for the first child and other children get £8.80 a week. You should claim on leaflet CH1 from your local Social Security office. In Northern Ireland, ask for a Child Benefit 'Claim Pack' at a post office or Social Security office. You need to send your baby's birth certificate (which will be returned).

Preparing to Leave Your Job

Whatever your plans – leaving work a few months early, working until the day you deliver – *be prepared* to leave by the end of the eighth month. You will need to prepare your replacement to step into your job temporarily, schedule times at which to call the office and take care of other details.

Think Ahead

Think about how to be prepared in case your water breaks or you have some other problem at work. Keep a towel and some sanitary pads available. Carry medical information cards and identification with you at all times. Check with the personnel department to make sure that the paperwork for your maternity leave is in order.

Have your suitcase packed and ready at home in case you need to go from your office to the hospital. I have seen some very unusual items brought in by partners who had to pack a bag to take to the hospital when the mother-to-be was unexpectedly ready to give birth!

> Tina's water broke at work, and she went directly to the hospital. When she got there, she called her husband and asked him to pack some things for her and come right away. Tina's delivery went well. In her room later, she opened her overnight bag to look for a hairbrush. Was she surprised! She wished she'd taken the time to pack for herself. The nightgown Kevin brought was one of her flimsiest, as was the underwear he had chosen. And he had forgotten her dressing-gown. Luckily the hospital provided her with a toothbrush, toothpaste and a comb. She was able to get her sister to bring her a dressing-gown, some make-up and other things she needed. At least the orange and apple Kevin packed came in handy after the delivery.

Prepare Your Replacement

Save yourself problems later by training the person who will handle your job to do the work the way you would. Initiate the relief worker to office procedures, rules and regulations, and particular ways to do your job efficiently. It is a good idea to have the person perform your duties while you are still on the scene so you can evaluate the work.

Before you leave, arrange to talk with your replacement, your boss and your co-workers one last time about details that must be taken care of while you are gone. Together, review the plans you have prepared.

Schedule times to call the office. Discuss with co-workers how to keep in touch with you. (Will you call them? When can they call you?) It is a good idea to schedule times to call the office. That enables your co-workers to have information available for you and to have questions ready when you call. Few annoyances are worse than having various people at your office call you every day asking questions when you are trying to concentrate on your baby! Letting them know in advance when you will call sets guidelines and puts you in more control.

CHAPTER 4

Will You Be a Single Mother?

Some women, especially those in their late 30s and early 40s, choose to have a child without a spouse. The situations I have seen vary from woman to woman. Some women are deeply involved with their partner, the baby's father, but have chosen not to marry. Some women are pregnant without their partner's support. Still other single women have chosen donor (artificial) insemination as a means of getting pregnant.

I have come to realize that no matter what the personal situation for each woman, many concerns are shared by all of them. This chapter reflects many of the issues they have raised with me.

Information in the first part of this chapter is general and deals with situations single mothers face frequently. Questions I list at the end of the chapter have no absolute answers. They are of a legal nature that I am not qualified to answer. However, I include them because the decision to have a baby as a single woman has legal ramifications of which you should be aware. If you are single and pregnant, use them as a basis for formulating questions about your own situation, then seek the advice of a social worker, your Community Health Council, your doctor, a solicitor or family members.

People may ask why you chose to be a single mother as your pregnancy begins to show. Answers to this question vary greatly. Marriage does not meet the needs of many women, but their desire to be a mother – to give birth to a child and to be a parent – is very strong.

In many situations – whether a mother is single, widowed or divorced – a child's overall environment is more important than the presence of a man in the household. Eighty-six per cent of single-parent households are headed by women. Recent studies indicate that if a woman has other supportive adults to depend on, a child can fare well in a home headed by a single woman.

Concerns about Your Decision

You may find people ask you the most intimate questions during your pregnancy, especially if you are single. If you believe you need to answer their questions, decide early how detailed an explanation you want to provide.

Some people may think your choice is unwise and tell you that you are 'crazy' to have a baby alone. However, your true friends won't treat you this way. Once they understand your situation, they will be supportive. If anyone gives you a hard time, change the subject. Don't discuss your reasons for having a baby with anyone unless you want to.

Even if you are 'alone', you are not really alone. Seek support from family and friends. Mothers of young children can identify with your experiences – they have had similar ones recently. If you have friends or family members with young children, talk with them. You would probably share your concerns with these people even if you were married. Try not to let your particular situation alter this.

Sometimes a single woman's family is against her decision to have a baby. If you are comfortable with your decision, ask family members to talk to you about the reasons they are uncomfortable with your pregnancy. You may not change their minds; you have no control over that. You *do* have control over your response; learn to live with their disapproval or ignore it.

Some women choose not to marry their partner. If this is your situation, you may find that people assume that you and your partner are married, especially if you are pregnant and together. In most cases, it is nobody's business; however, do tell your doctor about the situation.

Emotional upheavals are not uncommon for many women during pregnancy. If coping with emotions is hard for you, talk with your doctor. He or she will know about support groups or will be able to direct you to a counsellor, if that is what you need. Check the resource section of this book starting on page 292 for the name and telephone number of a group you can contact that deals with the issues of single motherhood.

Deciding Who Can Help You

Finding someone to count on for help during your pregnancy and after your baby arrives is a concern for many single pregnant women. One patient told me that she thought abc . whom she would call at 2am if her baby were crying uncontrollably. When she answered that question, she had the name of someone she believed she could count on in any type of emergency – during or after pregnancy!

You may want to choose someone to be with you when you labour and deliver, and who will be there to help afterward. The only part of labour and delivery that might require special planning because you are single is your plan to get to the hospital to deliver. One woman wanted her friend to drive, but couldn't reach her when the time came. Her next option (all part of the plan) was to call a taxi, which got her to the hospital in plenty of time.

Finding a Labour Companion

Finding a labour companion probably won't be difficult. Not all women choose their partner for the job; you can ask a good friend or a relative. A woman who has given birth using the method you have chosen is an excellent choice. She understands your feelings and can identify closely with your experience.

If you can't think of someone, discuss the matter with your doctor. He or she may suggest other single mothers who might volunteer to be with you during labour.

Going Home from Hospital

If you are a single mother without a partner, going home from hospital may seem overwhelming at first. You will be fine if you plan ahead and enlist a little help.

A new baby is an incredible challenge in any situation. You may need some support from family and friends because you will have total responsibility for your new baby. Ask for their help! If you feel you can't ask others for their time, consider employing someone to stay with you at night for the first few weeks until you get on your feet.

Your 'Unusual' Situation

Today, being a single mother isn't that unusual – many mothers are divorced, widowed or unmarried. Women of all ages have made the same decision you have. Some people may treat you differently; others won't care. Good friends and family members should draw closer to you.

Some women have chosen donor insemination to conceive a child. This can create unusual situations but families today are different from the way they were in the past. Many families are 'unusual' now. Many children don't have a complete set of parents or grandparents, even in the closest family units. I have found in these situations that an older family friend can be just as loving as a grandparent. Encourage older friends to take an active part in your child's life. Support groups for single parents can also be a valuable source of information and help. Ask your doctor for the names of groups in your area.

As a single parent, you do need an alternative childcare plan in case you become ill or there is an emergency. Plan ahead for this. Ask a family member or close friend if they can be called upon to help out in case this happens. Providing for this event should give you peace of mind.

Legal Questions

The following questions have been posed to me and other physicians by women who chose to be single mothers. I repeat them here without answers because they are legal questions that should be reviewed with a Citizen's Advice Bureau or a solicitor in your area who specializes in family law. They can help you to clarify the kinds of questions you need to consider as a single mother:

- A friend who's had a baby by herself told me I'd better consider the legal ramifications of this situation. What was she talking about?
- I've heard that if I'm unmarried, I have to get a special birth certificate. Is that true?
- I'm having my baby alone, and I'm concerned about who can make medical decisions for me and my expected baby. Can I do anything about this concern?
- I'm not married, but I am deeply involved with my baby's father. Can my partner make medical decisions for me if I have problems during labour or after the birth?

- If anything happens to me, can my partner make medical decisions for our baby after it is born?
- What are the legal rights of my baby's father if we are not married?
- Do my partner's parents have legal rights in regard to their grandchild (my child)?
- My baby's father and I went our separate ways before I knew I was pregnant. Do I have to tell him about the baby?
- I chose to have donor (artificial) insemination. If anything happens to me during my labour or delivery, who can make medical decisions for me? Who can make decisions for my baby?
- I got pregnant by donor insemination. What do I put on the birth certificate under 'father's name'?
- Is there a way I can find out more about my sperm donor's family medical history?
- Will the sperm bank send me notices if medical problems appear in my sperm donor's family?
- As my child grows up, he or she may need some sort of medical help (such as a donor kidney) from a sibling. Will the sperm bank supply family information?
- I had donor insemination and I'm concerned about the rights of the baby's father to be part of my child's life in the future. Should I be concerned?
- What type of arrangements must I make for my child in case of my death?
- Someone joked to me that my child could marry its sister or brother some day and wouldn't know it because I had donor insemination. Is this possible?
- Are there any other things I should consider because of my unique situation?

CHAPTER 5

Concerns You and Your Partner May Have

At the beginning of your pregnancy, you won't know all the questions and concerns you will have. As your pregnancy progresses, many of the issues I cover here will become important to you. In this chapter, we will look at some of the common concerns couples expecting a child often have.

The Due Date

Most women don't know the exact date their baby was conceived, but they usually know the first day of their last menstrual period. Because ovulation occurs about the middle of a woman's cycle, or about two weeks before the beginning of the next period, a doctor uses the date of the last period and adds two weeks as an estimate of when conception occurred. By doing this, your doctor can determine your due date.

You can calculate when your baby is due another way. Begin with the date of the onset of your last menstrual period; add seven days and count back three months. This gives you the *approximate* date of delivery. For example, if your last period began on 20 January, your estimated due date is 27 October.

Gestational age or *menstrual age* is one way to date a pregnancy. If your doctor says that you are 12 weeks pregnant, he is referring to gestational age. He means that your last menstrual period began 12 weeks ago; however, you actually conceived 10 weeks ago.

Fertilization age, also called *ovulatory age*, is two weeks shorter than gestational age and dates from the actual day of conception. This is the age of the fetus. In the case of '12 weeks pregnant', the fetus is actually 10 weeks old.

Your doctor may also refer to your pregnancy by *trimesters*. Trimesters divide pregnancy into three stages, each about 13 weeks long. This division helps to organize the stages of development.

The Emotions of Pregnancy

When a woman discovers that she is pregnant, she may feel many different emotions – excitement, fear, anxiety, joy. You may be surprised by the emotions you feel when you learn you are pregnant. Even if you and your partner have been anticipating your pregnancy, the emotions you may feel may not be the ones you thought you would have.

If you are not immediately thrilled about pregnancy, don't feel alone. It is common to feel conflict about the news and to question your condition. Some of this may be attributed to the anxiety you feel if you are not sure what lies ahead.

It is normal to become very emotional about many things during pregnancy. You may feel moody, cry at the slightest thing or daydream. Emotional changes during pregnancy are discussed in more detail beginning on page 82.

You may feel attached to your developing baby immediately, or it may not happen for a while. Some women begin to feel attached as soon as they know they are pregnant. For others, it occurs when they hear their baby's heartbeat, at around 12 or 13 weeks, or the first time they feel their baby move, at between 16 and 20 weeks.

Stress, Fatigue and Rest

High levels of stress during pregnancy can increase a woman's chance of having a premature baby or giving birth to a baby that has a low birth weight. Studies have shown that the more anxious a woman is during pregnancy, the greater is the chance of premature birth.

Making some lifestyle changes may help to minimize the effects of stress on you and your baby. Eat a healthy diet. Practise stress-reducing exercises, such as yoga. Get enough rest.

You can't always eliminate stress, but you can learn to cope with it. The following suggestions may help you to deal with everyday stressful situations.

Accept what you cannot change. Turn off your anger, resentment or impatience, and tune out. When you feel anxious or upset, practise deep breathing or relaxation exercises learned in childbirth-education classes.

Talk about it. Instead of bottling up your problems, talk them through. Be specific, and listen to what others tell you in response. Work together towards practical solutions.

Take time out. When stress gets to be too much for you, take time out. Go into the bathroom or your bedroom – a quiet place. Stretch, practise breathing exercises or listen to soothing music.

Let go of the little stresses. Do your best – then relax! If you make a mistake, acknowledge it and go on. Be kind to yourself.

Set realistic priorities. Manage your time with priorities in mind. Use a daily calendar. Learn to say 'no'.

Get some exercise. Exercise is a great stress reliever. Walk, swim or ride an exercise bicycle to deal with stress.

Seek help. You many need outside help to make it through a difficult time or to change behaviour patterns. If necessary, ask your doctor for a referral.

Fatigue and Rest

During the first stages of your pregnancy, you may find that getting enough rest is utmost in your mind. Do yourself a favour by taking it easy and resting when possible.

Try not to lie on your back or stomach when you sleep or rest. As your uterus grows, it presses on important blood vessels that run down the back of your abdomen. When you lie on your back, the pressure decreases circulation to your baby and to the lower parts of your body. You may notice that it is harder to breathe when you lie on your back. Lying on your stomach puts a lot of pressure on your uterus, which can become a comfort problem later.

Learn to sleep on your side early in the pregnancy – you will be glad you did as you get bigger. Elevate your feet to keep blood moving throughout your body, especially your legs. Rest your top leg on a pillow. Many women find that 'pregnancy pillows' that support the entire body can offer great relief.

Some pregnant women can't sleep enough at night to make them feel rested. If you can, nap during the day. If you can't nap, sit down and relax – listen to music or read, if that helps. When you relax, prop your feet above your chest or lie on your side to help to ease the swelling and discomfort in your legs.

*Use extra pillows to support your abdomen or your legs as your
pregnancy progresses*

Childbirth Education Classes

Childbirth education classes help you and your partner to prepare for
the birth of your baby. I have found that if a couple, especially the
woman, is prepared for labour and delivery, the entire experience is
usually more relaxed, even enjoyable. Childbirth education classes
have been developed for couples in their 30s and 40s to meet their
specific needs.

What to Look for in a Class

Every class has a different style. The list below can help you evaluate
if a childbirth class is right for you:

- The class was recommended by my doctor.
- The class uses a philosophy shared by my doctor and childbirth
  team.
- The class begins when I need it, in the seventh month of my
  pregnancy (earlier if you are having more than one baby).
- The class size is small – no more than 10 couples.
- Patients who have been to the classes are enthusiastic. (Locate some
  and ask about the class.)
- The class outline is informative and interesting.
- The class covers caesarean section, different types of anaesthesia
  and emotional issues.
- The class includes the time and the opportunity to ask questions, to
  practise techniques and to talk to parents who have recently given
  birth.

How Classes Help to Prepare You for Childbirth

Classes help to prepare a woman and her partner for labour and delivery. Studies have shown that women who take childbirth-education classes need less medication, have fewer forceps deliveries and feel more positive about the birth than women who do not take classes.

Classes cover many aspects of labour and delivery, including vaginal birth, caesarean section, hospital procedures, ways to deal with the discomfort and the pain of labour and delivery, various pain-relief methods and the puerperium or recovery period. Having this information available beforehand can make you feel more confident and prepared to cope with the birth experience. The majority of all first-time expectant parents attend some type of childbirth education class.

Major Childbirth Philosophies

Patients often ask me if one type of delivery method covered in childbirth education classes is better than another. Any method can be the right one for a couple, but I always suggest that both parties agree on the method. If the woman chooses a method that involves her partner greatly and the partner is not able to provide that level of involvement, it could lead to disappointment and anxiety.

Childbirth preparation methods are usually divided among three major philosophies – Lamaze, Bradley and Grantly Dick-Read. Each philosophy offers its own techniques and methods.

Lamaze is one technique of childbirth preparation. It conditions mothers, through training, to replace unproductive labouring efforts with effective ones. It emphasizes relaxation and breathing as ways to relax during labour and delivery. In recent years, partners have been included in Lamaze classes.

Bradley classes teach the Bradley method of relaxation and inward focus; many types of relaxation are used. Strong emphasis is put on relaxation and deep abdominal breathing to make labour more comfortable. Classes begin when pregnancy is confirmed and continue until after the birth. Bradley class members typically have decided they do not want to use any type of medication for labour-pain relief.

Grantly Dick-Read introduced a method that attempts to break the fear-tension-pain cycle of labour and delivery. These classes were the first to include fathers in the birth experience.

Choosing Your Class

At around 20 weeks of pregnancy, begin looking into classes that are offered in your area. You should be signed up or just beginning classes by the beginning of the third trimester (about 27 weeks). Plan to finish the classes at least a few weeks before you are due. The following ideas can help you and your partner find the right class for you.

Find out what classes fit into your schedule and your partner's. Talk to friends and relatives who have taken different childbirth classes. Decide whether you want a drug-free birth or whether you are willing to consider pain relief if it is necessary. Learn about the instructor's qualifications. Visit some classes in your area.

Childbirth classes are offered in many settings. Most hospitals that deliver babies offer antenatal classes on site. They are often taught by a labour-and-delivery midwife.

Classes are not only for first-time pregnant women. If you have a new partner, if it has been a few years since you have had a baby, if you have questions or if you would like a review of labour and delivery, I encourage you to consider taking these classes.

Ask your doctor to recommend classes in your area. He or she is familiar with what is being offered. Friends can be good sources.

Paediatricians

These are doctors who specialize in the care of babies and children. With normal pregnancy and delivery, a paediatrician should check your baby after delivery, care for the baby if there are any problems while you are in hospital, and review the baby before you go home. Hospitals often have a paediatric infant follow-up clinic and see your baby a few weeks after delivery and, if there are any problems, at intervals thereafter.

If you have a problem pregnancy, the paediatrician may see you in hospital before labour to discuss the outlook for the baby. If there are any problems in labour, a paediatrician should be present at the birth. If there are any difficulties with the baby after delivery, a paediatrician will be called at once if he is not already present. He will look after your baby and, if necessary, will arrange a transfer to a neonatal intensive care unit. For example, with a premature baby, senior paediatricians will be responsible for the baby's care there.

When your baby is discharged home, your family doctor will be responsible for managing any medical problems with the baby. You should bear this in mind when selecting a general practitioner, giving preference to one who has, or has a partner with, paediatric experience, and whom you trust. Discuss this with your doctor during the pregnancy.

In utero and postpartum transfer

If a baby is likely to need very specialized neonatal care which cannot be provided at your local hospital, it may be decided to transfer you to a hospital with such facilities, before you are delivered – 'in utero transfer'. An example is a very premature baby. The transfer may even take place after you have started in labour. Also, if the baby is in danger after delivery, he or she may be transferred to a specialist hospital after delivery. If this is possible, you should be transferred with the baby, and you should press strongly for this to happen.

The Cost of Having a Baby in a Private Hospital

No doubt about it – it costs a lot of money to have a baby with a private obstetrician in a private hospital, no matter where you live. Costs vary depending on how long you stay in hospital, what type of anaesthesia you have, whether you or your baby have complications and where you live.

The costs will be the fees charged by the obstetrician and the paediatrician plus the hospital charges. Most obstetricians give a 'package deal' and do not vary this if delivery has to be by forceps or caesarean section. In and around London, the obstetrician's fee varies from £1,000 to £2,500, but you may have to budget for as much as £750 for special antenatal tests. In areas outside London, charges may be less. You should telephone the secretary of an obstetrician in your area to enquire what his or her charges are. You family doctor will know which obstetricians provide private care. Hospital charges for a normal delivery and a stay of two or three days are £1,500 to £2,500 in London, but if you have an operative vaginal delivery with forceps or a caesarean section, you may have to pay up to £1,500 more. Again, provincial hospitals may charge less and you should check by telephone with the private patients department at your local hospital or with a nearby private maternity hospital. Your family doctor will be able to advise on which hospitals provide a private service. There may be an additional charge of up to £50 a day for the care of the newborn baby.

If you want to select a private paediatrician, you will have to check with his or her secretary to find out the daily fee. The care your baby will get will not be very different from that provided by the hospital paediatrician.

You may also need to check with the hospital and your health insurance company. When you communicate with an insurance company, it helps to have a list of questions ready. Write down the answers so that you can refer to them later, especially if you need to discuss them with your doctor.

Driving during Pregnancy

Driving a car is important to most women, but some wonder if it is safe to drive during pregnancy. It is usually safe to drive throughout pregnancy, but it may become uncomfortable for you to get in and out of the car as pregnancy progresses. However, your increasing size should not interfere with your ability to drive.

Many women are confused about whether they should or should not wear seat belts during pregnancy. These safety restraints are just as necessary during pregnancy as they are when you are not pregnant.

For your protection, and the protection of your developing fetus, *always wear your safety belt when driving or riding in a car!* There is no evidence that use of safety restraints increases the chance of fetal or uterine injury. You have a better chance of survival in an accident when you are wearing a seat belt than when you are not wearing one.

There is a correct way to wear your safety belt during pregnancy. Place the lap-belt part of the restraint under your abdomen and across your upper thighs so that it is snug but comfortable. Adjust your sitting position so that the belt crosses your shoulder without cutting into your neck. Position the shoulder harness between your breasts; don't slip this belt off your shoulder. The lap belt cannot hold you safely by itself.

Taking Others to Your Clinic Visits

If you want to bring your partner with you to your antenatal visits, do so. These visits can help him to realize what is happening to you and help him to feel that he is a part of your pregnancy. And it is nice for your partner and your doctor or midwife to meet before labour begins.

It is all right to take your mother or mother-in-law, too. If you want to bring anyone else, discuss it with your doctor first.

Many doctors don't mind if you bring your children with you; others ask that you do not bring children to your clinic visit. If you have a problem and need to talk with your doctor, it can be difficult to do if you are trying to take care of a young child at the same time. If you do bring children, observe the following rules of etiquette:

- Ask about clinic policy ahead of time.
- Bring only one child to a visit.
- Don't bring a child on your first visit, when you will probably have a pelvic examination.
- If you want your child to hear the baby's heartbeat, wait to bring him or her until after you have heard it.
- Bring something to 'entertain' your child with in case you have to wait. Not all clinics have toys or books for children.
- Be considerate of other patients; if your child has a cold or is ill, don't bring him or her.

Some Pregnancy Precautions

Your baby relies on you to maintain correct body temperature. An elevated body temperature in a pregnant woman for an extended period may harm a developing fetus. For this reason, avoid hot baths, saunas, steamrooms and spas.

Nearly all doctors agree that douching can be dangerous during pregnancy because it can cause an infection or bleeding, or even break your bag of waters (rupture your membranes). It can also cause more serious problems, such as an air embolus which results when air gets into your circulation from the pressure of douche. It is rare but can be a serious problem.

There is some controversy about the safety of using electric blankets during pregnancy. Until we know more, stay warm other ways, such as with a duvet, extra blankets or a well-protected hot-water bottle. Do not use an electric blanket.

Feeding Your Baby

It is never too early to think about whether you want to breast-feed or bottle-feed. Even after you have decided on a method, you may have to make adjustments after your baby is born.

Early in life, most babies feed every three to four hours, although some babies feed as often as every two hours. It may help your baby to get on a regular schedule if you time feedings. Or let your baby set the schedule – some babies need to nurse more often than others.

Sometimes a baby needs to feed more often than normal. See how often your baby wants to feed and whether she is growing properly. A baby usually waits longer between feeds and feeds longer each time as she grows older.

A baby is usually the best judge of how much should be taken at each feeding. Usually a baby turns away from the nipple once full.

We do know that breast-feeding is best for your baby. Breast milk contains all the nutrients a baby needs, and it is easy to digest. Breast-fed babies have lower rates of infections because of the immunological content of breast milk. Breast-feeding can also give the baby a sense of security and the mother a sense of self-esteem. However, if there are reasons why you cannot or choose not to breast-feed, be assured that your baby will do well if bottle-fed on formula.

The Bottle-feeding Option

It will not harm your baby if you choose to bottle-feed. I don't want any mother to feel guilty if she chooses bottle-feeding. Sometimes a woman cannot breast-feed because of a physical condition or problem. Some women want to breast-feed and try to, but it doesn't work out. If breast-feeding doesn't work for you, please don't worry about it.

> At her 37-week visit, Lily wanted to talk about breast-feeding and bottle-feeding. With her first child, she had tried breast-feeding and had a miserable experience, giving up after two weeks. This time she planned to bottle-feed from the start and wanted to know if this was all right. Friends and family had been giving her a hard time about it. I reassured her that bottle-feeding was fine and not to feel guilty. I told her that breast-feeding wasn't for everyone – it's an individual decision.
>
> Lily left my clinic feeling better. She realized that giving birth to, caring for and rearing a baby carries a lot of decisions. Some aren't easy to make.

Statistics show that more women choose to bottle-feed than to breast-feed their babies (about two to one). We know that with iron-fortified formula, your baby receives good nutrition if you bottle-feed. There are advantages to bottle-feeding:

• Some women enjoy the freedom that bottle-feeding provides; someone else can help to care for the baby.

- Bottle-feeding is easy to learn; it never causes the mother discomfort if it is done incorrectly.
- Fathers can be more involved in caring for the baby.
- Bottle-fed babies are often able to last longer between feedings because formula is usually digested more slowly than breast milk.
- A day's supply of formula can be mixed at one time, saving effort.
- You don't have to be concerned about feeding your baby in front of other people.
- It is easier to bottle-feed if you are planning to return to work soon after your baby is born.
- If you feed your baby iron-fortified formula, he or she won't need iron supplementation.
- If you use fluoridated tap water to mix formula, you may not have to give your baby fluoride supplements.

The Benefits of Breast-feeding

Breast-feeding is an excellent choice for feeding your baby. Breast-fed babies contract fewer infections than those who are bottle-fed because breast milk is bacteria free and actively helps newborn avoid disease. One study showed that breast-fed babies are much less likely to develop ear infections than bottle-fed babies.

All babies receive from their mother some protection against disease before they are born. During pregnancy, antibodies are passed from the mother to the fetus through the placenta. These antibodies circulate through the baby's blood for up to a few months after the baby is born. However, breast-fed babies continue to receive protection from breast milk.

Breast milk is easily digested by a baby; for a premature baby, it is often the best nourishment. It cannot become contaminated, be mixed incorrectly or served at the wrong temperature. There are also benefits for you – breast-feeding helps to metabolize fat deposits your body laid down during pregnancy.

Breast-fed babies are less likely to develop allergies and asthma; research has shown that this protection can last until a child is a teenager. Studies show that babies fed only breast milk for six months had fewer instances of asthma, food allergies and eczema into their teens.

You can usually begin breast-feeding your baby within hours after birth. This provides your baby with *colostrum*, the first milk your breasts produce. Colostrum contains important factors that help to boost the baby's immune system. Baby's breast-feeding also causes your pituitary gland to release oxytocin, which helps the uterus to contract and decrease bleeding. Breast milk comes in 12 to 48 hours after birth.

> Jane was due to deliver soon and wanted to breast-feed, but she was scared she couldn't do it. She had read books, talked to friends and knew lots of information. I think her biggest fear was that she would be left alone with this new baby and wouldn't know what to do. I told her it didn't work that way, and there would be a lot of help available. One of the best places to learn to breast-feed is in hospital after the baby is born. The midwives are experienced in helping new mothers learn how to start breast-feeding, and they are available to help after you go home. Patients have told me that after they went home, they called the hospital nursery and even went back for help.

Breast-feeding is an excellent way to bond with your baby. Closeness between mother and child can be established during the feeding process. Don't be discouraged if breast-feeding doesn't feel natural to you at first. It takes some time to find out what works best for you and your baby. Hold your baby so she can easily reach the breast while nursing; hold her across your chest or lie in bed. She should take your nipple into her mouth fully, so that her gums cover the aerola. She can't suck effectively if your nipple is only slightly drawn into her mouth.

For the first few weeks, feed your baby 8 to 10 times a day, for 20 to 30 minutes at each feeding. Take more time if your baby needs it.

You may be concerned about how much breast milk your baby gets at a feed. You will know that your baby is getting enough to eat if he nurses frequently, such as every 2 to 3 hours or 8 to 12 times in 24 hours; has 6 to 8 wet nappies and 2 to 5 bowel movements a day; gains 4 to 7oz (100 to 200g) a week or at least 1lb (450g) a month, and appears healthy, has good muscles and is alert and active.

How Breast-feeding Affects You

The nutrients your baby receives while breast-feeding depend on the quality of the food you eat. Breast-feeding places more demands on your body than pregnancy. Your body burns up to 1,000 calories a day just to produce milk. If you breast-feed, you need to eat an extra 500 calories a day. You also need to keep up your fluid intake.

While you are breast-feeding, you may not have menstrual periods and you may not ovulate, meaning you won't get pregnant. However, don't rely on breast-feeding alone if you don't want another pregnancy right away. *Take precautions.*

Do not use oral contraceptives because hormones in oral contraceptives can get into the milk and be passed to your baby. Choose some other form of birth control until you are finished breast-feeding. You may choose a 'minipill' or progesterone-only birth control pill, condoms, a diaphragm or an intra-uterine contraceptive device. Norplant (levonorgestrel implant) birth control is also safe to use if you nurse.

Most substances you eat or drink (or take orally, as medication) can pass to your baby in your breast milk. Spicy foods, chocolate and caffeine are some things your baby may react to when you ingest them. Be careful about what you eat and drink when you breast-feed.

Pumping Breast Milk

Many women pump their breast milk for use at a later time, especially when they return to work. Many types of breast pumps are available; ask your doctor or midwife which is best for what purposes. Pumps are hand, battery or electrically operated.

Other Breast-feeding Facts

Many women are surprised when they experience milk let-down. Soon after a baby begins to nurse, a woman feels a tingling or cramping in her breasts; this means that milk is flowing into breast ducts. It occurs several times during feeding; sometimes a baby chokes a bit when the rush of milk comes too quickly. You may also experience this let-down when it is time for your baby to nurse or when you hear a baby crying – your own or any other baby!

It is best to avoid bottles for the first month of breast-feeding for two reasons. Your baby may come to prefer feeding from a bottle (it is not as hard to suck), and your breasts may not produce enough milk.

Women who have had breast-enlargement surgery with silicone implants are often able to breast-feed successfully; ask your doctor or midwife about it if this concerns you. You should also be able to breast-feed after a breast reduction. Milk production may be less after such surgery, but it is usually enough to satisfy the baby.

If you need help with breast-feeding your baby, ask friends and family members for help. Call your doctor or midwife – they may be able to refer you to someone knowledgeable. You can also look in the telephone book for the La Leche League, an organization that promotes breast-feeding. Someone from a local branch can give you advice and encouragement.

PART TWO

Your Medical Health

CHAPTER 6

Your Health and Medical History

If possible, see your doctor before you become pregnant so that you can take care of any existing medical problems and routine examinations. If you know that you are in good health before you get pregnant, you will feel more secure about your growing baby. You will know that your cervical smear is normal, your breast examination is all right and any medical conditions are under control. If a preconception visit is not possible, make an appointment to see your doctor as soon as you realize that you are pregnant.

Your health affects the health of your growing baby. Good nutrition, proper exercise, sufficient rest and attention to how you take care of yourself are all important to your baby. These matters also affect you and how well you tolerate being pregnant.

Antenatal Care

Antenatal care is the care you receive throughout your pregnancy. Special care from professionals during pregnancy is designed to help to identify any pregnancy problems or conditions before they become serious. Always feel free to ask questions about your pregnancy at your antenatal check-ups.

If you have confidence in your doctor, you will be able to relax and enjoy your pregnancy. Pregnancy really is a special time in a woman's life; good antenatal care helps to ensure that you do everything in your power to make it the best nine months possible for your growing baby, too.

Your First Antenatal Visit

Your first antenatal visit to your doctor may be one of the longest. He or she will ask questions, order laboratory tests and give you a physical examination.

To take a complete medical history, your doctor will ask about your menstrual periods, recent birth control methods, previous pregnancies and other details. Tell him or her about any miscarriages or abortions you have had. Include information about hospital stays or surgical procedures.

Tell your doctor about any medicines you take or those you are allergic to. Your family's past medical history may be important, as in the case of diabetes or other chronic illnesses. Tell your doctor about any chronic medical problems you have. If you have medical records, bring them. (*See* the discussion of your medical history on pages 74 and 75.)

On your first visit, you will probably have a pelvic examination, which helps your doctor to determine if your uterus is the appropriate size for how far along you are in your pregnancy. A cervical smear is done if you have not had one in the last year, and other tests may be required. Tests are discussed in Chapter 9.

Normal Antenatal Care

In most cases, you will visit a doctor or midwife every four weeks for the first seven months, then every two weeks until the last month, then once a week. You may be scheduled for visits more frequently if necessary. On every visit, your weight and blood pressure should be checked to give valuable information about how your pregnancy is progressing.

Choosing a Doctor and a Hospital

You have a choice when it comes to selecting your obstetrician, family practitioner or midwife to oversee your antenatal care.

An *obstetrician* is a medical doctor who works in a maternity unit and specializes in the care of pregnant women, including delivering babies. He or she completed training in obstetrics and gynaecology after medical school.

A *perinatologist* is an obstetrician who specializes in high risk pregnancies. Only about 10 per cent of all pregnant women need to see a perinatologist. If you see a perinatologist, you may still be able to deliver your baby normally. You may have to deliver at a hospital other than the one you had chosen because of its specialized facilities or the availability of specialized tests for you or your baby.

A *family practitioner*, usually called a *general practitioner*, is a physician who provides care for the entire family. Some family practitioners deliver babies and are very experienced at it. If problems arise, your family practitioner may refer you to an obstetrician or perinatologist for antenatal care.

A *certified midwife* is a trained professional who cares for women with low-risk, uncomplicated pregnancies and delivers their babies. These professionals are registered nurses who have additional professional training and certification in midwifery. Supervised by a doctor, they will call him or her if antenatal or delivery complications occur.

A midwife may serve as your regular healthcare provider at antenatal visits, if your pregnancy is normal. They are certified by national organizations in their speciality and practise under rules and regulations under the supervision of a physician. They can provide antenatal care and family planning services. At delivery, a midwife, family practitioner or obstetrician delivers the baby.

If you have a maternity hospital you like, you may be all set. If you don't, ask your doctor for a referral. Ask friends who have recently had a baby about their hospital. Sometimes another doctor, such as a paediatrician, can advise you on a hospital.

Make an effort to communicate with your doctor so that you can comfortably ask him or her questions about your condition. Read articles and books such as this one and my other books, *Your Pregnancy Week-by-Week* and *Your Pregnancy Questions and Answers*. They will help you to prepare questions to ask your doctor. However, never substitute information you receive from other sources for information instructions or advice you receive from your own doctor. He or she knows you, your history and what has occurred during your pregnancy.

Don't be afraid to ask any question. Your doctor has probably already heard it, so there is no need to be embarrassed. Check out even the smallest details. Your doctor would be the first to tell you that it is better to ask a thousand 'silly' questions than to risk overlooking a single important one.

Your Health Affects Your Baby

Your health directly affects your baby's health and well-being. Some illnesses, diseases and conditions women experience during pregnancy can affect their babies; it is a good idea to be informed about them.

Asthma

Most women with asthma have a safe pregnancy. If you have had severe asthma attacks before pregnancy, you may have them during pregnancy. Usually you can use the medication you are accustomed to, but discuss the matter with your doctor.

I have found that many women feel better and have fewer problems with their asthma if they increase their fluid intake during pregnancy. Try it – you should increase your fluid intake during pregnancy anyway.

Cytomegalovirus

Cytomegalovirus (CMV) is a member of the herpes-virus family. It is transmitted in humans by contact with saliva or urine. Day care centres are a common source of the infection; CMV can also be passed by sexual contact. Most infections do not cause symptoms. However, when there are symptoms, they include fever, sore throat and joint pain.

Cytomegalovirus can affect a developing baby, causing low birth weight, developmental problems, jaundice, enlarged liver, enlarged spleen and anaemia, among other problems.

Diarrhoea during Pregnancy

Diarrhoea during pregnancy can raise concerns. If the diarrhoea does not go away in 24 hours, or if it keeps returning, contact your doctor. He or she may prescribe medication for the problem. Do not take medication for diarrhoea without discussing it with your doctor first.

One of the best things you can do for yourself if you experience diarrhoea during pregnancy is to increase your fluid intake. Drink a lot of water, juice and other clear fluids, such as broth. (Avoid apple juice and prune juice because they are laxatives.) You may be happier eating a bland diet, without solid foods, until you feel better.

It is all right to avoid solid food for a few days if you keep up your fluid intake. Solid foods may actually cause you more gastrointestinal distress when you have diarrhoea. Avoid milk products while you have diarrhoea; they can make it worse.

Epilepsy

Epilepsy can be a serious problem during pregnancy. If you suffer from the disease you should see your doctor and discuss management before becoming pregnant. If you become pregnant unexpectedly, call your physician immediately. Most medication to control seizures can be taken during pregnancy; however, some medicines are safer than others.

During pregnancy, phenobarbitone is often used to control seizures. Phenytoin (Dilantin) may not be the best drug for seizure control in pregnancy because it can cause birth defects if preconception folic-acid tablets have not been taken. Discuss this important issue with your doctor as soon as possible.

Some people have expressed concern about the safety of taking phenobarbitone during pregnancy. During pregnancy, phenobarbitone is used mainly to prevent seizures in women with a history of seizures or at the end of pregnancy to treat pre-eclampsia (toxaemia) and prevent seizures. If you take phenobarbitone, do not stop taking it without first checking with your physician. In most cases, doctors will administer the lowest possible amount of phenobarbitone to control seizures during pregnancy.

Fever

Fever commonly accompanies some illnesses. A fever, especially a high one, can be serious because your baby relies on you for its temperature control. A prolonged high fever, especially in the first trimester, may affect a developing fetus and cause limb (arm and leg) defects. To bring down a high fever, drink lots of liquids (1 pint of fluid a day for every degree above 98.6°F [37°C]), take paracetamol (Panadol) and dress appropriately to help you cool down. If your physician prescribes medication for an infection or other illness that may be causing the fever, take it as prescribed.

Fifth Disease (Parvo Virus 19)

Fifth disease, also called *parvo virus 19*, received its name because it was the fifth disease to be associated with a certain kind of rash. Fifth disease is a mild, moderately contagious airborne infection that spreads easily through groups, such as classrooms or day care centres.

The rash looks like skin reddening caused by a slap. Reddening fades and recurs, and can last from 2 to 34 days. There is no treatment for fifth disease, but it is important to distinguish it from rubella, especially if you are pregnant.

This virus is dangerous during pregnancy because it interferes with the production of red blood cells. If you believe you have been exposed to fifth disease during pregnancy, contact your doctor. A blood test will determine whether you have had the virus before; if you have, you are immune. If you have not, your doctor can monitor you to detect fetal problems. Some fetal problems can be dealt with before the baby is born.

Group-B Streptococcus Infection

Group-B streptococcus (GBS) infection is found in 15 to 35 per cent of all healthy women. GBS in a pregnant woman does not affect the fetus, but it is the most common cause of life-threatening infections in newborn, including pneumonia, meningitis, lung damage, kidney damage, loss of sight, hearing loss, cerebral palsy and developmental problems. The infection is transmitted to the baby during delivery.

GBS is often transmitted from person to person by sexual contact; it is found in the mouth or lower digestive, urinary or reproductive organs. In women, GBS is most often found in the vagina or rectum. It is possible to have GBS in your system and not have any symptoms.

We do not have an ideal screening test for GBS, but your doctor may recommend taking a swab of your vagina or rectum towards the end of the pregnancy. The culture test identifies 90 per cent of all women who will carry the bacteria at the time of birth. (Faster tests that can be used during labour to detect GBS are not as accurate.)

If you become at high risk during labour because of your symptoms or if you have had GBS recently or in the past, your doctor tests you at that time. He or she may administer antibiotics to help prevent transmission of the bacteria to your baby.

Hepatitis

Hepatitis, a viral infection of the liver, is one of the most serious infections that can occur during pregnancy. Your doctor will probably test you for hepatitis antibodies at the beginning of your pregnancy. Hepatitis B is responsible for nearly half of the cases of hepatitis. It is transmitted from one person to another by sexual contact and the reuse of intravenous needles. Symptoms include flu-like symptoms, nausea and pain in the liver area or upper right abdomen. The person may appear yellow or jaundiced, and urine may be darker than normal. This form of hepatitis is transmitted to the baby during birth or through breast-feeding.

If a mother tests positive for hepatitis during pregnancy, the baby may receive immune globulin to treat hepatitis after it is born. This is different from hepatitis vaccine. Hepatitis vaccine is given to *prevent* hepatitis from occurring. It is now recommended that all newborns receive hepatitis vaccine shortly after birth. Ask your doctor if the vaccine is available in your area.

Lyme Disease

Lyme disease is an infection carried and transmitted to humans by ticks, and it crosses the placenta. Complications include preterm labour, fetal death or a rashlike illness in the newborn.

The disease appears in stages. In most people, a skin lesion with a distinctive look, called a *bull's eye*, appears at the site of the bite. Flu-like symptoms appear next, and four to six weeks later, heart or neurological problems may develop. Arthritis may be a problem much later.

Treatment for Lyme disease includes long-term antibiotics. Many medicines used to treat Lyme disease are safe to use during pregnancy.

To avoid exposure to Lyme disease, you should refrain from going to places that are known to have ticks, such as heavily wooded areas. If you can't avoid these areas, wear long-sleeved shirts, long pants, socks and boots or closed shoes. Keep your head and hair covered with a hat or scarf. Check your hair for ticks; they often attach themselves to the hair or the scalp.

Rubella (German Measles)

Rubella is a viral infection that causes few problems in the non-pregnant woman. It is more serious during pregnancy, especially in the first trimester. There may be no symptoms, or you may have a rash or flu-like symptoms; the most common symptom of rubella is a skin rash. Rubella infection in a mother-to-be can increase the rate of miscarriage and cause malformations in the baby, especially heart defects.

One of the blood tests you have at your first or second antenatal visit is a rubella titre. It determine whether you have been vaccinated against rubella or if you have previously contracted the disease. Most women have had rubella, but if you have not, you will be vaccinated after pregnancy to safeguard you in the future.

Sickle-cell Anaemia

Sickle-cell anaemia occurs when a person's bone marrow makes abnormal red blood cells. It occurs most often in people of African and Mediterranean descent.

Sickle-cell anaemia can cause anaemia during pregnancy. It can cause abrupt pain in the abdomen or limbs of the pregnant woman, called a *sickle crisis*. (A sickle crisis can happen at any time in a woman's lifetime, not just during pregnancy.) In addition to a painful sickle crisis, the pregnant woman may suffer from infections more frequently and may even have congestive heart failure. Risks to the fetus include a higher incidence of miscarriage and stillbirth.

A relatively new treatment for sickle-cell disease relieves severe pain and is called *hydroxyurea*. It does pose some risk and is not for all sickle-cell sufferers. Because we do not know the long-term effects of the drug, women who are pregnant are advised not to use it.

Toxoplasmosis

Toxoplasmosis is a disease caused by the microbe *toxoplasma gondii*. It is spread by eating infected raw meat, drinking infected raw goat's milk, eating infected raw eggs, eating food that has been contaminated by insects or by contact with an infected cat or its faeces. You can pick up the protozoa from the cat's litter-box, from work surfaces or other surfaces the cat walks on or from the cat itself when you pet it.

Infection in the mother-to-be during pregnancy can lead to miscarriage or an infected baby at birth. Usually an infection in a pregnant women has no symptoms. An infected baby may appear normal at birth. Between 80 and 90 per cent develop serious eye infections months to years later. Some lose their hearing, suffer from mental retardation, experience seizures or have learning disabilities. Babies whose mothers had toxoplasmosis in the first trimester are usually the most severely affected. About 1 in 1,000 babies is born with toxoplasmosis.

To prevent transmission of the micro-organism, cook foods thoroughly and use hygienic measures in the kitchen. Get someone else to change the cat's litter. Keep cats off work surfaces, tables and other areas where you could pick up the microbe. Wash your hands thoroughly after every contact with your cat, and don't nuzzle or kiss it.

Varicella

Herpes is a family of viruses that includes the herpes-simplex virus, herpes varicella-zoster virus and cytomegalovirus. The word *varicella* is used interchangeably with chicken-pox. (It is also used to describe the rash seen with chicken-pox.) The term *herpes zoster* is used interchangeably with shingles.

When adults contract chicken-pox, they can become very ill. The most serious times for you to get chicken-pox are during the first trimester or around the time of delivery. The baby can get the virus during delivery, which can cause a serious infection.

Shingles occurs mainly in adults whose immune systems are deficient. During pregnancy, shingles can be a severe illness, with sharp pain and even breathing problems. Fortunately, it rarely occurs then. Exposure during the first trimester, when major organs are developing in the fetus, can cause defects such as heart problems.

Allergies

Allergy sufferers may notice that their allergies change with pregnancy. They may improve or get worse. If you have allergies, drink plenty of fluid, especially during hot weather.

You may have to treat your allergy problems differently during pregnancy. Before taking any medicine, ask your doctor or pharmacist whether it is safe to take during pregnancy; don't presume that it is all right to take it. If you ask before you use any medication, you will not have to sort out any problems later.

Nasal Congestion

Some women complain of nasal stuffiness during pregnancy. We believe this occurs because of circulation changes and hormone changes in pregnancy that can cause mucous membranes of the nose and nasal passages to swell and to bleed more easily.

Do not use decongestants or nasal sprays to relieve stuffiness without first checking with your doctor. Many preparations are combinations of several medications that should not be used during pregnancy. Use a humidifier instead. Increase your fluid intake and use a gentle lubricant, such as petroleum jelly, in nasal passages. Discuss the problem with your doctor if these remedies do not provide relief.

Anaemia

Anaemia is a common medical problem in pregnant women. Women who are anaemic don't have enough haemoglobin in their blood. Haemoglobin, the iron-containing pigment of red blood cells, is important because it carries life-sustaining oxygen to all the body's cells.

If you suffer from anaemia, you won't feel well during pregnancy. You will tire more easily. You may become dizzy. If you are anaemic during labour, you may need a blood transfusion after your baby is born. Pregnancy anaemia increases the risk of preterm delivery, growth retardation in the baby and low fetal birth weight.

Anaemia is a serious but preventable condition during pregnancy. If you are anaemic, your doctor can prescribe a course of treatment to deal with the problem.

Pregnancy Anaemia

Iron deficiency anaemia is caused or aggravated by the fetus' demands on your iron stores. While you are pregnant, your baby uses some of the iron stored in your body. Your body makes red blood cells but not enough of them, and you become iron deficient. Several factors can cause iron-deficiency anaemia. These include:

- bleeding during pregnancy
- multiple fetuses
- recent surgery on your stomach or small bowel
- frequent antacid use
- poor dietary habits

Iron deficiency anaemia is easy to control; iron is contained in most antenatal vitamins. If you can't take an antenatal vitamin, you may be given iron supplementation. Eating foods that are high in iron, such as a limited amount of liver or spinach, also helps.

Blood-sugar Problems

Pregnancy affects your blood-sugar levels; high blood sugar (hyperglycaemia) or low blood sugar (hypoglycaemia) can make you feel dizzy or faint. Many doctors routinely test pregnant women for blood-sugar imbalances during pregnancy. A blood-sugar problem caused by diet can be avoided or improved by eating balanced snacks and meals, by not skipping meals and by not going too long without eating.

Diabetes is a much more serious blood sugar condition. Doctors diagnose diabetes through a blood test called a *glucose tolerance test*. If you are diagnosed as having diabetes, you may be able to control it through dietary changes. A dietitian can help you. If diet changes alone are not enough, you may need insulin, which helps the body to process sugars. Your doctor or another specialist, usually a physician, prescribes this drug. *Also see* the discussion of gestational diabetes that begins on page 200.

Environmental Poisons

Be aware of your environment's effect on your health and that of your baby. Environmental poisons and pollutants that can harm a developing fetus include lead, mercury, PCBs (polychlorinated biphenyls) and pesticides.

Exposure to lead increases the chance of miscarriage. Lead is readily transported across the placenta to the baby; toxicity occurs as early as the twelfth week of pregnancy. Lead exposure may come from many sources, including some petrol, water pipes, solders, storage batteries, some construction materials, paints, dyes and wood preservatives. Workplace exposure is possible; find out if you are at risk.

Reports of mercury exposure have been linked to cerebral palsy and microcephaly. Exposure occurs with ingestion of contaminated fish; one report linked contaminated grain to mercury poisoning.

PCBs are mixtures of several chemical compounds used for industrial purposes. Most fish, birds and humans have small, measurable amounts of PCBs in their tissues. Humans are typically exposed through some of the foods we eat, such as fish. PCBs have been blamed for miscarriage and fetal-growth retardation.

Exposure to pesticides during pregnancy has been thought to be responsible for an increase in miscarriage rates and fetal growth retardation. Pesticides include a large number of agents. Human exposure is common because of the extensive use of pesticides; those of most concern include DDT, chlordane, heptachlor and lindane (Quellada). It is a good idea to stop using pesticides in your home and around your work area during pregnancy.

You may not be able to eliminate all contact with pesticides. To protect yourself against these agents, avoid exposure when possible. Thoroughly wash all fruits and vegetables before eating them. If you know that you will be near certain chemicals, wash your hands thoroughly after exposure.

Hypotension

It is normal for your blood pressure to change somewhat during pregnancy. It often decreases slightly during the second trimester and increases towards the end of pregnancy.

Hypotension (low blood pressure) during pregnancy can cause dizziness. The problem usually occurs during the second trimester for two reasons. First, an enlarging uterus puts pressure on the aorta and vena cava, major vessels leading away from and into the heart. Supine hypotension, a related condition, occurs when you lie down; it is alleviated or prevented by not sleeping or lying on your back.

Second, rising rapidly from a sitting, kneeling or squatting position causes postural hypotension. Your blood pressure drops when you get up rapidly, and gravity pulls blood toward your feet and away from your brain, making you light-headed. You can avoid postural hypotension by rising slowly from a sitting or a recumbent position.

Incompetent Cervix

An incompetent cervix describes a condition in which a woman's cervix dilates (stretches) prematurely. Usually the woman doesn't notice it. Membranes may rupture without warning, and the baby is usually delivered prematurely.

The problem is not usually diagnosed until after one or more deliveries of a premature baby without any pain before delivery. If it is your first pregnancy, you cannot know if you have an incompetent cervix.

Some researchers believe that the condition occurs because of previous trauma to the cervix, such as a miscarriage. It may occur if surgery has been performed on the cervix.

Treatment is usually surgical. A weak cervix can be reinformed by sewing the cervix shut, called a *cerclage*. At the end of the pregnancy or when the woman goes into labour, the surgical stitch is removed and the baby is born normally.

Rhesus Compatibility

If you have Rhesus-negative blood, you may require additional attention during pregnancy and after your baby is born. Your blood type contains a factor that determines if it is positive or negative. When you are 'Rhesus negative,' your blood contains the negative factor. Fifteen per cent of all women have Rhesus-negative blood.

In the past, a Rhesus-negative woman who carried a Rhesus-positive baby faced complications in pregnancy that could result in a very sick newborn. Today, many of these problems can be prevented.

When we did lab tests on Linda, we discovered that she was Rhesus-negative. Her mother was Rhesus-negative and had told Linda stories about pregnancy problems she had had 30 years before. Understandably, Linda was scared. I told her that years ago, it *was* a serious problem to be Rhesus-negative, but it is a problem we have solved. We had checked Linda for Rhesus-antibodies, and she was negative for them. I told her that we would check her again at 28 weeks and would give her anti-D immunoglobulin , a blood product, to help to ensure that she would not form antibodies during the last part of her pregnancy. If the baby was Rhesus-positive, we would give her the immunoglobulin again after the birth. I reassured Linda that it wasn't anything to worry about and explained that this is one reason we do all the blood tests that we do.

How It Occurs

Rhesus incompatibility occurs when a fetus inherits Rhesus-positive blood from its father; the mother, who is Rhesus-negative, develops antibodies to the fetus' antigens (substances that stimulate the body's immunities against antibodies). Antibodies are made only when the mother has Rhesus-negative blood and the fetus has Rhesus-positive blood. These antibodies circulate inside your system. They don't harm you, but they can cross the placenta and attack the blood cells of a Rhesus-positive fetus. This can lead to serious problems in the fetus, such as anaemia; however, it is rare.

If you are Rhesus-negative, you need to know it. You could become Rhesus-sensitized, also called *isoimmunized*, under many other circumstances. ('Rhesus-sensitized' means that your antibodies will recognize and attack your baby's Rhesus-positive blood.) These circumstances include:

- If you have had a blood transfusion with Rhesus-positive blood.

- If you received blood products of some kind.
  - during a previous pregnancy;
  - with a previous ectopic pregnancy;
  - when a previous pregnancy ended in miscarriage;
  - with a previous abortion.

The problem doesn't usually occur with a first pregnancy. A woman does not develop antibodies until her immune system comes in direct contact with Rhesus-positive blood. This usually does not happen until delivery, when the placenta separates from the uterus.

Treatment

Many problems can be prevented with the use of anti-D immunoglobulin. If you are Rhesus-negative and pregnant, you will be checked for antibodies at the beginning of pregnancy and at 28 weeks. An injection of the immunoglobulin is given at 28 weeks to prevent sensitization before delivery. It is also administered when you have amniocentesis, a miscarriage, an ectopic pregnancy, an abortion or bleeding during pregnancy.

Sometimes a baby needs a blood transfusion shortly after birth. In severe cases, transfusions are done *before* the baby is born.

Anti-D immunoglobulin is a blood product. If you have religious or ethical reasons for not using blood products, discuss the situation with your minister and your physician.

Some women have expressed concern about the risk of contracting hepatitis or HIV (the Aids virus), but no such problems have been reported. Donors for Rhesus-immunoglobulin are screened carefully to eliminate those in high risk groups for transmission of infectious diseases. Immune globulins have not been reported to transmit hepatitis, HIV/Aids or any other infectious diseases. If you are concerned, talk with your doctor.

If you baby is Rhesus-positive and you are Rhesus-negative, you will be given an injection of anti-D immunoglobulin within 72 hours after delivery. If your baby is Rhesus-negative, like you, an immunoglobulin injection is not necessary.

Sexually Transmitted Diseases

A sexually transmitted disease can be a serious health problem. Sexually transmitted diseases (STDs) are contracted during sexual activity, whether sexual, oral or anal intercourse. An STD during pregnancy can be even more serious because it can harm a developing fetus. If you have an STD, you must be treated as soon as possible!

Today, the incidence of STDs appear to be on the increase. As many as 1 in 5 Americans is currently infected with an STD. One out of every 20 American adults will contract an STD in the next 12 months. These conditions are not so widespread in Great Britain.

Sexually transmitted diseases are more common in women than in men. A woman is more susceptible to sexually transmitted diseases because her reproductive organs are inside her body, a fertile environment in which infections can grow. This also makes diagnosis in women more difficult than in men.

Left untreated, STDs can harm an unborn baby. Every year, thousands of babies are born early or suffer from infection because of undetected STDs passed to them by their mothers. Effects include early rupture of membranes, miscarriage, stillbirth and preterm birth. Other serious effects include blindness, mental retardation, neurological problems, brain damage and even death. In some cases, the effects are not evident until years after birth.

Some STDs are transmitted when the baby comes in contact with the virus during birth. Others are passed to the baby through the mother's blood and infect the baby during pregnancy or birth.

The most common sexually transmitted diseases include candidal vulvovaginitis, trichomonal vaginitis, condyloma acuminatum (venereal warts), genital herpes simplex infection, chlamydia, gonorrhoea, syphilis and HIV/Aids.

Some sexually transmitted diseases can be diagnosed and cured during pregnancy. With the exception of Aids, those that cannot be cured usually can be treated successfully. It is important to be tested for an STD if you believe that you might have been exposed. Discuss this important subject with your doctor.

Substance Use and Abuse

It is never too early to start thinking about how your every action will affect the baby growing inside you. Substance abuse is never healthy for you, but when you are pregnant, it can also harm your developing baby.

We usually cannot make exact statements about particular substances and their effects on the mother or developing baby. It is easier to identify substances that cause nutritional deficiencies and fetal growth problems than those that cause birth defects. However, much circumstantial evidence associates substance abuse with fetal problems.

Many substances that you normally use without adverse effects can adversely affect a developing fetus. Some substances readily cross the placenta and enter your baby's bloodstream, where they can cause problems. Alcohol, cigarette smoke and drugs are most dangerous for the fetus during the first trimester.

Cigarette Smoking

Cigarette smoke is the most commonly known harmful exposure in pregnancy, and it can have serious effects on a woman and her developing baby. Do stop smoking before or during pregnancy; fetal and infant mortality rates increase by more than 50 per cent in first-time pregnant women who smoke more than a packet of cigarettes a day.

Tobacco smoke contains harmful substances, including nicotine, carbon monoxide, hydrogen cyanide, tars, resins and some cancer-causing agents. When you inhale cigarette smoke, it crosses the placenta to your baby with all the additional substances, which may harm the fetus. The problem is so serious that warnings for pregnant women appear on some cigarette packages:

EC-Ministers of Health: SMOKING WHEN PREGNANT HARMS YOUR BABY

Effects of smoking on the fetus. A pregnant woman who smokes reduces a fetus' oxygen supply by as much as half because carbon monoxide in cigarette smoke displaces oxygen in the mother's bloodstream, and toxins in cigarette smoke narrow blood vessels. Smoking can damage the placenta and hinder the baby's growth.

Babies born to mothers who smoke may weigh less than other babies, which can cause problems. Increased incidence of reading disorders has been noted in children born to mothers who smoked during pregnancy. Hyperactivity (minimal-brain-dysfunction syndrome) is also more common in children born to women smokers.

If a woman smokes during pregnancy, the substances she inhales interfere with her body's absorption of vitamins B and C and folic acid, and increase her risk of pregnancy-related complications. Smoking has been associated with specific birth defects, including cleft palate, heart defects and neural tube defects, such as spina bifida.

Effects of smoking on the pregnant woman. Serious pregnancy complications are more common among pregnant women who smoke than among women who don't. The risk of developing placental abruption increases by 25 per cent in moderate smokers and 65 per cent in heavy smokers. Placenta praevia occurs 25 per cent more often in moderate smokers and 90 per cent more often in heavy smokers. (For further information on these problems, *see* pages 206 and 207.)

Cigarette smoking increases the risk of miscarriage, premature rupture of membranes and fetal death or death of a baby soon after birth. The risk is directly related to the number of cigarettes a woman smokes each day. The risk can increase as much as 35 per cent for a woman who smokes more than a packet of cigarettes a day.

The best thing to do is to quit smoking completely before and during pregnancy. If you can't quit totally, reduce the number of cigarettes you smoke to help to reduce the risks.

Effects of secondary smoke. Exposure to secondary smoke has been thought to increase a non-smoker's risk of giving birth to a low birth weight baby. Researchers have found significant levels of nicotine in the hair of newborn exposed to passive smoke for at least three hours a day during pregnancy. Ask your husband, family members, friends and co-workers to stop smoking around you while you are pregnant.

Alcohol

When you drink, so does your baby – the more you drink, the more your baby 'drinks'.

Alcohol use by a pregnant woman carries considerable risk to her developing baby. Alcohol inhibits the transport of amino acids and glucose in the placenta. The fetus is especially vulnerable to the effects of alcohol in early pregnancy.

Your developing baby may be harmed by an alcohol level that has little apparent effect on you. A fetus cannot metabolize alcohol as quickly as an adult, so alcohol remains in the fetus' system longer. Moderate use of alcohol has been linked to a greater risk of miscarriage. Studies show that spina bifida is up to 60 times more common in babies exposed to alcohol before birth than in babies that were not exposed to alcohol.

Before pregnancy, Ruth drank socially but she hadn't missed alcohol during her pregnancy. She felt that by abstaining from alcohol, she was doing something good for her baby. At a party, she was offered a glass of wine. The pregnancy was going well, and she hadn't had any problems; what would be the harm? She wasn't sure, so she decided to stay with fruit juice.

At her next visit with me, she wanted to know how much alcohol she could drink safely. I supported her in her decision not to drink during her pregnancy at all. I told her that no research has identified a 'safe' amount of alcohol to consume during pregnancy. The more we learn, the more it appears that even a little alcohol may be harmful.

The word is spreading about alcohol use during pregnancy. Today in North America, nearly 80 per cent of pregnant women abstain from alcohol during pregnancy.

Excessive alcohol consumption during pregnancy often results in abnormalities in the baby. However, drinking as little as two drinks a day has been thought to be associated with fetal alcohol effects. Chronic use of alcohol during pregnancy can lead to fetal alcohol syndrome (FAS), which is characterized by abnormal fetal development.

Fetal alcohol syndrome. Fetal alcohol syndrome (FAS) is a collection of problems that affect children born to alcoholic women. The complete syndrome occurs in 1 or 2 of every 600,000 births.

FAS is characterized by growth retardation before and after birth. Defects in the heart and limbs, and unusual facial characteristics, such as a short, upturned nose, a flat upper jawbone and 'different' eyes, have also been seen in FAS children. These children may have behavioural problems, impaired speech and impaired gross motor functions.

At this time, we don't know how much alcohol causes FAS, so I advise women that any amount of alcohol is too much. Most studies indicate that four or five drinks a day can cause some features of FAS, but mild abnormalities have been said to be associated with as little as two drinks a day (1oz [28g] of alcohol). It is best to avoid alcohol completely while you are pregnant.

Other facts about alcohol use. Taking drugs with alcohol increases the risk of damaging the fetus. Drugs that cause the greatest concern include analgesics, antidepressants and anticonvulsants.

Be very careful about substances you use that may contain alcohol. Over-the-counter cough medicines and cold remedies often contain alcohol – as much as 25 per cent of the preparation!

Drug Use and Abuse

Drug abuse usually refers to drugs prohibited by law, but it can also include recreational use of legal substances, such as alcohol, caffeine and tobacco. Legal medications, such as benzodiazepines or barbiturates, may also have harmful effects, whether they are used for legitimate or illegal reasons.

Drug use can affect your pregnancy greatly. A woman who abuses drugs may have more pregnancy complications because of her lifestyle. Women who abuse certain substances commonly display nutritional deficiencies; anaemia and fetal-growth retardation can occur as a result. A pregnant woman who abuses drugs may increase her risk of pre-eclampsia.

Marijuana. Marijuana contains tetrahydrocannabinol, which crosses the placenta and enters the baby's system. Exposure can cause attention-deficit disorders, memory problems and impaired decision-making ability in children; these problems can appear in a child between 3 and 12 years of age.

Central nervous system drugs. Central nervous system stimulants, such as amphetamines, are associated with an increase in cardiovascular defects in babies when they are used during pregnancy. These babies frequently show signs of withdrawal, poor feeding, seizures and other problems.

Tranquillizing agents include benzodiazepines (Valium and Librium) and newer agents. Heavy use in pregnancy is associated with infant withdrawal after birth.

Narcotics include morphine, pethidine, heroin and codeine. Habitual use can lead to physical dependence.

A pregnant woman who uses narcotics is subject to pre-eclampsia, preterm labour, growth problems in the fetus and narcotic withdrawal in a baby following birth. The incidence of cot death (sudden infant death syndrome – SIDS) is ten times higher among babies born to mothers who used narcotics during pregnancy than to babies whose mothers did not.

Intravenous drug use is frequently accompanied by health problems, such as Aids, hepatitis and endocarditis. Any of these problems is considered extremely serious during pregnancy.

One of the most difficult discussions I have had was with Sue. She came to see me for her yearly examination and cervical smear, and she was upset and discouraged. Adam, her 10-year-old pride and joy, was having trouble in school and had been diagnosed with attention deficit disorder. Her pregnancy had seemed to go all right ten years ago. She hadn't been able to talk about it then, but she said she had continued using cocaine through the first part of her pregnancy. She was now contemplating another pregnancy. Sue realized that although there was nothing she could do now to change her pregnancy with Adam, she would do things differently for this baby.

Mind-altering drugs. Hallucinogens, such as LSD, mescaline, hashish and peyote, are still used by many people. Phencyclidine (PCP, angel dust) falls into this group. It is thought that PCP may cause abnormal development in human babies, although it has not been definitely proved.

Cocaine and crack. Cocaine use definitely complicates a pregnancy. Often a user consumes the drug over a period of time, such as several days. During this time, the user may eat or drink very little, with serious consequences for a developing fetus.

Among other problems, continual use of cocaine or its stronger form, crack, can affect maternal nutrition and temperature control, which can harm the fetus. Cocaine use has been linked with miscarriage, preterm labour, bleeding complications, placental abruption and congenital defects. A woman who uses cocaine during the first 12 weeks of pregnancy faces an increased risk of miscarriage. Cocaine can damage the developing baby as early as three days after conception.

Infants born to mothers who use cocaine during pregnancy often have long-term mental deficiencies. Cot death (sudden infant death syndrome – SIDS) is more common among these babies. Many babies are stillborn.

Urinary Tract Infections

A urinary tract infection (UTI) refers to an infection anywhere along the urinary tract, which includes the bladder, the urethra, the ureters and the kidneys. Your doctor usually does a urine analysis and a urine culture for UTIs at your first visit. He or she may also check your urine for infections on subsequent visits.

UTIs are common during pregnancy because of the changes in a woman's urinary tract and increased pressure on the area. The uterus sits directly on top of the bladder and on the tubes, called *ureters*, that lead from the kidneys to the bladder. An enlarging uterus puts increasing pressure on the bladder and ureters.

Symptoms of a bladder infection include frequent or burning urination, blood in the urine (if the infection is severe) or the urge to urinate, although nothing comes out.

Pyelonephritis is an infection of the urinary tract that also involves the kidneys; it occurs in 1 to 2 per cent of all pregnant women. Symptoms of pyelonephritis include many of those associated with a bladder infection. The infection may require hospital admission and treatment with intravenous antibiotics.

Kidney stones occur about once in every 1,500 pregnancies. Symptoms usually include severe back pain and blood in the urine. In pregnancy, ultrasound is usually used to diagnose a kidney stone. A kidney stone in pregnancy is usually treated with pain-relieving drugs and by drinking lots of fluid or receiving intravenous fluids to hydrate you to enable you to pass the stone.

Genetic Counselling May Be Recommended

If you are older than 35, your doctor may recommend genetic counselling for you and your partner. This is different from your medical history. With genetic counselling, your doctor interprets information gathered from interviews, tests and health histories.

Genetic counselling seldom provides exact information. Instead, information is described in terms of percentages and odds. Most genetic counsellors will not tell you what to do; they provide you with information and support so that you can make your own decision.

Genetic counselling can help you to understand your current situation, its diagnosis and prognosis. It can help you in family planning and provide support to your family. Counsellors can help you to explore options for now and the future.

Genetic counselling is advised in a number of situations. It is usually recommended:

- if there is a family history of birth defects, mental retardation, chromosome abnormality or neurological disorders
- when the woman is 35 or older at the time of birth
- if a woman has had three or more miscarriages
- when a woman has been exposed to teratogens (environmental factors that are harmful to the fetus)
- with consanguinity (the couple is related)
- for high-risk ethnic groups

Genetic counselling is complicated and requires input from several different healthcare professionals. These professionals can include a medical geneticist, genetic counsellor, social worker, psychologist or psychiatrist, laboratory specialists, clergy, parent groups and others.

It is critical that you and your partner feel free to ask your genetic counsellor questions about the information you are given. This person can help you to use all the resources available and help you to understand what is involved in making important decisions.

As information is gathered, it may be necessary to share it with other members of your family. If a gene abnormality is identified, your sister, for example, will probably want to know about it before she starts her own family.

Incidence of Genetic Disease

The hoped-for and anticipated outcome for every pregnant couple and their healthcare provider is a normal, healthy infant. It is expected and taken for granted. However, that is not always the case – about 1 per cent of all babies born have a chromosome abnormality; 4 to 7 per cent of perinatal deaths (death after birth) are attributed to chromosome problems. Almost half of all first-trimester miscarriages are caused by some type of chromosome abnormality.

Among newborn, 3 to 5 per cent are born with a major congenital malformation, such as a heart defect; many of these birth defects are found to have a genetic component. In the USA, this represents more than 250,000 children each year.

Mental retardation is another area of concern; about 3 per cent of the general population is mentally retarded. It is estimated that 70 per cent of mental retardation is caused by genetic problems. Genetic counselling can offer an indication that some of these cases might occur.

Basic Genetics

Human cells contain 46 chromosomes each (diploid number); each sperm and each egg contain 23 chromosomes (haploid number). Chromosomes are composed of DNA and proteins that contain genes. Each cell contains 23 pairs of chromosomes – one chromosome of each pair is inherited from each parent. Of the 23 pairs, 22 are autosomes (non-sex chromosomes), and one pair is the sex chromosomes, X and Y. In a normal woman, the sex chromosomes are represented by two X (XX) chromosomes, and in the normal man by X and Y (XY) chromosomes.

Blood cells are usually used for chromosome analysis. Chromosomes are viewed through a microscope, then photographed and enlarged. They are then arranged in pairs, called a *karyotype*; a karyotype is used to identify abnormalities in the number of chromosomes.

With recent advances, individual chromosomes can also be examined for abnormalities. We have learned that too much chromosome material or too little chromosome material can cause an abnormality.

Preconception Counselling

In the past, genetic counselling was offered only after the birth of a child with a defect. With increased awareness and advances in technology, today we can provide couples with information before conception. The three major areas we focus on to provide a couple with information before they conceive include reproductive history, family history and consanguinity (you and your partner are related).

Reproductive History

When a genetic counsellor asks questions about your reproductive history, he or she seeks information on any type of pregnancy loss, miscarriage, stillbirth or perinatal death (death of the baby at the end of pregnancy or after birth). Other important information can include fertility problems, the type and duration of contraception and environmental exposures (as from your job). The information is evaluated so recommendations can be made.

Family History

Your family history can be important in determining a high risk situation. Information essential to your genetic counsellor includes a description of the health status of you, your partner and siblings, cause of death of any relatives, the age at death of these relatives and any birth defects in relatives. Your family history helps to identify abnormalities that occurred in the past in those related to you and helps to predict the likelihood of these defects occurring with your child.

Ethnic background can be an important aspect of family history. For example, if both partners are of Ashkenazi Jewish descent, there is an increased risk of giving birth to a baby with Tay-Sachs disease. Some people of African and Mediterranean descent are at an increased risk for having a baby with sickle-cell anaemia.

If you are unsure of all the information a family history requires, ask your parents and other family members for help. By working together, you will be able to provide the data necessary for the most thorough evaluation.

Consanguinity

Consanguinity (being related by birth to your partner, such as a cousin) can create problems. A related couple may have a very high risk of having a child with a genetic birth defect, especially if there is a family history of genetic defects. (First cousins have one-sixteenth of their genes in common.) If you are related to your partner, be sure to advise your genetic counselling team of the fact.

Antenatal Diagnosis

A couple should consider antenatal diagnosis in a variety of situations. These include:

- The mother is older than 35 at the time of delivery.
- A couple has previously given birth to a child with a chromosome abnormality.
- A family history of chromosome abnormalities.
- One parent has a chromosome abnormality.
- Either parent is a carrier of a chromosome disorder.
- There is a family history of neural tube defects (such as spina bifida).

Amniocentesis, ultrasound, chorionic villus sampling, fetoscopy and X-ray are all techniques that help to identify chromosome abnormalities. The tests are discussed in Chapter 9.

How Antenatal Diagnosis Can Help You

Antenatal testing does not guarantee the birth of a normal baby. It only provides information about malformations or disorders that can be specifically tested for. Some malformations cannot be found or are difficult to find before a baby is born, such as phenylketonuria, cleft lip and cleft palate.

Testing for a fetal abnormality allows for termination of a pregnancy, if that is desired. Sometimes an antenatal diagnosis may call for antenatal surgery in utero (in the uterus) to correct various conditions, such as kidney blockage or omphalocoele (congenital hernia of the navel).

Results learned from antenatal genetic counselling can be used to make special arrangements for care of the baby, if necessary, after it is born. Results may also influence which method of delivery is chosen.

Counselling and support of the couple or family can help to prepare them for what lies ahead after the baby's birth. This support can include social services, mental health counselling (psychiatrist, psychologist, social worker) and spiritual guidance.

For some couples, antenatal genetic counselling is the beginning of the grieving process over the loss of the 'perfect baby'. Counselling can help a couple to begin to deal with the possible death of the fetus or baby, or the challenges associated with a child with special needs.

Postconception Counselling

Counselling may be provided to a couple after the couple achieves pregnancy or after their baby is born. Some couples expecting a child have a specific reason for an antenatal diagnosis, as in the case of an older mother. In this situation, diagnostic testing is done during pregnancy.

When a couple gives birth to a child with a birth defect or a genetic disorder, genetic testing of the couple may be recommended after the birth, especially if they desire more children. Testing may alert the couple to problems that could arise in subsequent pregnancies.

Postnatal Diagnosis

Most infants with problems are identified at birth or shortly afterward. Babies born with genetic malformations or birth defects are usually grouped in one of three categories:

- Babies with obvious malformations at the time of birth.
- Babies who are 'sick' or have a difficult time immediately after birth.
- Babies who appear normal at birth but develop abnormalities later.

An important goal with postnatal diagnosis is an accurate diagnosis. Sources of information that are helpful in making a diagnosis include family history, laboratory results, physical examinations, pregnancy history (including medicines, complications and environmental exposures), growth and development history during the pregnancy and after the birth, and photographs of the baby.

The information can provide guidance about what lies ahead and various treatments that might be available. Genetic counselling after a baby is born with a birth defect is most helpful in answering the question, 'What are the chances of it happening again?'

If the risk of recurrence of a problem is low, some families choose to have more children. If the risk is high or if antenatal diagnosis is not available, a couple may decide not to have children or to choose sterilization.

In some cases, a couple may opt for donor insemination, if that might prevent a recurrence of a problem. This choice is not for every couple. Donor insemination uses donor sperm to achieve pregnancy. The partner's sperm is not used if he has a chromosome disorder or is a carrier of a chromosome disorder.

Your Medical History

To give you and your baby the best care possible, your doctor will ask you for a lot of information at your first antenatal visit. You can help your doctor a great deal by gathering the information before you meet.

Stilboestrol Use by Pregnant Woman's Mother

In the 1940s and 50s, a non-steroidal synthetic oestrogen, stilboestrol (DES) was given to some women to prevent miscarriage. The compound was even included in some antenatal vitamins. Research proved later that stilboestrol caused problems in some of the female offspring of women who used it. Daughters born to women given stilboestrol during the first trimester of their pregnancies have higher rates of vaginal cancer.

Stilboestrol has been shown to cause other problems for female offspring, including an increased risk of miscarriage and premature labour when the women become pregnant. A higher rate of ectopic pregnancy is blamed on stilboestrol-related fallopian tube deformities and uterine deformities. Stilboestrol affects uterine muscle development, resulting in an abnormally shaped uterus.

Because stilboestrol was prescribed in the 1940s and 50s, most affected women have passed through their years of conception. However, as an older pregnant woman, it could be significant for you.

Ask your mother if she knows if she received stilboestrol while she was pregnant with you. If you were exposed to stilboestrol through your mother being given the drug, some researchers recommend antenatal counselling before pregnancy about the risks of miscarriage, premature delivery and ectopic pregnancy.

Preparing Your Medical History

Check family records, and ask family members if anyone in the family has suffered from problems listed on pages 76 and 77. Be sure that your partner does the same with his family. This information may help your doctor to address potential problems.

> Ella didn't fill out all of the forms at her first clinic visit; she left the family history portion blank. She said she didn't realize that it mattered. We discussed how her family history could affect her and her pregnancy. The next month, she told me that she had spoken to her mother, and there was a family history of diabetes and twins, both important pieces of information for her pregnancy.

Medical History Chart

Directions: If a problem applies to you, your partner or another family member, tick the appropriate column.

Problem	You	Partner	Family
Aids/HIV	☐	☐	☐
Alcohol abuse	☐	☐	☐
Allergies	☐	☐	☐
Anaemia	☐	☐	☐
Cancer	☐	☐	☐
Cleft lip/palate	☐	☐	☐
Cystic fibrosis	☐	☐	☐
Diabetes	☐	☐	☐
Down's syndrome	☐	☐	☐
Drug abuse	☐	☐	☐
Epilepsy	☐	☐	☐
Group B streptococcus infections	☐	☐	☐
Genital herpes	☐	☐	☐
Haemophilia	☐	☐	☐
Heart disease	☐	☐	☐
Huntington's disease	☐	☐	☐

Problem	You	Partner	Family
Hypertension	☐	☐	☐
Miscarriage	☐	☐	☐
Multiple pregnancies	☐	☐	☐
Muscular dystrophy	☐	☐	☐
Rubella (German measles)	☐	☐	☐
Sexually transmitted diseases	☐	☐	☐
Sickle-cell anaemia	☐	☐	☐
Spina bifida	☐	☐	☐
Stilboestrol use by pregnant woman's mother	☐	☐	☐
Systemic lupus erythematosus	☐	☐	☐
Tay-Sachs disease	☐	☐	☐
Thyroid disease	☐	☐	☐
Urinary tract infections	☐	☐	☐

CHAPTER 7

How Your Body Changes during Pregnancy

Pregnancy is exciting, and it may be a little unsettling, too. You will see yourself change – your abdomen will grow, your breasts will enlarge, and hands and feet may swell, among other changes. If you are aware of these changes before they occur, you may be more comfortable with the situation.

During the first trimester, you may notice little change in yourself, although your baby is growing and changing quite rapidly. You may not even realize that you are pregnant until the middle or close to the end of this trimester. You gain little weight – probably no more than 5lb (2.3kg) for the entire 13 weeks. Your abdomen grows a little; you may be able to feel your uterus about 3in (8cm) below your belly-button. You won't feel the fetus move during this time.

During the second trimester, others begin to notice that you are pregnant. At the beginning of the second trimester, you will be able to feel your uterus about 3in (8cm) below your belly-button. By the end of the second trimester, you will feel your uterus about 3in (8cm) above your belly-button. Average weight gain at the end of this trimester is 9 to 20lb (4 to 9kg), including weight gained in the first trimester. During this time you will begin to feel your baby move!

The greatest change during the third trimester is the growth of your baby. By delivery, you will be able to feel the uterus $6\frac{1}{2}$ to 8 inches (16 to 20cm) above your belly-button. Your baby gains a great deal of weight during this time, although you may not. The average total weight gain for a normal weight woman by delivery is between 24 and 28lb (11–13kg).

Your abdominal muscles are stretched and pushed apart as your baby grows. Muscles attached to the lower portion of your ribs may separate

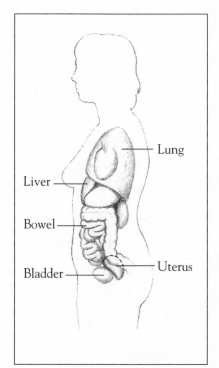
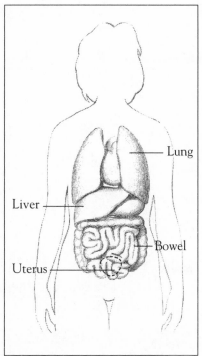

During the first trimester of pregnancy, you will notice very few changes in your body.

in the midline, called a *diastasis recti*. The condition isn't painful and does not harm the baby. Diastasis recti may still be present after the birth of your baby, but the separation will not be as noticeable. Exercising can strengthen the muscles, but a small bulge or gap may remain.

Skin Changes

Most women experience some changes in their skin while they are pregnant. Some women find that their skin becomes less oily and softer. Other women develop acne. Skin changes of this type are due to the hormones of pregnancy; skin usually returns to normal after your baby is born.

Many patients tell me they believe their skin becomes more alive and glowing while they are pregnant. While there is no medical fact to back this belief, I have seen women who do seem to 'glow' during pregnancy.

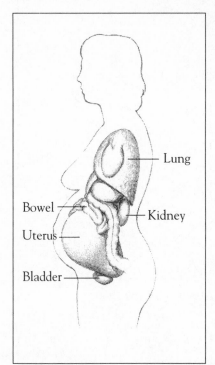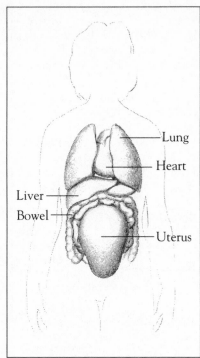

Your body undergoes fantastic changes later in pregnancy. Close to delivery, your uterus takes up a great deal of room and 'rearranges' various organs.

Surface Skin Changes

In some women, a vertical line appears along the midline of the abdomen, called the *linea nigra*. The linea nigra fades markedly after pregnancy but does not usually fully disappear.

Occasionally irregular brown patches appear on the face and neck of a pregnant woman, called *chloasma* or *mask of pregnancy*. We believe that this change is caused by the hormone changes of pregnancy. Usually dark patches disappear completely or get lighter after your baby is born. (Oral contraceptives can cause similar pigmentation changes.)

During pregnancy, you may develop small red elevations with branches extending outward on your skin. These changes are called *vascular spiders*, *telangiectasias* or *angiomas*. They usually occur on the face, neck, upper chest and arms. After pregnancy they will fade, but may not disappear completely.

The palms of your hands may turn red during your pregnancy. The condition is called *palmar erythema* and is fairly common. Palmar erythema is probably caused by increased oestrogen and has no other symptoms. It is safe to use lotions on your hands, but the redness may not disappear until after delivery. Vascular spiders and red palms often occur together.

Moles

Pregnancy can cause moles to appear for the first time or cause existing moles to grow larger and darken. If a mole changes, make sure that a doctor checks it.

Itching Skin

Itching, also called *pruritus gravidarum*, is a common problem that occurs later in pregnancy. About 20 per cent of all pregnant women suffer from it. The itching is harmless but can be annoying. As your uterus grows and fills your pelvis, abdominal skin and muscles stretch to accommodate it. Stretching the skin can cause itching.

Scratching can make itching worse. Use lotions to help reduce itching; occasionally cortisone creams may be advisable. Discuss it with your doctor if it continues to trouble you.

Stretch Marks

Stretch marks, also called *striae distensae*, or *striale gravidarum*, are areas of stretched skin that may become discoloured. Marks usually occur as your uterus grows larger and stretches abdominal skin. They can also occur on the breasts, hips or buttocks.

Stretch marks usually fade and aren't as noticeable after your pregnancy, but they don't disappear completely. To date, no one has found a reliable way of avoiding stretch marks. Women have tried many kinds of lotions with little success. There is certainly no harm in using lotion products, but they probably won't help.

Dental Care

Be sure that you have regular dental check-ups and take very good care of your teeth during pregnancy. Good dental care at this time is important because the hormone changes of pregnancy may cause dental problems.

If possible, avoid dental X-rays while you are pregnant. If you must have one, be sure that your abdomen and pelvis are completely shielded by a lead apron. Tell your dentist that you are pregnant when you check in at the surgery.

Pregnancy may cause sore, bleeding, swollen gums. Gums are more susceptible to irritation during pregnancy and may bleed more often when you brush your teeth. The condition usually clears up by itself after the baby is born. Talk to your dentist if the problem becomes uncomfortable.

You may develop small nodules on your gums that bleed when you brush your teeth or eat. This condition is called a *pyogenic granuloma* or *pregnancy tumour*. It usually clears up after pregnancy, but don't ignore it if it causes you problems.

Emotional Changes

Crying easily, mood swings, energy 'lows' and fatigue can be normal aspects of pregnancy. During the first trimester of pregnancy, hormone production increases to support your body's pregnancy needs. Some women are more sensitive to these changes, especially those who are sensitive to similar hormone shifts before menstruation. If you become weepy or edgy around your menstrual period, you may experience similar emotions as your body adjusts to pregnancy. Let your partner and other family members know that you may experience these mood swings.

Antidepressant medication is not usually prescribed during pregnancy because it is not considered safe. However, if it is necessary, most physicians prefer to use tricyclic antidepressants such as amitriptyline (Lentizol and Tryptizol). Treatment is always individualized to the patient. Your doctor and possibly a psychiatrist or psychologist will discuss the situation with you.

You may feel more emotional in your third trimester. Mood swings may occur more frequently, and you may be more irritable. You may be feeling anxious about the forthcoming labour and delivery. Relax and let go of your feelings. Talk to your partner about how you are feeling and what you are experiencing, and ask for his help and understanding. This may be a good time to practise relaxation exercises (*see* page 18).

Feeling Your Baby Move

One of the greatest joys of pregnancy is feeling your baby move inside you. It's a positive sign! The first time you feel your baby move is different for every woman. It can be different from one pregnancy to another.

When You First Feel Your Baby Move

Many women describe the first feelings of fetal movement as a gas bubble or fluttering in their abdomen. It may be something you notice for a few days before you realize what it is. Movements become more common and occur fairly frequently – that's how you will know that what you are feeling is your baby moving. Movement can be felt below your belly-button. If it is your first baby, it may be 19 or 20 weeks before you are sure that you feel the baby move.

At first you probably won't feel your baby move every day – that's normal. As your baby grows, movements become stronger and probably more regular.

Babies' Movements Are Different

The movement of every baby is different. One baby will move less than another. If your baby has been very active, then is very quiet for a long while, you may want to discuss it with your doctor. He or she will determine if there is cause for concern.

Some women complain that their baby is extremely active during the night, and it keeps them awake. There really isn't much you can do about it, but you can try to change your position in bed. Avoid exercising just before bed – it may cause your baby to move more. Taking paracetamol (Panadol) or relaxing in a warm (not hot) bath may help. Between 20 and 32 weeks of pregnancy, the fetus can move between 200 and 500 times a day, kicking, rolling or wiggling!

> When Veronica came in for her 28-week visit, she was tired and concerned. She had been up all night because the baby was kicking her. She wanted to know if this was all right. Was it a bad sign about the baby? Could it be moving too much? I reassured her that this wasn't bad and told her that I'd rather have a baby move a lot than not enough.

Occasionally you might feel pain or pressure from your baby's position in the uterus. For relief, rest on your opposite side for a while. For example, if you feel pressure under your right ribs, lie on your left side.

I have had women ask if some of the pressure they feel low in the uterus means that the baby is falling out of the birth canal. Your baby can't 'fall out' of the birth canal. If you experience this sensation, what you are probably feeling is the pressure of your baby as it moves lower in the birth canal. If this occurs, tell your doctor about it. He or she may want to do a pelvic examination to check how low the baby's head is.

A doctor may ask a pregnant woman to monitor the baby's movements if she has had a difficult pregnancy, if she had a previous childbirth or if she has a medical condition, such as diabetes. Recording the movements at certain times each day may provide the doctor with additional information about the baby's status.

Some Discomforts of Pregnancy

Along with the many joys of pregnancy, there are some discomforts. Most of the them are minor (although it may not seem that way at the time!). At the beginning of pregnancy, you may have the urge to urinate frequently. As you progress through pregnancy, you may have to deal with constipation. Towards the end of pregnancy, swollen hands and feet may be a problem, along with more frequent heartburn. Let's look at some of these common complaints and see what you can do to relieve them.

Uterine Tightening

Your uterus tightens and contracts throughout pregnancy. (If you don't feel this, don't worry.) As your uterus grows, you may feel slight cramping or even pain in the lower abdominal area, on your sides; this is normal. However, if contractions are accompanied by bleeding from the vagina, *call your doctor immediately.*

Braxton-Hicks contractions during pregnancy are painless, non-rhythmical contractions you may feel when you place your hands on your abdomen. You may also feel them in the uterus itself. These contractions may begin early in pregnancy and are felt at irregular intervals throughout pregnancy. They are *not* signs of true labour.

Some women experience tingling, numbness or pressure in the uterine area or abdomen. These feelings are associated with increased pressure as the baby moves lower in the birth canal. To help decrease pressure in your pelvic area, lie on your left side. This position helps to relieve pressure on pelvic nerves, veins and arteries.

Round Ligament Pain

Round ligaments lie on either side of the uterus; as your uterus gets bigger, these ligaments stretch, becoming longer and thicker. Quick movements can overstretch the ligaments, causing round ligament pain. This is not harmful to you or your baby, but it can be uncomfortable.

Be careful about making quick movements. If you feel pain, lie down and rest. Most doctors recommend paracetamol (Panadol) if the pain bothers you. Tell your doctor if it gets worse.

Urinary Discomfort

One of the first symptoms of early pregnancy is frequent urination. The problem continues off and on throughout pregnancy; you may have to go to the bathroom at night when you never did before. It usually lessens during the second trimester, then returns during the third trimester, when the growing baby puts pressure on the bladder.

Some women experience urinary-tract infections during pregnancy; they are also called *bladder infections, cystitis* and *UTIs. See* the discussion of urinary problems beginning on page 68.

You will do yourself a favour by not 'holding' your urine. Empty your bladder as soon as you feel the need. Drink plenty of fluids; cranberry juice helps to kill bacteria and may help you to avoid infections. For some women, urinating after having intercourse is helpful.

During pregnancy, urinary tract infections may cause premature labour and low birth weight infants. If you think you have an infection, discuss it with your doctor. If you do, take the entire course of antibiotics prescribed for you.

Increased Vaginal Discharge

It is normal to notice an increase in vaginal discharge or vaginal secretion during pregnancy. It is called *leucorrhoea*. The discharge is usually white or yellow and fairly thick; it is not an infection. We believe that the discharge is caused by the increased blood flow to the skin and muscles around the vagina.

Do not douche if you have a heavy vaginal discharge during pregnancy. Wear sanitary pads if necessary. Avoid wearing tights and nylon underwear – choose underwear with a cotton lining.

The discharge that accompanies a vaginal infection is often

foul-smelling, has a greenish or yellowish colour, and causes itching or irritation around or inside the vagina. If you have these symptoms, notify your doctor. Treatment is often possible; many medicinal creams and ointments are safe to use during pregnancy.

Other Changes

Changes in your hair are often triggered by pregnancy hormones circulating through your body. You may notice less hair loss than usual. After your baby is born, the hair you retained during pregnancy falls out. If it happens to you, don't worry about it – you're not going bald!

The same hormones that encourage the growth of your hair also influence your nails. You may find during pregnancy that you have problems keeping your nails filed to a practical length. Enjoy them!

Some women find they experience increased facial hair during pregnancy. Usually it is not a problem, but check with your doctor if it worries you. Facial hair will probably disappear or decrease after pregnancy, so wait before making any decisions about permanent hair removal.

Pregnancy hormones can elevate your body temperature slightly, which may lead to greater perspiration. If you perspire heavily, keep up your fluids to avoid dehydration.

Breast Changes

Your breasts undergo many changes during pregnancy. After about eight weeks, breasts normally start to get larger; you may notice that they are lumpy or nodular. Tenderness, tingling and breast soreness early in pregnancy are common. These are all normal changes at this time.

Your breasts may change colour slightly. Before pregnancy, the areola (the area surrounding the nipple) is usually pink, but it can turn brown or red-brown and may enlarge during pregnancy and lactation.

During the second trimester, a thin yellow fluid called *colostrum* is formed; it is the precursor to breast milk. Sometimes it leaks from the breasts or it can be expressed by squeezing the nipples. This is normal. Leave your breasts alone; don't express the fluid.

Inverted Nipples

Some women have inverted nipples, which are flat or retract (invert) into the breast. Women with inverted nipples may find it more difficult to breast-feed, but breast-feeding is not impossible.

To determine if you have inverted nipples, place your thumb and index finger on the areola, the dark area surrounding the nipple. Gently compress the base of the nipple; if it flattens or retracts into the breast, you have inverted nipples.

Plastic breast shells worn under your bra during the last few weeks of pregnancy create a slight pressure at the base of the nipple that helps to draw out the nipple. Ask your doctor or midwife for further information.

Lightening

Often a few weeks before labour begins or at the beginning of labour, the head of your baby begins to enter the birth canal, and your uterus seems to 'drop' a bit. This is called *lightening*. Don't be concerned if it happens to you.

A benefit of lightening is that it allows you more room to breathe. As your baby descends into the birth canal, you may notice more pressure in your pelvis, bladder and rectum, which can be uncomfortable.

When Your Doctor Measures Your Abdomen

As you progress in your pregnancy, your doctor needs a point of reference from which to measure the growth of your uterus. Some doctors measure from the belly-button. Some measure from the pubis symphysis, the place where pubic bones meet in the middle – in the lower part of your abdomen.

These measurements can reveal a great deal. A higher than expected measurement at 20 weeks, for example, may alert your doctor to the possibility of twins or an incorrect due date. A lower than expected measurement at this point may mean that your due date is wrong or that there may be some other problem. In either case, your doctor would probably have you evaluated further by ultrasound.

CHAPTER 8

How Your Baby Grows and Develops

During the time your baby grows inside your uterus, it goes through the most incredible changes of its life. From a few small cells, it grows into a fully developed baby.

The first 13 weeks of pregnancy represents the most critical period of development for the fetus. During this time, the fetus is most susceptible to effects from outside influences, such as medicines you may take or other substances you might ingest or be exposed to.

By the end of the first half of your pregnancy – 20 weeks – your baby has developed nearly all of its organs. During the last half of pregnancy, these organs mature, and your baby grows and gains weight, until it is ready to be born.

Your baby goes through an early period of development, sometimes called *embryonic development*, which lasts from fertilization through week 8 of fetal development. The *fetal development* period lasts from week 9 of fetal development until your baby is born.

Normal Fetal Development

During the first eight weeks of pregnancy, your baby is sometimes called an *embryo*. During the rest of your pregnancy, the developing baby is referred to as a *fetus*.

Trimesters of Pregnancy

Your pregnancy is divided into 13-week periods called *trimesters*. The first trimester is the one of greatest change for the developing baby. During this time, your baby grows from a collection of cells the size of the head of a pin to a fetus the size of a grapefruit. Organs begin to develop, and your baby begins to look like a baby.

At the beginning of the second trimester, your baby weighs less than 1oz (28g) and is only about 4in (10cm) long. By the beginning of the third trimester, he or she is almost 16in (40cm) long and weighs more than 2lb (1kg). At delivery, your baby will weigh close to 7¹/₂lb (3.4kg) and be about 21¹/₂in (55cm) long.

Very few, if any, structures in the fetus are formed after the twelfth week of pregnancy. This means that your baby has formed all of its major organ systems by the end of the first trimester. However, these structures continue to grow until your baby is born.

If a baby is born before 37 weeks of pregnancy, it is called a *preterm baby*. A fetus born between 37 and 42 weeks of pregnancy is called a *term baby* or a *full term baby*. A baby delivered after 42 weeks of pregnancy is called a *postdates baby* (*see* page 249).

Your Baby's Sex

The sex of the baby is determined at conception. If a sperm carrying a Y chromosome fertilizes the egg, a male child is created. A sperm carrying an X chromosome results in a female child.

The Baby's Size

Sometimes my patients express concern about giving birth to a large baby. Many factors affect how big your baby will be. If you are in good health, have no medical problems and take good care of yourself during pregnancy, you will probably have an average-size baby. Although weight varies greatly from baby to baby, the average baby at term weighs 7 to 7¹/₂lb (3.2 to 3.4kg).

> Sally said she weighed 9lb at birth, and all her brothers and sisters were big, too. She was worried that her baby would be too big, and she would need a caesarean section. I reassured her that her pregnancy growth had been normal and told her it was difficult to estimate the size of the baby. She laughed and relaxed a little when I told her that if 100 doctors tried to guess the weight of her baby, the guesses would range from 6 to 8lb. When she delivered the baby, it weighed 8lb and Sally did fine.

Some factors do affect the size of a baby at birth, including hypertension and diabetes, which are more common in older pregnant women. Hypertension during pregnancy causes intra-uterine growth retardation, which results in smaller babies. Diabetes can influence the development of a larger or smaller baby. Blood sugar levels are higher in those with gestational diabetes or mild diabetes that is not controlled. Diabetes exposes the baby to higher sugar levels, and larger babies are the result. In cases of insulin-dependent diabetes, the result may be a smaller baby. Women with insulin-dependent diabetes may have circulation problems, which can result in decreased blood flow to the baby and intra-uterine growth retardation.

Can a Baby Hear Inside the Womb?

A baby can hear inside the womb. It may be similar to living near a busy airport – the developing baby hears a constant murmur of digestive noises and the maternal heart beat. The fetus hears its mother's voice, too, but it may not hear higher pitched tones.

There is evidence that by the third trimester the fetus responds to the sounds it hears. Researchers have noted fetal heart rate increases in response to tones heard through the mother's abdomen.

Newborns have been found to prefer their mother's voice to a stranger's, which suggests that they recognize her voice. They have also been found to prefer their mother's native language, and they respond strongly to a recording of an intra-uterine heart beat.

Too much noise may be harmful to an unborn baby. A baby exposed *in utero* to noise levels between 85 and 95 decibels (common at rock concerts and dance clubs) is three times more likely to suffer from high frequency hearing loss.

The Fetal Environment

Your baby is growing and developing inside a complex system within your body. There are three major parts to this system, and each relies upon the others to work together as a complete unit. Your baby's first home consists of the placenta, the umbilical cord and the amniotic sac. Together they provide nourishment, warmth and protection while your baby matures and prepares to live on its own, outside your uterus.

The Placenta

The placenta is a soft, round or oval organ that grows with your baby. At 10 weeks, it weighs about $^1/_2$oz (14g); by the time your baby is born, its weight has multiplied almost sixtyfold to about 1½lb (700g).

When the early pregnancy implants in your uterus, the placenta grows and sends blood vessels into the uterine wall. These blood vessels remove nourishment and oxygen from your blood for use by your baby. Your baby's waste products pass back into your bloodstream through these vessels for disposal by your body.

We once believed that the placenta acted as a barrier to all outside substances, but we know that this is not the case. In some instances, the placenta cannot keep your baby from being exposed to substances that you are exposed to or that you ingest. We know that alcohol, most medicines, other substances (such as nicotine) and many vitamins and minerals cross the placenta to your baby. This is one reason that women are warned to avoid various substances during pregnancy.

The placenta is important to your pregnancy and remains so until the birth of your baby. At that time, when your uterus begins to shrink after your baby is born, the placenta detaches from it and is delivered on its own.

The Umbilical Cord

The umbilical cord is the connection between your baby and the placenta. It is usually about 24in (60cm) long. The cord is grey or white, coiled or lumpy, and contains two arteries that carry the baby's blood to the placenta, where it absorbs oxygen and nutrients. A vein in the umbilical cord carries blood and nutrients back to the baby.

Occasionally knots form in an umbilical cord, but it is unusual. Doctors believe that knots form as the baby moves around early in pregnancy. A loop forms in the umbilical cord, and when the baby moves through the loop, a knot is completed. You can't do anything to prevent it.

You may have heard about saving blood from your baby's umbilical cord for future use. Umbilical cord blood banking is a fairly new technology that is not available everywhere. Since 1989, cord blood has been used as an alternative to bone marrow transplants. Cord blood has been used to treat some forms of anaemia (such as Fanconi's anaemia), Wiskott-Aldrich syndrome, Hunter's syndrome, some forms of leukaemia, neuroblastoma and breast cancer. Talk with your doctor about cord-blood banking if you are interested in learning more.

The Amniotic Sac

The amniotic sac is a bag inside your uterus that contains your baby and the amniotic fluid that surrounds it. Early in pregnancy, amniotic fluid comes from the amniotic membrane that covers the placenta and cord. Later in pregnancy, the fluid is partly composed of fetal urine and fluid excreted by fetal lungs.

As your pregnancy progresses, the amount of amniotic fluid produced increases. This continues until close to the time of delivery, when it begins to decrease.

Amniotic fluid keeps the sac from collapsing and enables the baby to move around so that muscles and joints can develop. Fluid regulates temperature and cushions the fetus from injury. It also helps a baby's lungs to mature as fluid passes into and out of fetal lungs when the baby's chest moves in and out.

By 21 weeks, the fetal digestive system has developed enough to enable the fetus to swallow the fluid. The fetus absorbs much of the water contained in the swallowed fluid.

Swallowing amniotic fluid may encourage development of the fetal digestive system. It may condition the digestive system to function after birth. By term, a baby may swallow large amounts of amniotic fluid, as much as 18fl oz (500ml) of amniotic fluid in 24 hours.

Amniotic fluid is an important gauge of fetal well-being. If you have amniocentesis, amniotic fluid is removed from your uterus for study. The amount of fluid can also be an indication of fetal health; ultrasound is used to evaluate the amount of fluid in the sac. Too much fluid may indicate a malformation in the spinal cord or digestive system. Too little may signal fetal bladder or kidney problems.

The Presence of Meconium

The term *meconium* refers to undigested debris from swallowed amniotic fluid in the fetal digestive system. Meconium is a greenish-black to light-brown substance that your baby may pass from its bowels into the amniotic fluid. This can happen before or at the time of delivery.

The presence of meconium in amniotic fluid may be caused by fetal distress. When meconium is present, it does not always mean distress, but the possibility must be considered. Meconium in the amniotic fluid can be swallowed by the baby just before birth or at the time of birth. If it is inhaled into the lungs, meconium may cause pneumonia or pneumonitis.

Meconium can be detected when your water breaks. Before then, the only way to know about it is by amniocentesis. If meconium is present at the time of delivery, an attempt is made to remove it from the baby's mouth and throat with a small suction tube so that the baby will not swallow it.

Problems for the Developing Fetus

The embryonic period (the first eight weeks of the baby's growth) is a time of extremely important development for your baby. During this time, the embryo is most susceptible to factors that can interfere with its development. Most malformations originate during this period.

Teratogenic Effects on a Fetus

Teratology is the study of abnormal fetal development. When a birth defect occurs, we want to know why it happened. This can be frustrating because in most instances we are unable to determine a cause. A substance that has been identified as causing birth defects is called a *teratogen* or is said to be *teratogenic*.

Some things that have a bad effect (are teratogenic) at one point in pregnancy are safe at other times. The most critical period appears to be early in pregnancy, during the first trimester or first 13 weeks. Rubella is an example. If the fetus is infected during the first trimester, abnormalities such as heart defects can occur. Infection later can be less serious for the fetus. The box overleaf shows critical periods of fetal development (gestational age).

Maternal Medicine Use

Some medicines a pregnant woman takes can harm a developing fetus; other are safe at any time during pregnancy. Still others are safe for one part of pregnancy but not advised for another. It is best to avoid medicines during pregnancy unless you discuss them with your doctor first. *See* the discussion of medication during pregnancy that begins on page 177.

Premature Birth

It is hard to believe, but today a baby born at only 25 weeks gestational age may survive. Some of the greatest advances in medicine have been

Critical Periods of Fetal Development	
Time Period **Gestational Age**	**Fetal Development Affected**
3 to 5½ weeks	Central nervous system
3½ to 5½ weeks	Heart
3½ to 7 weeks	Upper and lower limbs
3½ to 7½ weeks	Eyes
3½ to 8½ weeks	Ears
5½ to 8 weeks	Teeth
5½ to 8½ weeks	Palate
6½ to 9 weeks	External genitalia
20 to 36 weeks	Brain

in the care of premature babies. Because of advances in technology, fewer than 10 deaths per 1,000 are reported in premature births.

However, babies born extremely early are in the hospital a long time and often have serious problems. Physical and mental handicaps are more common in babies born too prematurely. The average hospital stay for a very premature baby in 1997 ranges from 50 days to more than 100 days.

Intra-uterine Growth Retardation

Intra-uterine growth retardation (IUGR) means that a newborn baby is small for its gestational age. By medical definition, the baby's weight is 'below the 10th percentile' for the baby's gestational age. This means that 9 out of 10 babies of the same gestational age are larger.

The word 'retardation' frequently causes prospective parents some concern. Retardation in this sense does not apply to the development or function of the baby's brain. It means that the growth is slow ('retarded'), and the fetus is inappropriately small.

Causes of Intra-uterine Growth Retardation

Conditions that increase the chance of IUGR include:

• maternal anaemia

- maternal smoking during pregnancy
- poor weight gain by the mother
- maternal vascular disease, including high blood pressure
- maternal kidney disease
- alcoholism or drug abuse by the pregnant woman
- multiple fetuses
- fetal infections
- abnormalities in the umbilical cord or the placenta

A small woman is more likely to have a small baby, but this would probably not be a cause for alarm. A woman who has previously delivered a very small baby is more likely to do so in subsequent pregnancies.

IUGR is usually suspected when the size of the uterus does not change over a period of time. If you measure 10.5in (27cm) at 27 weeks of pregnancy and at 31 weeks you measure 11in (28cm), your doctor might want to look into the situation. Checking for IUGR is one important reason to keep all your antenatal appointments.

Risks with IUGR

The greatest risk associated with IUGR is stillbirth (the baby dies before delivery). Delivery of the baby before full term may be required to avoid this serious problem. The baby may be safer outside the uterus than inside. Because infants with IUGR often do not tolerate labour well, a caesarean section delivery is more likely.

Hydrocephalus

Hydrocephalus causes an enlargement of the fetus' head. It occurs in about 1 in 2,000 babies and is responsible for about 12 per cent of all severe fetal malformations found at birth.

The organization and development of the brain and central nervous system of the baby begin early. Cerebral spinal fluid circulates around the brain and spinal cord, and must be able to flow without restriction. If openings are blocked and the flow of fluid is restricted, it can cause hydrocephalus (sometimes called *water on the brain*). Fluid accumulates and the baby's head becomes enlarged.

Hydrocephalus is only a symptom, and it can have several causes. Once hydrocephalus is diagnosed, a cause is sought; these causes include spina bifida, meningomyelocoele and omphalocoele.

Sometimes intra-uterine treatment – performed while the fetus is still in the uterus – is possible. See the discussion in the following section.

Antenatal Treatment

In this discussion, 'antenatal treatment' refers to treatment of the baby, not treatment of the pregnant woman. Today, physicians can treat many fetal problems before a baby is born. Some procedures that are available today were unknown even a few years ago.

Treatment of a fetus *in utero* has proved to be a valuable tool in saving the lives of some babies. Today, abut ten specific problems can be dealt with by treatment of the fetus *in utero* or with fetal surgery.

Transfusions before Birth

The earliest form of *in utero* treatment was done in 1963 and involved blood transfusions to fetuses with a life-threatening form of anaemia. Today we have developed more refined blood transfusion techniques. Cordocentesis is a transfusion procedure by which blood is introduced directly into the fetal bloodstream, through the umbilical cord. *See* page 109 for a detailed discussion.

Antenatal Medication in Utero

The greatest use of medication *in utero* is to hasten development of fetal lungs. If you are at high risk for a preterm birth, your doctor may recommend this treatment to ensure that your baby's lungs are adequately developed before birth. If a baby is born before its lungs are mature, it can develop respiratory distress syndrome.

If your doctor believes that you are at risk of delivering your baby before 34 weeks of pregnancy, you may be advised to receive injections of corticosteroids. This medication passes from your bloodstream into the fetus' bloodstream, reducing the risk of infant death or the risk of complications, such as breathing problems. It appears safe for both mother and fetus.

A less common problem that can be treated before birth with medication is a heart-rhythm disturbance. One of a number of drugs is given to the mother to treat her baby. In some cases, doctors deliver medication directly to the fetus via cordocentesis.

Other problems for which cordocentesis is used include inherited inborn errors of body chemistry. Treatment of these problems with medication given to the mother has been very successful.

Fetal Surgery

Fetal surgery can treat various problems while the baby is still growing inside the mother. Open surgery or closed-uterus surgery may be performed.

Most operations on the fetus, whether open or closed-uterus, are not performed until around 28 weeks of pregnancy. The operations treat a variety of problems, including urinary-tract blockages, tumours and fluid in the lungs.

Open surgery. With open surgery, the surgeon makes a caesarean section-like incision in the mother's abdomen and partially removes the fetus. The fetus is operated upon and returned to the uterus. The surgery carries risks for mother and baby, and only about 50 have been performed since the first one was done in 1981. One problem with open surgery is that it may stimulate uterine contractions, which can lead to premature birth. The surgery exposes the mother to all the risks of surgery, including anaesthesia problems and infections. After open surgery, the mother must have a caesarean section delivery.

Closed-uterus surgery. Closed-uterus procedures are more common than open surgery today. With this approach, a needle-thin, fibre optic instrument is guided by miniature cameras into the fetus' body. The fetus remains inside the uterus. The most successful closed-uterus operations are associated with the opening of urinary tract blockages.

CHAPTER 9

Tests for You and Your Baby

Tests for you and your baby during pregnancy are an important part of antenatal care. From weighing you to amniocentesis, every test provides your doctor with information. Doctors use the information to plan the best course of treatment for you and your developing baby. Tests described in this chapter can help reassure you that your baby is doing well as it develops and that anything that might need to be done, can be done.

Pregnancy Tests

The first challenge of pregnancy may be to find out if you really are pregnant! Before you invest in a home pregnancy test or go to your doctor's surgery to have a pregnancy test, look for the signs and symptoms of pregnancy, which include:

- missed menstrual period
- nausea, with or without vomiting
- fatigue
- breast changes and breast tenderness
- frequent urination

If you think that you are pregnant, then have a home pregnancy test. If the test is positive, contact your doctor to make your first antenatal appointment. Pregnancy tests have become increasingly sensitive and can show positive results even before you miss a menstrual period. Most tests are positive seven to ten days after you conceive. Most doctors recommend that you wait until you miss your period before having a test to save you money and emotional energy.

A special type of pregnancy test, called a *quantitative HCG test*, is a blood test done in the first trimester; it is ordered when there is concern about miscarriage or ectopic pregnancy. The test measures the hormone HCG (human chorionic gonadotropin), which the pregnancy produces early in pregnancy in rapidly increasing amounts. Two or more tests done a few days apart identify the change in the amount of the hormone. An ultrasound scan may also be done.

Tests at Your First Antenatal Visit

Your doctor will probably order a battery of tests during your first or second visit. These may include:

- a complete blood count to check the amount of iron and to look for infections
- urine analysis and culture
- a test for syphilis
- cervical cultures, as indicated
- rubella titres, for immunity against rubella
- blood type
- rhesus-factor
- a test for hepatitis-B antibodies
- alpha-fetoprotein
- cervical smear

The results of these tests give your doctor the information that he or she needs to provide the best care for you. For example, if testing shows that you have never had rubella (German measles) or rubella vaccine, you know that you need to avoid exposure during this pregnancy and receive the vaccine before your next pregnancy. *See* the discussion about rubella starting on page 55.

Later in pregnancy, your doctor may repeat some tests or order new tests. For example, the 28th week of pregnancy is the best time to pick up blood sugar problems.

Routine Tests

Every time you visit your clinic during your pregnancy, you are weighed and your blood pressure is checked. Simple as they are, these two tests provide your doctor with a great deal of information. Checking your weight is an easy way to check your well-being. Not gaining enough weight, or gaining too much, can indicate problems. High blood pressure (hypertension), discussed on pages 203 to 204, can be very significant during pregnancy, especially as you near your due date. By taking your blood pressure throughout the pregnancy, your doctor establishes what is normal for you. Changes in blood pressure readings alert him or her to potential problems.

As your baby grows, you are checked to see how much your uterus has grown since your last visit. Your doctor or midwife also listens to the fetal heart beat.

Third-trimester Tests

If you are like most women, your pregnancy progresses normally and you are in good health in your third trimester. You continue to have your weight and blood pressure checked at each antenatal visit. You may undergo urine analyses as well. Checking your blood pressure and urine are important during the last trimester to help to detect *pre-eclampsia*, a condition that is more common in first-time pregnancies and in older pregnant women. *See* the discussion of pre-eclampsia that begins on page 208.

In this last trimester, your physician may do an internal examination to see whether your cervix has begun to thin and dilate, to evaluate the size of your pelvis and to see if the baby is in the head-down position. This examination is usually done in the last few weeks of pregnancy. It *cannot* predict when you will go into labour.

Other tests may be ordered by your doctor if your baby is post-term (overdue), if your pregnancy is considered high risk or if your physician believes that your baby might have a problem. Possible tests include cardiotocography, recording the fetal heartbeat and uterine contractions, ultrasound and a biophysical profile. These tests help to determine the well-being of mother and baby or the kind of problem you or your baby may be experiencing.

Tests for the Mother Expecting Multiples

If you are carrying more than one baby, your pregnancy is different. Even the number of tests you receive, and when you receive them, is different.

Some researchers recommend that if you are at least 32 years old and your doctor determines that you are carrying more than one baby, you should be offered chromosome testing, such as amniocentesis or chorionic villus sampling. Research indicates that there is a slightly greater chance of an abnormality when a woman is carrying two babies or more.

In many cases, screening tests are the first indication that a woman is carrying more than one baby. Sometimes these tests give an 'abnormal' result. Be assured that an abnormal test result does not necessarily indicate that the babies have a problem; it alerts the doctor to perform follow-up tests.

Often with a multiple pregnancy, blood tests are repeated around week 28 to check for gestational diabetes. Tests can also reveal if the mother-to-be is anaemic, which is more common in women carrying multiples.

Tests may be performed if other problems develop. Amniocentesis may be done to check lung maturity in the babies if there is indication of preterm labour or pre-eclampsia in the mother. Premature lung disease is a serious complication for multiples who are delivered too early.

Ultrasound

An ultrasound examination may be one of the most exciting tests you have during pregnancy! You and your partner can actually see your growing baby inside your uterus. The test is also a valuable tool for your doctor because it enables him or her to check for many details of fetal development. (*Ultrasound*, *sonogram* and *sonography* refer to the same test.)

Many doctors routinely perform ultrasound examinations on their pregnant patients, but not every doctor does them with every patient. Some doctors perform ultrasounds only when there is a problem.

Katie had done most of the talking at her antenatal visits. I mainly listened to this bubbly, excited first-time mother-to-be. I don't think her husband, Ron, had said a word. They both came for her 18-week visit, when we were doing an ultrasound scan. Katie had been a little unsure about her last period, an I thought her uterus was larger than expected, so we hoped her ultrasound would help us to determine if we had the right due date. The scan told us a lot – her due date was right, but she was carrying twins! Katie was in shock; all she could do was gasp. Ron was ecstatic – he whooped with joy. They left with Katie shaking her

head and Ron grinning from ear to ear. At her next visit, Katie and I
talked about twins and twin pregnancies.

Ultrasound scans pose no threat to you or to your baby. The possibility
of adverse effects has been studied many times without any evidence of
problems.

How the Test Is Performed

Ultrasound is a test that gives a two-dimensional picture of the
developing embryo or fetus. It involves the use of high frequency sound
waves made by applying an alternating current to a device called a
transducer. The transducer sends and receives sound waves. While this
happens, you lie on your back. The transducer moves over gel that has
been spread over your abdomen. The transducer picks up echoes of
sound waves as they bounce off the baby, then a computer translates
them into a picture. This can be compared to 'radar' used by aeroplanes
or ships to create a picture of the terrain under a night sky or the ocean
floor.

Before the test, you may be asked to consume 1½pt (850ml) of
water. Drinking all that water makes it easier for the technician to see
your uterus. The bladder lies in front of the uterus; when it is full, the
uterus is pushed up and out of the pelvic area and can be seen more
easily by the ultrasound. When your bladder is empty, your uterus lies
further down in the pelvis and is harder to see.

Reasons for an Ultrasound

An ultrasound scan can help to confirm or determine your due date,
determine if there is one baby, not multiples, and determine if major
physical characteristics of the fetus are normal. An ultrasound scan can
be done just about any time during pregnancy.

Whether you have a scan during your pregnancy depends on several
factors, including problems such as bleeding, or previous problem
pregnancies. Many doctors like to do at least one ultrasound scan
during pregnancy. If your pregnancy is 'high risk', you may have
several.

A doctor may order an ultrasound to learn vital information about a
fetus' brain, spine, face, major organs, limbs or sex. A scan can show
where the placenta is, so it is used with other tests, such as
amniocentesis. The test can also provide information on fetal growth,

the condition of the umbilical cord and the amount of amniotic fluid in the uterus.

Doctors generally perform an ultrasound scan for the following reasons:

- to identify an early pregnancy
- to show the size and rate of growth of the embryo or fetus
- to measure the fetal head, abdomen or femur to determine the duration of pregnancy
- to identify some fetuses with Down's syndrome
- to identify fetal abnormalities, such as hydrocephalus
- to identify the location, the size and the maturity of the placenta or placental abnormalities
- to detect an IUD (intra-uterine contraceptive device)
- to differentiate between miscarriage, ectopic pregnancy and normal pregnancy

If you are 18 weeks or more when you have an ultrasound scan, you may be able to determine the sex of your baby, but don't count on it. It isn't always possible to tell the sex if the baby has its legs crossed or is in a breech presentation. Even if your doctor makes a prediction as to the sex of your baby, keep in mind that ultrasound is only a test, and tests can sometimes be wrong.

Vaginal Ultrasound

Another type of ultrasound scan is called *vaginal probe ultrasound* or *transvaginal sonography*; it can be very helpful in evaluating problems early in pregnancy, such as possible miscarriage or ectopic pregnancy. The instrument (probe transducer or other device) is placed just inside the opening of the vagina; it does not touch the cervix and will not cause bleeding or miscarriage. This type of ultrasound sometimes gives better information earlier in pregnancy than an abdominal ultrasound.

Ultrasound in Late Pregnancy

If your doctor orders an ultrasound scan in the third trimester, he or she is looking for particular information. Performed later in pregnancy, this test can:

- evaluate the baby's size and growth

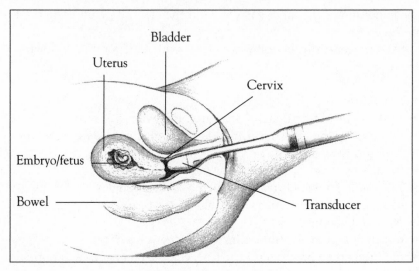

Vaginal probe ultrasound

- determine the cause of vaginal bleeding
- determine the cause of vaginal or abdominal pain
- detect some fetal malformations
- monitor a high risk pregnancy
- measure the amount of amniotic fluid
- help to decide which delivery method to use

The test can also be used to evaluate the fetus, including its size. Breathing movements, body movements and muscle tone can be checked. If the baby is too big, it may need to be delivered by caesarean section. If the baby is very small, other decisions can be made.

Other Facts about Ultrasound

You may be able to get a videotape of your ultrasound; ask about it when your ultrasound is scheduled to find out if you need to bring a videotape cassette. Most ultrasounds do include black-and-white photographs that you may keep.

You can usually take your partner with you to the examination, so arrange to have the ultrasound scan when he can join you. You may want to have others come, such as your mother or older children. Ask if that is possible when you book your ultrasound scan.

Amniocentesis

Amniocentesis is a test done on fetal cells and is usually offered to women over 35. However, this guideline is currently being challenged. The age threshold for amniocentesis is discussed beginning on page 4.

What the Test Can Predict

Most women who have amniocentesis are being screened for chromosome defects, such as Down's syndrome, Turner's syndrome or neural tube defects (spina bifida). The test can pick up some specific gene defects, including cystic fibrosis and sickle cell disease. Other problems a physician can identify include:

- skeletal diseases, such as osteogenesis imperfecta
- fetal infections, such as herpes or rubella
- central nervous system disease, such as anencephaly
- blood diseases, such as erythroblastosis fetalis
- chemical problems or deficiencies, such as cystinuria or maple-syrup urine disease

Amniocentesis can determine the baby's sex. The test is not used for this purpose, except in cases in which the sex of the baby could predict

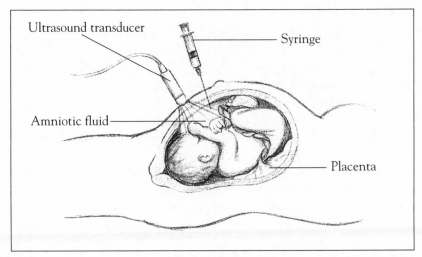

Amniocentesis performed near the end of pregnancy can determine if your baby's lungs are mature

a problem, such as haemophilia. Amniocentesis may be performed to see if the baby of a Rhesus-negative woman is having problems, and it may be done to determine fetal lung maturity before delivery.

Who Receives Amniocentesis?

Amniocentesis does not need to be performed on every pregnant woman. It is often performed on women:

- who will deliver after their 35th birthday
- who have had a previous baby with a birth defect
- with a family history of birth defects
- who have a birth defect themselves
- whose partners have a birth defect

How the Test Is Performed

Ultrasound is used to locate a pocket of fluid where the fetus and placenta are not in the way. Skin over the mother's abdomen is cleaned and numbed with a local anaesthetic. A needle passes through the abdomen into the uterus, and fluid is withdrawn with a syringe. About 1oz (28ml) of amniotic fluid is needed to perform the tests. The test can identify about 40 different fetal abnormalities.

Risks with Amniocentesis

The risks of amniocentesis include trauma to the fetus, to the placenta or to the umbilical cord, infection, miscarriage or premature labour. Although the risks are relatively small, there is some risk associated with the procedure. Fetal loss from complications is estimated to be about 0.3 per cent.

Discuss the risks with your doctor before the test. Only someone with experience, such as a doctor at a maternity unit, should perform amniocentesis.

In a multiple pregnancy, genetic testing can be a complicated procedure. In most multiple pregnancies, for example, each baby lies in its own sac. Double abdominal punctures are required to withdraw fluids in each of these sacs, which can increase the risk of complications. In the case of one sac shared by the two babies, only one amniocentesis is performed.

Disadvantages of the Test

The greatest disadvantage of the test is the time at which it is performed. Amniocentesis is usually performed for antenatal evaluation at around 16 weeks of pregnancy, making legal abortion (if that is what the woman chooses) more difficult. Some doctors are now performing the test at around 11 or 12 weeks. This is considered experimental.

Alpha-fetoprotein Testing

The alpha-fetoprotein (AFP) test is a blood test done on the mother-to-be. Alpha-fetoprotein is produced in the baby's liver, and it passes in small quantities into your bloodstream. Measurement of the amount of alpha-fetoprotein in your blood can help your doctor to predict problems in your baby, such as spina bifida or Down's syndrome. (AFP detects only about 25 per cent of Down's syndrome cases. If Down's syndrome is suggested, additional detailed diagnostic tests will probably be ordered.)

At this time the AFP is not performed on all pregnant women. If the test is not offered to you, discuss it with your doctor.

The test is usually performed between 16 and 20 weeks of pregnancy. Test results must be correlated with the mother's age and weight, and the gestational age of the fetus. If AFP detects a possible problem, more definitive testing is usually ordered.

What the Test Can Predict

AFP can detect neural tube defects, severe kidney or liver disease, oesophageal or intestinal blockage, Down's syndrome, urinary obstruction and osteogenesis imperfecta (fragility of the baby's bones).

False Positive Results

One problem with the AFP test is a very high number of false-positive results – that is, the results say there is a problem when there isn't one. Currently, if 1,000 women take the AFP test, 40 test results come back as 'abnormal'. Of those 40, only one or two women actually have a problem.

If you have an AFP and your test result is abnormal, don't panic. You will take another AFP test, and an ultrasound scan will be performed. Results from these second tests should give you a clearer answer.

The Triple-screen and Quad-screen Tests

Tests that go beyond alpha-fetoprotein testing are available now to help your doctor to determine if your child might have Down's syndrome and to rule out other problems in your pregnancy.

The Triple-screen Test

The triple-screen test helps to identify problems using three blood components: alpha-fetoprotein, a pregnancy hormone called *human chorionic gonadotropin* (HCG) and a form of oestrogen produced by the placenta called *unconjugated oestriol*.

Abnormal levels of these three blood chemicals can indicate Down's syndrome. For older mothers, the detection rate is higher than 60 per cent, with a false-positive rate of nearly 25 per cent. Abnormal results of a triple-screen test are usually double-checked with ultrasound and amniocentesis.

The Quad-screen Test

The quad-screen test is similar to the triple-screen but adds a fourth measurement – the blood level of inhibin-A, a chemical produced by the ovaries and the placenta. This fourth measurement raises the sensitivity of the standard triple-screen test by 20 per cent in determining if a fetus has Down's syndrome. The quad-screen test identifies almost 80 per cent of fetuses with Down's syndrome. It has a false-positive rate of 5 per cent.

Chorionic Villus Sampling

Chorionic villus sampling (CVS) analyses chorionic villus cells, which become the placenta. The test detects genetic abnormalities; sampling is undertaken early in pregnancy.

The advantage of CVS is that a doctor can diagnose a problem earlier in pregnancy with it. The test can be done at 9 to 11 weeks instead of 16 to 18 weeks, as with amniocentesis. Some women choose CVS so they can make a decision about their pregnancy earlier. If a woman wishes to have an abortion, the abortion procedure may carry fewer risks when performed earlier in the pregnancy.

How the Test Is Performed

An instrument is placed through the cervix or through the abdomen to remove a small piece of tissue from the placenta. The procedure carries a small risk of miscarriage; it should be performed only by someone who is experienced in doing the test.

Fetoscopy

Because of advances in fibre optics, today we can look at a fetus or placenta as early as ten weeks into its development. Ultrasound cannot provide the same degree of detail. Fetoscopy enables the doctor to look through a fetoscope to detect even very subtle abnormalities and problems.

How the Test Is Performed

A small incision is made in the mother's abdomen, and a scope similar to the one used in laparoscopy is placed through the abdomen. The doctor uses the fetoscope to examine the fetus and the placenta.

The test is specialized and is not done very often. It is usually recommended if you have given birth to a child with a birth defect that cannot be detected by any other test. If your doctor suggests fetoscopy to you, discuss it with him or her. The risk of miscarriage is 3 to 4 per cent. The procedure should be done *only* by someone who is experienced at it.

Percutaneous Umbilical Blood Sampling

Percutaneous umbilical blood sampling, also called *cordocentesis*, is a fairly new test that is done on the fetus. The test has improved the diagnosis and treatment of Rhesus-incompatability and other blood disorders. The advantage of the test is that results can be available within a few days. The disadvantage is that it carries a slightly higher risk of miscarriage than amniocentesis.

How the Test Is Performed

Guided by ultrasound, a fine needle is inserted through the mother's abdomen into a tiny vein in the umbilical cord of the fetus. A small sample of the baby's blood is removed for analysis. Blood disorders, infections and Rhesus-incompatability are detectable by cordocentesis.

If the fetus is found to be Rhesus-positive and its mother is Rhesus-negative, doctors have time to give it a blood transfusion, if necessary. This procedure can help to prevent life-threatening anaemia that can develop if the mother is isoimmunized (she has antibodies that attack her baby's blood). *See* the discussion of Rhesus-compatibility on page 61.

Other Tests for the Mother-to-be

Listening to the Baby's Heart Beat

A special listening machine, called a *doppler*, magnifies the sound of the baby's heart beat so that it can be heard. It is possible to hear the baby's heart beat around your 12-week visit.

Radiation Tests

There is no known safe amount of radiation from X-ray tests for a developing fetus. The baby may be harmed by exposure. Avoid exposure to X-rays during pregnancy, unless it is an emergency. The medical need for the X-ray must always be weighed against its risk to your pregnancy. Discuss the procedure with your physician before *any* X-ray is taken when you are pregnant. This warning also applies to dental X-rays.

Computerized tomographic scans, also called *CT scans* or *CAT scans*, are a very specialized X-ray. The test involves the use of X-rays with computer analysis. Many researchers believe the amount of radiation received from a CT scan is far lower than that from a regular X-ray. It is probably wise to avoid even this amount of exposure, if possible.

Unless you have a good reason for having a mammogram during pregnancy, such as a breast lump, don't expose your developing baby to this type of radiation.

With radiation examinations, risk to the fetus appears to be the greatest between 8 and 15 weeks of pregnancy (between the fetal ages of 6 and 13 weeks). Some physicians believe that the only safe amount of radiation exposure for a fetus is *no* exposure.

Magnetic resonance imaging, also called *MRI*, is a diagnostic tool widely in use today. No harmful effects have been reported from its use in pregnancy, but pregnant women are advised to avoid MRI during the first trimester of pregnancy.

Cervical Smear

Often on your first antenatal visit, you will have a cervical smear if it has been a year or more since your last test. If you have had a normal cervical smear in the last few months, you won't need another one.

A cervical smear is done to look for abnormal cells, called *precancerous*, *dysplastic* or *cancerous* cells, in the cervical area. The goal of the smear is to discover problems early so they can be dealt with more easily. If you have an abnormal smear, it usually identifies the presence of an infection, a pre-cancerous condition or some other condition.

If your test reveals an infection, it is treated immediately. If the first test reveals a pre-cancerous condition, called *dysplasia*, the next step is usually a *colposcopy*.

In a colposcopy, a microscope is used to examine your cervix and to look for abnormal areas. If any are found, a sample of the tissue is removed, called a *biopsy*. Usually a biopsy is not done while you are pregnant; your doctor will usually wait until after your pregnancy for further testing. An abnormal cervical smear during pregnancy is a special situation and must be handled carefully.

Home Uterine Monitoring

Some women are monitored during pregnancy with home uterine monitoring. Contractions of a pregnant woman's uterus are recorded while she is at home and are transmitted by telephone to her doctor. This type of testing or monitoring is used to identify women at risk of premature labour. With it, labour can often be stopped to prevent premature delivery.

Pelvic Examination

A pelvic examination is usually done at the first or second antenatal visit and again in late pregnancy. It is done early in pregnancy to evaluate the size of the uterus and to help your doctor to determine how far along you are in pregnancy. It is needed late in pregnancy because it tells your doctor many things, including:

- the presentation of the baby – whether the baby is head first or breech
- the dilatation of the cervix – how much the cervix is opened (if at all)
- effacement – how much the cervix has thinned
- station – how low the baby is in your birth canal
- shape and size of your birth canal or pelvic bones

After a pelvic examination late in pregnancy, your doctor may tell you some numbers, such as '2 and 50 per cent'. This means that your cervix has dilated 2cm and is halfway thinned out. (*See* the illustration on page 232.)

The information collected during the examination is helpful if you go to hospital thinking you are in labour. At the hospital, you will be checked again. Knowing the measurements from your last pelvic examination can help your doctor to determine if you are in labour.

A pelvic examination does not tell your doctor when you will go into labour. Labour can start at any time, regardless of the condition of your cervix.

Cardiotocography on the Baby

This is a simple, non-invasive procedure done at 32 weeks' of pregnancy or later; it is performed in the clinic or in the labour and delivery ward at the hospital. This test measures how the fetal heart responds to the fetus' own movements. The test evaluates fetal well-being in late pregnancy and is commonly used in post-term and high risk pregnancies. The information gained from the test gives reassurance that your baby is doing well.

How the Test Is Performed

While you are lying down, a nurse attaches a monitor to your abdomen. Every time you feel the baby move, you push a button to make a mark on the monitor paper. At the same time, the fetal monitor records the baby's heart beat on the same paper.

Test Results

Each time the baby moves, the heart rate should accelerate by about 15 beats a minute for about 15 seconds. When this occurs twice in a

20-minute period, the test is considered normal or *reactive*. If the baby doesn't move or if the heart rate does not react to movement, the test is called *non-reactive*. This doesn't necessarily mean that there is a problem – the baby may be sleeping. In more than 75 per cent of non-reactive tests, the baby is healthy.

If the test is non-reactive, it could be a sign that the baby is not receiving enough oxygen or is experiencing some other problem. In this case, you will probably have to repeat the test in 24 hours or have additional tests, including a biophysical profile.

A slowed heart rate after a spontaneous uterine contraction may be a sign of foetal distress. The baby may not be receiving enough oxygen or may be experiencing another difficulty. The doctor may recommend delivery of the baby. In other cases, the doctor may repeat the test the next day or order a biophysical profile. (A discussion follows.) If the test shows no sign of a slowed fetal heart rate, the test result is reassuring.

Biophysical Profile of the Baby

A biophysical profile is a comprehensive test that helps to determine the fetus' health status. The test is commonly performed in high risk situations, overdue pregnancies or pregnancies in which the baby doesn't move very much. It is useful in evaluating a fetus with intra-uterine growth retardation.

A biophysical profile measures five areas, which are identified and scored: fetal breathing movements, gross body movements, fetal tone, reactive fetal heart rate and amount of amniotic fluid.

How the Test Is Performed

Ultrasound, external monitors and direct observation are all used to take the various measurements. Each area is given a score between 0 and 2. A score of 1 in any test is a middle score; a total is obtained by adding the five scores. The higher the score, the better the baby's condition.

A baby with a low score may need to be delivered immediately. Your doctor will evaluate the scores, your health and your pregnancy before any decisions are made. If the score is reassuring, the test may be repeated at intervals. Sometimes a doctor will repeat the test the following day.

Fetal Monitoring during Labour

In many hospitals, a baby's heartbeat is monitored throughout labour with external fetal monitoring and internal fetal monitoring. Fetal monitoring enables doctors to detect problems early.

External fetal monitoring can be done before your membranes rupture. A belt with a recorder is strapped to your abdomen to pick up the baby's heart beat. Internal fetal monitoring monitors the baby more precisely. An electrode is placed on the fetal scalp to measure the fetal heart rate.

Fetal Blood Sampling during Labour

Fetal blood sampling is another way of evaluating how well a baby is tolerating the stress of labour. Before the test can be performed, membranes must be ruptured, and the cervix must be dilated at least 2cm (about 1in). An instrument is passed into the vagina and through the dilated cervix to the top of the baby's head, where it is used to make a small nick in the baby's scalp. The baby's blood is collected in a small tube and its pH (acidity) is checked.

Knowing the baby's pH level helps doctors to determine if the baby is having trouble during labour and is under stress. The test helps the doctor to decide whether labour can continue or if a caesarean section is needed.

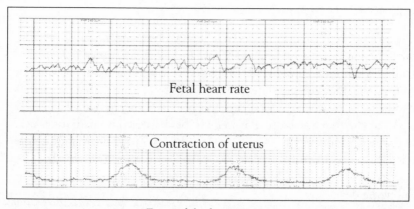

Fetal heart rate

Contraction of uterus

External fetal monitoring

Evaluating Fetal Lung Maturity

The respiratory system is the last fetal system to mature. Premature babies commonly experience respiratory difficulties because their lungs are not yet mature. Knowing how mature the baby's lungs are helps your doctor to make a decision about early delivery, if that must be considered.

If the baby needs to be delivered early, fetal lung maturity tests can determine whether the baby will be able to breathe without assistance. The two tests used most often to evaluate a baby's lungs before birth are the L-S ratio and the phosphatidyl glycerol (PG) tests. Fluid for the tests is obtained by amniocentesis.

CHAPTER 10

When You're Expecting More Than One Baby

A multiple pregnancy almost always surprises expectant parents. Because of today's advanced testing techniques, especially ultrasound, most parents know about it early enough to prepare for their new arrivals.

The rate of multiple births increased between 1980 and 1992; today 1.5 per cent of all births are multiple births. This increase is due to the use of fertility drugs and because more women are having babies at an older age.

A multiple pregnancy occurs when a single egg divides after fertilization or when more than one egg is fertilized. Twins from one egg, called *identical* or *monozygotic twins*, occur about once in every 250 births around the world. Twins from two eggs, called *fraternal* or *dizygotic twins*, occur in 1 out of every 100 births in white women and 1 out of 79 births in black women. In certain areas in Africa, twins occur once in every 20 births! Hispanic women also have a higher incidence of twins. The occurrence of twins in Asian populations is less common – about 1 in every 150 births.

Today, we are also experiencing more triplet births. However, a triplet birth is not common. It happens naturally about once in every 8,000 deliveries.

Causes of Multiple Births

The increase in multiple births among older women has been attributed to higher levels of gonadotropin, the hormone that stimulates the ovaries to develop and release eggs. As a woman ages, the level of gonadotropin increases, and she is more likely to produce two eggs during one menstrual cycle. Most twin births in older women are fraternal twins (babies are born from two different eggs).

The incidence of twin births can run in families, on the mother's side. One study showed that if a woman is a twin, her chance of giving birth to twins is about 1 in 58. If a woman is the daughter of a twin, she also has a higher chance of having twins. Another study reported that 1 out of 24 (4 per cent) of twins' mothers was also a twin, but only 1 out of 60 (1.7 per cent; about the population average) of the fathers was a twin.

Multiple births are also more common with *in vitro* fertilization. This may be due to the frequent use of fertility drugs to increase the chance of pregnancy or the introduction of several fertilized eggs in the hope that at least one will implant.

Signs of a Multiple Pregnancy

Most multiple pregnancies are discovered well before delivery. A doctor or midwife usually finds out a woman is carrying more than one baby because of various signs, including a larger than expected uterus, more severe nausea and vomiting, and more than one fetal heart beat.

When a doctor suspects that a woman is carrying more than one baby, an ultrasound is usually ordered. A scan almost always detects a multiple pregnancy.

Increased Risks Associated with a Multiple Pregnancy

If a woman is pregnant with more than one baby, her risk of problems during pregnancy increases. Risks can be minimized and possibly avoided with good antenatal care and careful attention to the woman's health. Possible pregnancy problems include:

- increased miscarriage
- fetal death
- fetal malformations
- low birth weight or growth retardation
- pre-eclampsia
- maternal anaemia
- problems with the placenta
- maternal bleeding or haemorrhage
- problems with the umbilical cords
- hydramnios in one sac or both

- labour complicated by breech or transverse presentation
- premature labour

If you are pregnant with more than one baby, take very good care of yourself during pregnancy. Pay strict attention to your eating plan; eat wisely and nutritiously for all of you. Extra rest is essential. Most pregnant women need at least two hours of rest during each day.

When you are pregnant with more than one baby, you are monitored more closely during pregnancy. You will probably have more frequent check-ups, and more tests may be ordered for you.

Beginning at 20 weeks, you may need to visit your doctor every other week until 30 weeks. Then you may be seen once a week until delivery. You may have an ultrasound scan more frequently to monitor the babies' growth. Your blood pressure is monitored very closely because of pre-eclampsia, which is twice as common in multiple pregnancies.

Take Care of Yourself during Pregnancy

One of the most important things to remember with a multiple pregnancy is to take things more slowly, from the beginning of your pregnancy until delivery. Taking care of yourself is the best way to take care of your developing babies.

Eat more – a woman carrying more than one baby needs to eat at least 300 more calories per baby each day than she would if she were carrying one baby. That means she must consume more protein, minerals, vitamins and essential fatty acids. For a normal weight woman, a weight gain between 25 and 40lb (11 to 18kg) for a twin birth is recommended.

A multiple pregnancy is more stressful for your body than a single pregnancy, and your needs increase in many areas. Often women pregnant with more than one baby have iron-deficiency anaemia. Iron supplementation is often necessary.

You may need bed rest in your second trimester, even hospital admission, if you experience complications. With some multiple pregnancies, planned admission at 28 to 30 weeks may be recommended. Bed rest at home or in the hospital can help prevent or stop premature labour. It gives the babies the best chance to grow because bed rest increases blood flow to the uterus.

Coping with Discomfort

When you are expecting more than one baby, your discomfort may be more pronounced; you may experience more problems, or problems may last longer. When you are carrying twins, you get 'big' earlier, and you are larger than with a single pregnancy. This can cause you more problems, such as difficulty breathing, back pain, haemorrhoids, varicose veins, pelvic pressure and pelvic pain.

Treatment is often the same for you as for a woman with a single-fetus pregnancy. Refer to those discussions that appear elsewhere in this book, including morning sickness, page 130; backaches, page 125; digestion changes, page 129; heartburn, page 127; and sleep problems, page 11.

Exercising with a Multiple Pregnancy

As a general rule, I advise women who are carrying more than one baby *not* to exercise during pregnancy because of the extra stress their bodies must deal with. Walking and swimming may be permissible for you, but check with your doctor first.

If your doctor does approve of mild exercises, don't do anything that is strenuous – stop immediately if you feel overexerted. As much as you want to stay in shape, you may have to forgo all exercise programmes until after your babies are safely delivered.

Other Pregnancy Considerations

Working during Pregnancy

Often a doctor advises a woman expecting twins to stop working at least 8 weeks before her due date. Ideally, you should stop working at 28 weeks with a twin pregnancy – 24 weeks if your job requires standing or other physical exertion. Your doctor may recommend full or partial bed rest. These are general suggestions and may not apply in every case.

Childbirth-education Classes

It is a great idea to take childbirth-education classes for any pregnancy. If you are expecting twins, triplets or more, schedule your classes to begin at least three months before your due date. If you have time, a brief course in Caesarean section might also be worthwhile, if you can find a class in your area. *Also see* the discussion on childbirth-education classes that begins on page 36.

A Special Concern during Pregnancy

Some women are told early in pregnancy that they will give birth to twins, only to discover later that they are carrying one baby. Early ultrasound examinations reveal two babies; later ultrasounds of the same woman show that one baby has disappeared, but that the other baby is all right. We believe that one of the pregnancies dies and is then absorbed by the mother's body. This is one reason that many doctors prefer not to predict a twin birth before ten weeks of pregnancy.

Delivering More Than One Baby

Multiple fetuses are often delivered early. Most doctors try to delay delivery of twins until about the 37th week, but the average twin pregnancy is delivered at 35 weeks. Although the ideal time for delivery of triplets is 35 weeks, the average length of pregnancy for triplets is 33 weeks. Quadruplets are delivered, on average, at 29 weeks.

How multiple fetuses are delivered often depends on how the babies are lying in the uterus. All possible combinations of fetal positions can occur. When both twins are head first, a vaginal delivery is usually attempted. One baby may be delivered vaginally, with the second requiring a caesarean section if it turns, if the cord comes out first or if the second baby is distressed after the first one is born. Some doctors believe that two or more babies should always be delivered by caesarean section.

Breast-feeding More Than One Baby

It is possible to breast-feed twins or triplets. It may be more difficult and more demanding, but many women successfully breast-feed more than one baby. We know that breast milk is especially valuable for small or premature babies; often twins or triplets are both. If you want to breast-feed, do it! *See* the discussion of breast-feeding that begins on page 43.

Extra Help after the Babies Are Born

Even the most efficient woman discovers that having more than one baby can be exhausting. Extra help can make a tremendous difference in everyone's life. Your time of greatest need is immediately after your babies are born. Ask for help from family, neighbours and friends for the first four to six weeks after you bring your babies home. You may be fairly exhausted yourself, so it is very helpful to have extra pairs of hands available until you all settle into a routine.

Resources for Parents of Multiples

There are some wonderful resource groups for parents and families of multiples. Consult the resource list that begins on page 292.

PART THREE

While You're Pregnant

CHAPTER 11

Coping with Common Discomforts

In this chapter, let us look at how you can more easily cope with minor discomforts to which age contributes during pregnancy. Being pregnant. causes changes in your body; some of them are uncomfortable. Being aware of what they are before you experience them (if you do) may help to relieve anxiety.

Backaches

Nearly every woman experiences backaches and back pain at some time during pregnancy, especially as her abdomen gets bigger. You may experience backache after walking, bending, lifting, standing or excessive exercise. Be careful about lifting – do it correctly, with knees bent and back straight.

Backache is treated with heat, rest and analgesics, such as paracetamol (Panadol). Some maternity girdles may provide support. Keep your weight under control, and participate in mild exercise, such as swimming, walking and exercise-bike riding. Lie on your left side when resting or sleeping.

Lower-back pain is common during pregnancy, but occasionally it indicates a serious problem, such as a kidney stone. If pain is constant or severe, discuss it with your doctor.

Constipation

Your bowel habits may change during pregnancy. Many women notice constipation, often accompanied by irregular bowel habits and haemorrhoids. These problems are usually the result of a slowdown in the movement of food through the gastrointestinal system and the ingestion of iron as supplements or in antenatal vitamins.

You can take steps to help to relieve the problem. Increase your fluid intake, and exercise three or four times a week. Many doctors suggest prune juice or a mild laxative, such as milk of magnesia. However, avoid excessive use of *any* preparation that contains magnesium. Certain foods that are high in fibre, such as bran and prunes, increase the bulk in your diet and may help to relieve constipation.

Do not use laxatives, other than those mentioned above, without consulting your doctor. If constipation is a continuing problem, discuss it at your next clinic visit.

Headaches

Some women experience more headaches during pregnancy but hesitate to take medication for them. You can do a few things that are medicine-free to relieve headaches.

- Use deep-breathing exercises and relaxation techniques to help you to relax.
- Drink plenty of fluids so that you don't become dehydrated.
- Close your eyes and rest in a quiet place.
- Eat regularly.
- Avoid foods or substances, such as cheese, chocolate and caffeine, that sometimes cause headaches.
- Apply an ice-pack to the back of your head.
- Get enough sleep.

If your headache doesn't go away using these techniques, you may take regular or extra-strength paracetamol (Panadol). If this doesn't help, see your doctor.

Migraine Headaches

A migraine headache is characterized by severe throbbing pain and is aggravated by physical activity, such as walking. Some women experience nausea, vomiting or diarrhoea with a migraine headache.

Some women who experience migraines regularly do not suffer from them during pregnancy; others have worse migraine headaches, especially in the first trimester. For some, the second and third trimesters are migraine-free.

Try the techniques described above for headaches to deal with migraines. If they don't help, talk to your doctor; he or she will prescribe the safest medicine available. Do not take any medicine, other than paracetamol, for a migraine headache without discussing it first with your doctor.

Heartburn

One of the most frequent discomforts of pregnancy, especially among older pregnant women, is heartburn. Heartburn may begin early in pregnancy and often becomes more severe as pregnancy progresses.

Heartburn during pregnancy is caused by two things – a reflux (backing up) of stomach acids into the oesophagus and the hormone changes of pregnancy. During pregnancy, your body produces hormones that relax involuntary muscles; one such muscle normally prevents stomach acids from backing up into the oesophagus. Because the muscle is not doing its usual job, you experience heartburn. You may notice heartburn during the third trimester especially, when the expanding uterus crowds the stomach and the intestines somewhat. This can cause some stomach contents to back up into the oesophagus.

> Gina was having a hard time with heartburn. She loved to eat Italian food, Mexican food and other spicy foods, but she paid for it. She found that with a few modifications, she could eat the things she liked and not suffer from heartburn afterwards. She ate earlier in the evening, at least two hours before retiring. She ate smaller amounts, and she always carried antacids, such as Gelusil or magnesium trisilicate tablets.

Antacids may provide considerable relief. Follow your doctor's instructions or package directions relating to pregnancy. Don't overdo it and take too much in an effort to find relief. You can use some antacids, such as Gelusil, Milk of Magnesia, Gaviscon and Maalox, without too much concern. However, avoid excessive use of any product that contains sodium or magnesium. Sodium can contribute to water retention. Excessive use of magnesium antacids has been linked to magnesium poisoning.

In addition to taking antacids, try the following suggestions. (*Also see* the discussion of indigestion on page 129.)

- Eat smaller meals more frequently.
- Avoid carbonated beverages.

- Don't eat foods that you know give you heartburn, such as rich or spicy foods.
- Avoid eating before bedtime.
- When lying down, elevate your head and shoulders.

Haemorrhoids

Haemorrhoids are an annoying problem for many women during pregnancy. Haemorrhoids are dilated blood vessels (varicose veins) of the rectum that can itch, bleed and be painful. They appear around the area of the anus or inside the anus. Older women are especially vulnerable to haemorrhoids; they may have some dilated blood vessels around the rectum even before pregnancy.

Many patients ask me why they only have the problem during pregnancy. During pregnancy, your body tissue changes, with some loss of elasticity. Pressure from your enlarging uterus blocks blood flow in the pelvic area. These conditions encourage haemorrhoid formation.

Relieving the Discomfort of Haemorrhoids

If haemorrhoids are a problem, try any or all of the following suggestions for relief:

- Rest at least one hour every day with your feet and hips elevated.
- Lie on your side when you sleep at night.
- Eat adequate amounts of fibre, and drink lots of fluid.
- Take warm baths for relief.
- Suppositories, available without a prescription, may help.
- Stool softeners (Dioctyl, Fybogel) can prevent hard stools from forming, which can aggravate delicate tissues.
- At work, try to arrange a time every day to take off your shoes and put up your feet.
- Apply ice-packs or cotton-wool balls soaked in witch hazel to the affected area.
- Don't sit for long periods.

Discuss the situation with your doctor if haemorrhoids become a major problem. In rare cases, the problem is relieved with surgery.

Indigestion

My patients often ask me if there is a difference between heartburn and indigestion. There is. *Heartburn* is a burning discomfort related to the lower end of the oesophagus and is felt behind the lower part of the sternum. *Indigestion* refers to an inability to digest food or to difficulty in digesting food. (Heartburn is discussed starting on page 127.)

If you have indigestion, you can take steps to relieve it. Eat foods that agree with you; avoid spicy foods. Eat small meals frequently. If you need antacids after meals, use them but don't overmedicate yourself.

New medicines that are now available over the counter are advertised as being good to help indigestion and heartburn. Two popular medicines are famotidine (Pepcid) for acid control and cimetidine (Tagamet) for heartburn relief. The data we have advises women *not* to use these products during pregnancy unless there is a clear indication that they are needed. Do not take these or any other medicines without first discussing the situation with your doctor.

Leg Cramps

Leg cramps can be bothersome during pregnancy, especially if you experience them at night. Cramps are characterized by a sharp,

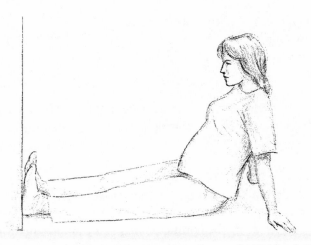

Stretching your legs can help to relieve leg cramps. Sit on the floor and place your feet flat against the wall. Pull your toes away from the wall, keeping your heels on the floor. Repeat six to eight times when you experience leg cramps.

grabbing pain in the calf. A cramp is a spasm in two sets of muscles that forces your foot to point involuntarily.

The best way to relieve a leg cramp is to stretch your muscles. Flex or bend your foot to stretch leg muscles in the opposite direction. You can do this by standing up or by gently pressing the knee down with one hand while you gently pull the upper part of the foot towards you with the other. Stretching exercises before you go to bed at night may help. Don't point your toes or stretch your legs before you get out of bed.

Some medical experts believe that leg cramps occur more frequently if there is an imbalance of calcium and phosphorus in the body. Do not consume more calcium than you need – 1,200mg is the recommended daily dose – about four cups of milk. (*Also see* the chart on page 152 for the calcium content of some foods.) Soft drinks, snack foods and processed foods are all high in phosphates; you may need to cut down on them or to eliminate them from your diet.

How to Cope with Leg Cramps

These suggestions may help to relieve leg cramps:

- Wear maternity support stockings during the day.
- Take warm baths.
- Ask your partner to massage your legs at the end of the day or whenever you feel like it.
- Take paracetamol (Panadol) for pain.
- Rest on your left side.
- Use a heated pad set on low for up to 15 minutes (no longer) on the cramp.

Your activities can also contribute to cramping. Avoid standing for long periods of time. Don't wear tight or restrictive clothing.

Morning Sickness

An early symptom of pregnancy for many women is nausea, sometimes with vomiting, often called *morning sickness*. Morning sickness is typically present at the beginning of pregnancy and is usually worse in the morning (it improves during the day). Morning sickness usually begins around week 6 and lasts until week 12 or 13, when it starts to subside.

Try the suggestions below to help you to deal with the nausea and vomiting related to morning sickness:

- Eat small portions of nutritious food throughout the day, instead of three larger meals.
- Eat a snack, such as dry crackers or rice cakes, *before* you get out of bed in the morning. Or ask your partner to make you some dry toast.
- Avoid heavy, fatty foods.
- Keep up your fluid intake – fluids may be easier on the stomach than solids and will help you to avoid dehydration.
- Alternate wet foods with dry foods. Eat only dry foods at one meal, then wet foods or liquids at the next.
- Try ginger – it's a natural remedy for nausea. Grate it on to vegetables and other foods.
- Avoid things that trigger your nausea, such as odours, movement or noise.
- Suck on a freshly cut lemon when you feel nauseated.
- Get enough rest.
- Avoid getting sweaty or overheated, which can contribute to nausea.
- Apply pressure to pressure points on your wrists. See the illustration and instructions below.

Hyperemesis Gravidarum

A woman who experiences severe vomiting and is unable to eat or drink suffers from *hyperemesis gravidarum*. She may be treated for several days in hospital if she becomes dehydrated and loses weight. In

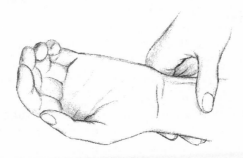

To help relieve nausea, find the pressure point that is three fingers above your wrist fold. Press on the point on each wrist at the same time – you will probably need help doing this. Hold for one minute; repeat three times.

hospital, she will be fed intravenously. Usually the patient can resume eating solid foods after a couple of days in hospital. Sometimes hypnosis treats the problem successfully.

Normal Swelling in Pregnancy

During the last few weeks of pregnancy, your ankles and feet may swell; some women also observe swelling in their hands and fingers. Swelling is caused by increased fluid in your bloodstream. It is more noticeable in your ankles and feet because the baby's weight puts pressure on the veins in your pelvis and slows the flow of blood from your legs back to your heart.

The best way to deal with the swelling is to improve your circulation through exercise and position changes. When possible, walk short distances. Do ankle circles while standing in line or sitting in a chair.

To deal with normal swelling in legs and feet, wear trainers, or shoes with low wedge heels (no higher than 2in/5cm) that fit comfortably. Choose the right kind of shoe for you. An ideal shoe has a 1in/2.5cm heel, good arch support, a roomy, box-shaped toe and adjustable straps or laces.

If swelling becomes extreme, especially during the last trimester, consult your physician; it could be a sign of problems. Rest lying on your left side as frequently as possible. You can also try the following:

- Take off your shoes when possible, and wiggle your toes to increase circulation.
- Don't stand for long periods.
- Don't wear ski pants.

Varicose Veins

Varicose veins, also called *varicosities* or *varices*, are dilated blood vessels that fill with blood. They occur to some degree in most pregnant women; however, varicose veins develop more often in older women.

There seems to be an inherited predisposition to varicose veins that can become more severe during pregnancy. If your mother had varicose veins, you are more likely to develop them.

Problems with varicose veins usually occur in the legs but also may be seen as haemorrhoids or appear in the birth canal and in the vulva. Pressure from the uterus and the change in blood flow during pregnancy can make varices worse. Varicose veins in the legs or varicose veins in the rectum (haemorrhoids) can cause great pain and discomfort.

Symptoms vary; for some women varicose veins are only a blemish or purple-blue spot on the legs that causes little or no discomfort, except in the evening. For other women, varices are bulging veins that require elevation at the end of the day or other measures.

Varicose veins may worsen during pregnancy. Increasing weight (from the growing baby, uterus and placenta), tight clothing that constricts at the waist or legs, and standing a great deal worsen varicose veins. If you continue to have problems with varicose veins after pregnancy, you may need surgery.

Preventing and Treating Varicose Veins during Pregnancy

The most effective way to prevent varicose veins is to improve circulation in your legs, especially through exercise and changes in position. Walk when possible, and do ankle circles while sitting and standing. Even sitting and rocking in a rocking chair can help – rocking contracts and relaxes leg muscles, which moves blood from your feet to your heart. Lie on your left side when you lie down to improve blood flow. Elevate your hips and legs when resting or lying down. Keep your total pregnancy weight gain within normal range – between 24 and 28lb (11–13kg) for a normal-weight woman.

If you suffer from varicose veins while you are pregnant, you can take steps to improve the problem. Many women wear support stockings to reduce swelling and ease leg pains. Many types of maternity support stockings or graduated-compression stockings are available. Quite a few of my patients have told me how much maternity support stockings have helped them, but they can be very difficult to get on. The following tips can help.

First, turn the stockings inside out. Starting at the toe, unroll the stockings up your leg. Second, put on your stockings before you get out of bed in the morning – your legs may tend to swell as soon as you get up. (You may need to change your habits and bathe before you go to bed.)

Clothes that don't restrict circulation at the knee or groin may be your best choices. Wear loose panties to help prevent vulvar varicosities (varicose veins in the vulva area) which can be very uncomfortable.

Spend as little time as possible on your feet. Wear flat shoes. Don't cross your legs at the knee and don't stand for long periods. If you must stand, bounce gently on the balls of your feet every few minutes.

Sciatic-nerve Pain

Some women occasionally experience a severe pain in their buttocks and down the back or side of either leg. This pain is called *sciatic-nerve pain*; it may occur more frequently as pregnancy progresses.

The sciatic nerve is located behind the uterus, in the pelvic area, and runs down into the leg. We believe that the pain is caused when the enlarging uterus puts pressure on the nerve.

The best way to deal with the pain is to lie on your opposite side which helps to relieve pressure on the nerve.

CHAPTER 12

Nutrition and Weight Management

The fetus growing inside you has many nutritional needs – needs that you must fulfil through the foods you choose to eat. A pregnant woman who eats a healthy diet during pregnancy is much more likely to give birth to a healthy baby. Eating well reduces the risk of complications and limits some pregnancy side-effects.

You can meet most nutritional needs by eating a well-balanced, varied diet. The *quality* of your calories is extremely important – if a food grows in the ground or on trees, it is better for you nutritionally than if it comes from a can or a box.

I am sure that you have heard the adage 'a pregnant women is eating for two'. Many women take this to mean that they can eat twice as much. Not true! The saying really means that you must be concerned about getting the best nutrition for yourself and for your growing baby.

Some women have the false idea that they can eat all they want during pregnancy. Don't fall into this trap. Don't gain more weight than your doctor recommends during your pregnancy – it can make you uncomfortable and it may be harder to lose the extra pounds after your baby is born.

A diet based on the recommended servings in the food-guide pyramid ensure good nutrition. *See* the illustration of the pyramid on page 137.

Your Calorie Needs in Pregnancy

If you are normal weight before pregnancy, your calorie intake should average about 2,200 calories a day during the first trimester of pregnancy. You need to add up to 300 calories to that number during the remainder of your pregnancy, depending on your pre-pregnancy weight. *See* the discussion of weight management during pregnancy that begins on page 156.

These extra calories are the foundation of tissue growth in you and your baby. Your baby uses the energy from your calories to create and to store protein, fat and carbohydrates, and to provide energy for its body processes to function. You use the extra calories to support the changes your body goes through during pregnancy. Your uterus increases in size many times, your breasts increase in size and your blood volume increases by 50 per cent, among other changes.

Calories aren't interchangeable. You can't eat whatever you want and expect to get the best nutrition for your baby and you; eating correctly takes care and attention. Where the calories come from is as important as the number you consume. You need to eat foods high in vitamins and minerals, especially iron, calcium, magnesium, folic acid and zinc. Fibre and fluids are also essential because constipation problems can be associated with pregnancy. Eating a wide variety of foods each day can supply you with the nutrients you need. Choose from dairy products, protein foods, fruits and vegetables, and breads and cereals.

During pregnancy, you will need to consume 6 to 7oz (170 to 200g) of protein every day to cover the growth or repair of the embryo/fetus, placenta, uterus and breasts. Carbohydrates are also important to your diet. There is no recommended dietary allowance (RDA) for daily carbohydrate intake during pregnancy. Most doctors believe that carbohydrates should make up about 60 per cent of the total number of calories in your diet. If you are eating 2,000 calories a day, you would consume about 1,200 carbohydrate calories.

You probably don't need to worry about an inadequate fat intake; in the British diet, fat intake is usually excessive. There is no recommended daily amount for fat intake during pregnancy. Don't avoid all fats, but use them sparingly; measure how much you use of each, and read the labels.

Eat a variety of foods throughout pregnancy. Suggested daily servings from each of the six food groups are listed in the box opposite. Serving sizes are described for each food group in the sections that follow.

Food Group Recommendations

Be good to you and your baby, and eat the recommended number of

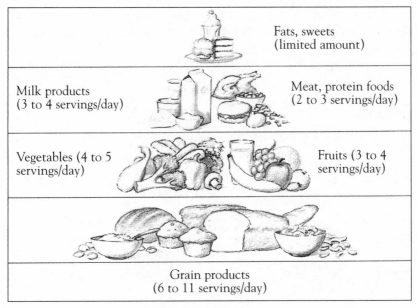

Fats, sweets
(limited amount)

Milk products
(3 to 4 servings/day)

Meat, protein foods
(2 to 3 servings/day)

Vegetables (4 to 5
servings/day)

Fruits (3 to 4
servings/day)

Grain products
(6 to 11 servings/day)

The food pyramid

servings from each food group every day. If you are carrying twins, you will need to eat at least one more serving each of dairy products and protein each day. Discuss your nutrition plan with your doctor or a qualified dietitian.

Dairy Products

Dairy products contain calcium, a mineral that is important for you

Daily Food Group Servings	
Food group	**Servings per day**
Dairy products	3 to 4
Meats, protein sources	2 to 3
Vegetables	at least 4
Fruits	3 to 4
Breads, cereal, pasta and rice	6 to 11
Fats and sweets	2 to 3

and your growing baby. The calcium content of many packaged foods is found on the nutrition label. Representative foods from this group, and their serving sizes, include:

6oz (170g) cottage cheese
2oz (60g) processed cheese
1¹/₂oz (40g) natural cheese (such as Cheddar)
1oz (30g) hard cheese (such as Parmesan or Romano)
8oz (230ml) pudding or custard
8oz (230ml) glass of milk
8oz (230ml) yogurt

If you need to keep the fat content low, choose skimmed milk, low-fat yogurt and low-fat cheese instead of whole milk and ice cream. The calcium content is unaffected in low-fat dairy products. Refer to the box on page 152 for other common foods which contain calcium.

Protein

Amino acids in protein are critical to the growth and repair of the embryo/fetus, placenta, uterus and breasts. The recommended amount of protein food in pregnancy is 6 to 7 ounces (170–200g) a day – about twice the amount normally recommended. Foods you might choose from this group, and their serving sizes, include:

2 tbsp (30g) peanut butter
4oz (120g) cooked dried beans
2–3oz (60–90g) cooked meat
1 egg

Poultry, fish, lean cuts of red meat, dried beans, eggs, nuts and seeds are all good protein sources. If you need to watch your calorie intake, skinless chicken and fish are better choices than beef or pork.

Vegetables

Vegetables are important in your nutritional plan. Because they change with the seasons, vegetables are also a great way to add variety to your everyday menu plans. Some vegetables are good sources of iron, folic acid, calcium and fibre; check a nutritional guide for particular information about vegetables you select. (Your greengrocer may be able to answer your questions.) Foods you might choose from this group, and their serving sizes, include:

6oz (170ml) vegetable juice
4oz (120g) broccoli, carrots or other vegetable, cooked or raw
1 medium baked potato
8oz (230g) raw, leafy vegetables (greens)

Eat a variety of vegetables for good nutritional balance in your diet. Eat at least one leafy, green or deep-yellow vegetable a day for extra iron, fibre and folic acid.

Fruits

Fruit is good for you, and tastes good, too. It is an excellent source of many important vitamins and minerals, so enjoy many types of fruit. Foods you might choose from this group, and their serving sizes, include:

6oz (170g) grapes
4oz (120ml) fruit juice
1 medium banana, orange or apple
2oz (60g) dried fruit
4oz (120g) tinned or cooked fruit

In your daily diet, be sure to include one or two servings of a fruit rich in vitamin C, such as orange juice or orange slices. Fresh fruits are also a good source of fibre, which can help to relieve symptoms of constipation.

Breads, Cereal, Pasta and Rice

Foods from this group are nearly interchangeable, so you shouldn't find it hard to get all the carbohydrates you need. If you don't like pasta, choose rice. If cereal isn't appealing, choose bread. Foods you might choose from this group, and their serving sizes, include:

1 slice bread
1 medium bread roll
1oz (30g) ready-to-eat cereal
4oz (120g) cooked pasta, cereal or rice
$^1/_2$ bagel

Fats and Sweets

Be careful with fats and sweets, unless you are underweight and need to add a few pounds. Current guidelines suggest that fat should make up no more than 30 per cent of your total daily calories. While sugar adds flavour to food, it has little nutritional value. Use it sparingly.

Be careful with butter, margarine, oils, salad dressing, nuts, chocolate and sweets. Foods in this group are often high in calories but low in nutritional value. Use them sparingly. Foods from this group, and their serving sizes, include:

> 1 tablespoon (15ml) sugar or honey
> 1 tablespoon (15ml) olive oil or other type of oil
> 1 pat of margarine or butter
> 1 tablespoon (15ml) jam
> 1 tablespoon (15ml) prepared salad dressing

Eat sweets in moderation during pregnancy. Eating sweets or junk foods full of empty calories will not do you or your baby any good. Instead, replace these treats with nourishing choices, such as a piece of fruit or a slice of fresh wholewheat bread. You will satisfy your hunger and your nutritional needs at the same time.

Other Food Facts

Junk Food

You may have to forgo most junk food while you are pregnant. 'Junk food' is high-calorie, high-fat food that contains little nutrition for you or your baby. It is probably fine to eat some now and then, but don't make it a regular part of your diet.

Avoid crisps, fizzy drinks, biscuits, pie, chocolate, sweets, cake and ice cream. Instead, select foods that are high in fibre and low in sugar and fat; choose fruits and vegetables, peas and beans, dairy products and wholegrain biscuits and breads.

Food Cravings

Cravings for particular foods during pregnancy are normal for many women. (Sometimes the chosen foods appear a little strange to other people!) Cravings can be both good and bad. If you crave foods that are nutritious and healthy, go ahead and eat them in moderate amounts. If you crave foods that are high in sugar and fat, loaded with empty calories, be very careful about eating them. Sometimes you can get rid of a craving by eating fresh fruits and vegetables.

We don't know why women sometimes crave unusual foods or food combinations during pregnancy. Hormone and emotional changes that occur during pregnancy may have something to do with it.

> Megan began having food cravings early in her pregnancy. Her craving for ice cream could have been a problem. She knew that if she ate it as often as she wanted to, her weight would be out of control. She found that by using self-control and by substituting low-fat yogurt for higher-calorie ice cream, she was able to have a treat once in a while and still manage her weight.

Some foods you love normally may make you feel sick during pregnancy. This is common. The hormones of pregnancy have a significant impact on the gastrointestinal tract, which can affect your reaction to certain foods.

Caffeine

Caffeine is a component of many beverages and foods, including coffee, tea, cola drinks and chocolate. Some medicines, such as cough medicines and headache preparations, contain a lot of caffeine. Caffeine is of no known benefit to you or the fetus.

Caffeine is a central nervous system stimulant that can affect calcium metabolism in both you and your baby. Four cups of coffee a day (800mg of caffeine) drunk by a pregnant woman have been thought to be associated with decreased birth weight and a smaller head size in newborns. An exact 'toxic' amount for caffeine has not

---

What do pregnant women crave?

A recent study of pregnant women found that they craved:

- Chocolate (33 per cent of the time they craved foods)
- Other desserts and ice cream (20 per cent of the time)
- Citrus fruits (19 per cent of the time)

been determined, but it makes sense to limit your caffeine intake.

Read labels on foods, beverages and over-the-counter medications to determine caffeine content. Eliminate as much caffeine from your diet as possible.

Herbal Teas

Some types of herbal tea are good for you and help to relieve certain pregnancy discomforts, which makes herbal tea a good alternative to coffee or regular tea. The herbal teas listed in the box below are delicious. Each is safe to use during pregnancy.

Some herbs and herbal teas are *not* safe to use during pregnancy because they could harm your developing baby. Herbs and teas to *avoid* during pregnancy include blue or black cohosh, penny-royal leaf, yarrow, goldenseal, feverfew, psyllium seed, mugwort, comfrey, coltsfoot, juniper, rue, tansy, cottonroot bark, large amounts of sage, senna, cascara sagrada, buckthorn, male fern, slippery elm and squaw vine.

Artificial Sweeteners

Studies to date have not shown any harm to pregnancy from aspartame

Herbal Teas and Their Benefits	
Tea	*Benefit*
Camomile	Helps digestion
Dandelion	Helps to reduce water retention and soothe an upset stomach
Ginger root	Helps ease nausea and nasal congestion
Nettle leaf	Rich in iron, calcium and other vitamins and minerals that are good for a pregnant woman
Peppermint	Relieves wind and calms stomach acids; can be used alone or mixed with camomile
Red raspberry	Helps to relieve nausea and stabilize hormones

(Canderel). The phenylalanine in aspartame contributes to phenylalanine in your diet, so if this is a problem for you, avoid foods and beverages sweetened with aspartame. Phenylalanine is discussed on page 144.

Saccharine is an artificial sweetener found in some foods and beverages; its effect on pregnancy is still being tested. My advice is to avoid artificial sweeteners or use them in moderation during pregnancy.

Late-night Snacks

Late-night nutritious snacks are beneficial for some women, especially if they must eat many small meals a day. However, many women should not snack at night because they don't need the extra calories. For others, food in the stomach late at night can cause distress, especially if heartburn or nausea and vomiting are problems.

Your Cholesterol Level

During pregnancy and lactation, the level of cholesterol in your blood rises naturally because of hormone changes. It probably won't make sense to have your cholesterol tested while you are pregnant or nursing.

Nausea during Pregnancy

Eating can be a problem if you suffer from nausea, also called *morning sickness*, during early pregnancy. Eating smaller meals frequently helps. You should be able to eat nutritious foods, even if you have morning sickness. For a few women, nausea becomes serious because it prevents from them eating an adequate amount of food or drinking enough fluid. *See* page 130 for further information about nausea and morning sickness.

Eating Out

Although there is no problem with eating out at restaurants, you should be careful about what you eat. Avoid raw meats or raw seafood, such as sushi. Avoid foods that may not agree with you right now.

May had a habit of going out for fast food every day for lunch before she got pregnant. But during her pregnancy, she found that she was very tired by midday and needed to rest. She discovered that if she brought a pack lunch to work she could eat a healthy meal, then lie down on a couch in the staff lounge for 45 minutes. She got some rest and enjoyed her afternoon work a lot more.

At a restaurant, your best choices may be fish, fresh vegetables and salads, but be careful with calorie-loaded salad dressings if you are concerned about excessive weight gain. Avoid highly spiced foods or foods that contain a lot of sodium. Chinese food often contains large amounts of monosodium glutamate (a sodium-containing product). You may retain water after eating these foods.

Other Special Precautions

Phenylketonuria (PKU). PKU is a condition in which the body is unable to use phenylalanine properly, and it accumulates in body fluids. The accumulation can lead to mental retardation and other nervous system disorders in you or your developing baby.

If you suffer from phenylketonuria, you will need to follow a diet that is low in phenylalanine. Avoid the artificial sweetener aspartame.

Salmonella poisoning. Salmonella are bacteria that can cause problems ranging from mild gastric distress to a severe, sometimes fatal, food poisoning. This situation can be serious for a pregnant woman and her developing baby if it prevents her from getting enough fluid or eating nutritiously. Almost 1,400 strains have been identified. Any form of salmonella could be dangerous to a pregnant woman.

We have long known that cracked raw eggs can be contaminated with salmonella organisms. These organisms are found in uncracked eggs as well, if a hen's ovaries are contaminated. Salmonella bacteria can be found in raw chicken and other raw poultry.

Salmonella are destroyed in cooking, but it is prudent to take additional precautions against salmonella poisoning.

- Clean work surfaces, utensils, dishes and pans with a disinfecting agent and wash your hands after preparing any poultry or products made with raw eggs. You could pick up salmonella from these surfaces on your hands and transfer it to your mouth or another surface.
- Thoroughly cook all poultry.
- Avoid foods made with raw eggs, including salad dressings (Caesar

salad), hollandaise sauce, homemade ice cream made with eggs or any other food made with raw or undercooked eggs.

- Boil eggs for seven minutes to make hard-boiled eggs.
- Poach eggs for five minutes.
- Fry eggs for three minutes on *each* side.
- Avoid 'sunny-side up' eggs (those not turned during frying). It is important to cook the entire egg thoroughly, not just part of it.

Facts About Fish

We know that eating fish is healthy, but it is particularly good for you during pregnancy. Fish contains omega-3 fatty acids, which help to prevent some heart problems; during pregnancy, this substance also seems to help prevent pregnancy-induced hypertension and pre-eclampsia, which are both greater risks for older pregnant women.

Women who eat a variety of fish during pregnancy have longer pregnancies and give birth to babies with higher birth weights, according to some studies. This is important because the longer a baby stays in the uterus, the better its chances are of being strong and healthy at delivery.

Many fish are safe to eat, and you should include them in your diet. Most fish is low in fat and high in vitamin B, iron, zinc, selenium and

---

Good Fish and Shellfish Choices

Below is a list of fish that are good choices for you during pregnancy. You can eat these fish as often as you like.

bass	plaice
cod	pollock
flounder	red snapper
haddock	salmon
halibut	sole
herring	sprats
mackerel	whitebait
perch	

You may eat the following shellfish as often as you like, if they are thoroughly cooked. You can steam, bake or broil any of them.

clams	oysters
crab	scallops
lobster	shrimps

copper. Many fish choices are an excellent, healthy addition to your diet, and you can eat them as often as you like. See the chart above for a list of good choices.

Omega-3 Fatty Acids

Some researchers now believe that eating fatty fish or ingesting omega-3 fatty acids in another form (such as fish-oil capsules) may enhance your baby's intellectual development. Studies have shown that fish oil is important to fetal neurological development. One recent study of pregnant women demonstrated that when a pregnant woman eats a fish oil, it actually reaches the brain of the developing fetus.

Include omega-3 fatty acids in your eating plan, but don't exceed 2.4g of omega-3 fatty acids a day. Fish high in these oils are salmon, mackerel, herring and tuna. Discuss the matter with your doctor.

Methyl-mercury Poisoning

Some fish are contaminated with a dangerous substance as the result of man-made pollution. People who eat these fish are at risk of methyl-mercury poisoning. Mercury is a naturally occurring substance as well as a pollution by-product. Mercury becomes a problem when it is released into the air as a pollutant. It settles into the oceans and from there winds up in some types of fish.

It has been determined that a certain level of methyl mercury in fish is dangerous for humans. However, we do not know if this level is harmful to a fetus. Researchers do know that methyl mercury can pass from mother to fetus across the placenta.

Doctors caution pregnant women and those trying to conceive against eating some kinds of fish more than once a month. These fish include shark, swordfish and tuna (fresh or frozen). If you are nursing, limit your consumption to once a week. Tinned tuna is safer but don't eat more than two 6oz (180g) tins a week.

Some freshwater fish, such as pike, may also be risky to eat.

Other Problems to Know About

Other environmental pollutants can appear in fish. Dioxin and PCBs (polychlorinated biphenyls) are found in some fish, such as lake trout; avoid them.

Parasites, bacteria, viruses and toxins can also contaminate fish.

Eating infected fish will make you sick, sometimes severely so. Sushi is a fish dish that could contain viruses or parasites. Raw shellfish, if contaminated, could cause hepatitis-A, cholera or gastroenteritis. Avoid *all* raw fish.

Drink Enough Fluids

Water enables your body to process nutrients, develop new cells, sustain blood volume and regulate body temperature – all very important during pregnancy! Your blood volume increases during pregnancy; drinking extra fluids helps you to keep up with this change. You may feel better during pregnancy if you drink more liquid than you normally do.

Research has shown that for every 15 calories you burn, your body needs about 1 tablespoon of water. If you burn 2,000 calories a day, you need 133 tablespoons – 4pt (1.9l) of water! Because you need more calories during pregnancy, you also need more water.

Drink six to eight or more glasses of liquid every day. Water is the best source of fluid; however, other fluids will satisfy your needs. Foods and drinks that can help you to get enough fluid include vegetables, milk and milk products, meats, grain products, fruits and juices. Avoid coffee, tea and diet cola as fluid sources – they can contain sodium and caffeine, which act as diuretics.

Two quarts a day may seem like a lot of liquid to consume, but you can do it. Some women drink water, one glass at a time, throughout the day. (Decrease your intake later in the day so you don't have to go to the toilet all night long.)

Many pregnant women who suffer from headaches, uterine cramping and other problems find that by increasing their water or fluid intake, they relieve some symptoms. Drinking plenty of water also helps to avoid bladder infections.

Water is important in regulating body temperature. In fact, for each degree above 98.6°F (37°C), drink an extra pint of water (or other fluid) each day to help bring down a fever.

To determine if you are drinking enough fluid, check your urine. When it is light yellow to clear, you are getting enough water. Dark-yellow urine is a sign that you need to increase your fluid intake.

Thirst is not a good indication of how much water you need. By the time you get thirsty, you have already lost 1 per cent of your body's water. Don't let yourself become thirsty!

When you exercise, drink a cup of water before you begin your routine. Then drink $^1/_2$ cup to 1 cup of water every 20 minutes while you are exercising to help prevent dehydration.

Salt, Sodium and Pregnancy

Sodium is a chemical that maintains the proper amount of fluid in your body. (Table salt, a compound comprised of sodium and chloride, is about half sodium.) During pregnancy, sodium can also affect your baby's system. Using too much or too little of it can cause problems. You need some sodium; you just don't need a lot.

Sodium is found in salty foods (such as potato crisps, nuts and pickled gherkins) and in many processed foods, from soups to meats. It can be found in carbonated beverages and sports drinks.

During pregnancy, keep your consumption of sodium under 3g (3,000mg) a day. Consuming too much sodium can cause fluid retention, swelling and high blood-pressure problems.

You can't avoid something unless you know where to find it. With sodium, that can be tricky. It is in the salt-cellar and in salty-tasting foods, such as pretzels, crisps and salted nuts. It is frequently used as a preservative in foods that do not taste salty, such as tinned and processed products, fast foods, cereals, desserts – even some medicines. Read nutrition labels. You can also buy inexpensive pamphlets at larger grocery stores and bookstores that list the sodium content of common foods and fast foods.

The Challenge of Being Vegetarian during Pregnancy

Some women choose to eat a meatless diet; other women find that during pregnancy, the sight of meat makes them feel sick. Many of my patients want to know if a vegetarian plan – a food plan without meat – is safe during pregnancy. Following a vegetarian diet while you are pregnant can be safe and healthy, if you pay close attention to the foods and combinations of foods you eat.

Most women who eliminate meat from their diets eat a more nutrient-rich variety of foods than those who eat meat. This may be true because these women make an extra effort to include more fruits and vegetables in their food plans when they eliminate meat products.

If you choose a vegetarian eating plan, be sure that you eat enough calories to fuel your pregnancy. During pregnancy, you need to consume between 2,200 and 2,700 calories a day, depending on your pre-pregnancy weight. *See* page 158 for a chart about weight gain during pregnancy.

Besides eating enough calories, be sure that you are eating the right kind of calories. Choose fresh foods that provide a variety of vitamins and minerals. Avoid too many fat calories because you may gain extra weight. If you are a vegetarian, discuss your daily diet with a doctor at your first antenatal visit. He or she may want you to see a nutritionist if you have any pregnancy risk factors.

Different Vegetarian Diets

There are different vegetarian nutrition plans, with unique characteristics. If you are a lacto vegetarian, your diet includes milk and milk products. If you are an ovo-lacto vegetarian, your eating plan includes milk products and eggs. A vegan diet includes only foods of plant origin, such as nuts, seeds, vegetables, fruits, grains and beans and peas. A macrobiotic diet limits foods to whole grains, beans, vegetables and moderate amounts of fish and fruits. A fruitarian diet is the most restrictive; it allows only fruits, nuts, olive oil and honey.

Macrobiotic and fruitarian diets are too restrictive for pregnant women. They do not guarantee the optimal intake of the vitamins, minerals, protein and calories you need for proper fetal development. Other vegetarian diets can provide complete nutrition for you and your growing baby; vegan diets, lacto diets or ovo-lacto diets can work if you eat a wide variety of foods in the right quantities.

Concerns When You Eat 'Vegetarian'

If you are vegetarian, your goal is to consume enough calories to maintain and to gain weight during pregnancy. You don't want your body to use protein for energy because you need it for your growth and your baby's growth.

Minerals are also a concern. By eating a wide variety of whole grains, peas and beans, dried fruit, Lima beans and wheat germ, you should be able to get enough iron, zinc and other trace minerals. If you don't drink milk or include milk products in your diet, you must find other sources of vitamins D, B_2, B_{12} and calcium. *See* the discussion of vitamins and minerals in the section that follows.

Vitamins and Minerals during Pregnancy

Vitamins and minerals – in the right quantities – are a major part of good nutrition. Eating a nutritious, varied diet helps to ensure that you get all the vitamins and minerals you need. Your doctor may ask you to take an antenatal vitamin pill every day. Vegetarians may need to pay special attention to getting enough of some vitamins and minerals.

Iron Supplementation

Iron is one of the most important elements for your body; women need more iron than men because of menstruation. However, most women do not get enough iron in their diet. Research has shown that between the ages of 20 and 50, many women consume only about two-thirds (10mg/day) of the Recommended Daily Allowance (RDA) of iron (15mg/day). The average woman's diet seldom contains enough iron to meet the increased demands of pregnancy (30mg/day).

It is very important that you meet your increased iron needs during pregnancy. Needs are higher because your blood volume increases by half to support the oxygen needs of your baby and the placenta. In the third trimester, your need for iron increases even more. Your baby draws on your stores of the mineral to create its own stores for the first few months of its life.

You will also need adequate iron reserves to draw on during your baby's birth. The uterus' oxygen requirements increase with labour contractions, and you will lose some blood during a normal delivery.

How can you recognize an iron deficiency? There are distinct symptoms. You feel tired, have trouble concentrating, feel sick easily or suffer from headaches, dizziness or indigestion. An easy way to check for iron deficiency is to examine the inside of your bottom eyelid – it should be dark pink. Or look at your nail beds; if you are getting enough iron, they will be pink.

In a healthy woman, only 10 to 15 per cent of the iron she consumes is absorbed by the body. To ensure that you have enough iron in your diet, eat a variety of foods that are rich in iron. These foods include:

- Chicken
- Dried fruits
- Egg yolks
- Lean red meat
- Organ meats, such as heart and kidneys

- Spinach
- Tofu
- Watercress

Your body stores iron efficiently, so you don't need to eat these foods every day. However, you do need to eat them on a regular basis. Eat vitamin-C foods and iron-rich foods together because iron is more easily absorbed by the body when it is consumed with vitamin C. (A spinach salad with orange sections is a nutritious example.)

Antenatal vitamins contain about 60mg of iron. You may not need extra iron if you eat a healthy diet and take your antenatal vitamins every day. Discuss it with your doctor.

The iron you ingest can cause constipation. Work with your doctor to minimize this side-effect while maintaining sufficient iron intake.

Vegetarians and others who eat very little meat are at great risk of iron deficiency during pregnancy. If you are a vegetarian, pay close attention to this aspect of your diet. Fish, poultry and tofu are all excellent sources of iron. Most beans and peas also contain significant amounts of the mineral. Some breakfast foods and breads are now iron fortified.

Dried fruit and dark leafy vegetables are good sources of iron. Cook in cast-iron pans because traces of iron will attach to whatever you are cooking. If you are a lacto or ovo-lacto vegetarian, do not drink milk with foods that are iron rich; calcium reduces iron absorption. Don't drink tea or coffee with meals because tannins present in those beverages inhibit iron absorption by 75 per cent.

Getting Enough Calcium

Calcium is important in the diet of every woman, especially women in their 30s and 40s. If you are pregnant, your needs increase because your developing baby requires calcium to build strong bones and teeth, and you need calcium to keep your bones healthy. The daily requirement for a non-pregnant woman is between 800 and 1,000mg of calcium. During pregnancy, your needs increase to 1,200mg a day.

Dairy products are excellent sources of calcium and vitamin D, which is necessary for calcium absorption in bones. It may be difficult for you to get enough calcium without eating dairy foods. Most prenatal vitamins contain only a small amount of the calcium you need. If your calcium intake is inadequate, your baby may draw needed calcium from your bones, which increases your risk of developing osteoporosis later in life.

Calcium Sources in Some Foods		
Food	*Serving Size*	*Amount of Calcium*
Almonds	¼ cup	95mg
Beans, dried, cooked	I cup	90mg
Milk	8oz	300mg
Orange juice, calcium-fortified	6oz	300mg
Sardines, with bones	3oz	324mg
Spinach, cooked	½ cup	140mg
Trout	4oz	250mg
Yoghurt, fruit	8oz	345mg
Yoghurt, plain	I cup	400mg

If you are lactose intolerant and unable to drink milk, a condition that is more frequent among older women, you may be able to eat hard cheeses and yoghurt. Lactose-reduced dairy products are also available. Discuss the situation with your doctor.

You may also choose non-dairy sources of calcium; it is found in beans, spinach, some fish, nuts and other foods. Read nutrition labels. The chart above lists some common calcium-containing foods.

If you need to watch your calories and avoid unnecessary fats, choose your calcium sources wisely. Select low-fat products and those with reduced-fat content. Skimmed or semi-skimmed milk and low-fat cheeses are better choices than whole milk and ordinary cheese.

Some foods interfere with your body's absorption of calcium. Be very careful about consuming salt, protein, tea, coffee and unleavened bread with a calcium-containing food.

Many women grow tired of drinking milk or eating cheese or yoghurt to meet their calcium needs during pregnancy. Below are some suggestions that can add calcium to your diet:

- Make milk shakes with milk and fresh fruit.
- Drink calcium-fortified orange juice, available commercially.
- Add non-fat dried-milk powder to recipes.
- Cook brown rice or oatmeal in low-fat or non-fat milk instead of water.

- Drink calcium-fortified skimmed milk.
- Make soups and sauces with undiluted evaporated non-fat milk instead of cream.
- Eat calcium-fortified breads.

If you and your doctor decide that calcium supplements are necessary, you will probably take calcium carbonate combined with magnesium, which aids calcium absorption. Avoid any supplement derived from animal bones, dolomite or oyster shells because they may contain lead.

Folic Acid

Some women may need folic acid (a term used interchangeably with *folate*) in addition to antenatal vitamins. Deficiency in folic acid can result in a type of anaemia called *megaloblastic anaemia*. Additional folate may be necessary for situations in which pregnancy requirements are unusually high, such as a pregnancy with twins or triplets, alcoholism or Crohn's disease.

Antenatal vitamins have 0.4mg to 1mg of folic acid in each dose, sufficient for a woman with a normal pregnancy. Some women do not need extra folic acid during pregnancy.

A neural tube defect called *spina bifida* afflicts 1 in 11,000 babies born in the UK every year. It develops in the first few weeks of pregnancy, when the fetus is highly susceptible to some substances or to the lack of them. Research has proved that nearly 75 per cent of all cases of spina bifida can be prevented if the mother takes 0.4mg of folic acid a day, beginning 3 or 4 months *before* pregnancy. Folic acid is required only through the first 13 weeks of pregnancy.

If a woman gives birth to a baby with spina bifida, she may need extra folic acid in subsequent pregnancies to reduce her chances of having another baby with the same problem. Some researchers now recommend that all women of child-bearing age take 0.4mg of folic acid a day, in the hope of significantly decreasing the chances of this serious problem.

Folic acid is obtained through many foods. Although it is difficult to get enough folic acid through food intake alone, a varied diet can help you to reach this goal. Common foods that contain folic acid are listed below.

Getting enough folic acid (vitamin B₉) is usually not a problem for vegetarians. Folic acid is found in many fruits, peas and beans and vegetables (especially dark leafy ones).

Foods with Folic Acid

Get the folic acid you need by enjoying any of these foods:

asparagus	green beans	spinach
avocados	lentils	strawberries
bananas	liver	wheatgerm
black beans	oranges and	wholewheat
broccoli	other citrus fruit	bread
egg yolks	peas	yoghurt
fortified cereals		

Eating a breakfast of 1 cup of fortified cereal, with milk, and a glass of orange juice supplies about half of your daily requirement of folic acid.

Vitamin A

Vitamin A is essential to human reproduction. Vitamin-A deficiency is rare in Great Britain; most women have adequate stores of the vitamin in the liver.

What concerns doctors now is the *excessive use* of vitamin A before conception and during early pregnancy. (This concern extends only to the retinol forms of vitamin A, often derived from fish oils. The beta-carotene form, usually derived from plants, is believed to be safe.) Studies indicate that elevated levels of the retinol form of vitamin A during pregnancy may cause birth defects, including cleft palate and hydrocephalus ('water on the brain').

The recommended daily allowance of vitamin A is 2,700 international units (iu) a day for a woman of child-bearing age (5,000 iu is a maximum dose). The requirement is the same whether a woman is pregnant or not. Most women get the vitamin A they need during pregnancy from the foods they eat. Supplementation during pregnancy is not recommended. Be cautious about taking *any* substances that you have not discussed with your doctor. This includes vitamin A. *See* pages 180 to 182 for particular cautions.

Vitamin B

The B vitamins – B_6, B_{12} and folic acid (B_9) – influence fetal development of nerves and red-blood-cell formation. If your vitamin

B_{12} level is low, you could develop anaemia during pregnancy. Milk and eggs provide vitamins B_6 and B_{12}. Other good sources of B_6 include bananas, potatoes, cabbage, avocados and brown rice.

Vitamin E

Vitamin E is important during pregnancy because it helps to metabolize polyunsaturated fats and contributes to building muscles and red-blood cells. Vitamin E appears in adequate quantities in meats, but if you don't eat meat, it can be harder to come by in the rest of the diet. If you are a vegetarian, you may need to pay particular attention to getting enough of it to meet the minimum requirements.

Unbleached, cold-pressed vegetable oils (such as olive oil), wheat germ, spinach and dried fruits are all good sources of vitamin E. Ask your doctor if your antenatal vitamin contains 100 per cent of the recommended daily allowance for vitamin E.

Zinc

Zinc stabilizes the genetic code in cells and ensures normal tissue growth in the fetus. It helps to prevent miscarriage and premature delivery and can help to regulate blood sugar in you and your baby.

Some women, especially thin ones, can increase their chances of giving birth to bigger, healthier babies by taking zinc supplements during pregnancy. In one study, babies born to thin women who took zinc during pregnancy were an average 4.5oz (130g) heavier, and head circumference was 0.16in (0.4cm) larger. Zinc also plays a critical role in immune functions.

Zinc is found in many foods, including seafood, meat, nuts and milk. Antenatal vitamins include 15 to 25mg of zinc, an adequate amount for most women.

If you are a vegetarian, you are more likely to have a zinc deficiency, so pay close attention to getting enough zinc every day. Lima beans, wholegrain products, nuts, dried beans, dried peas, wheat germ and dark leafy vegetables are all good sources of this mineral.

Fluoride

The benefit of fluoride supplementation during pregnancy is controversial. Some researchers believe that fluoride supplementation during pregnancy results in improved teeth in your child, but not everyone agrees. Fluoride supplementation during pregnancy has not been found to harm the baby. Some antenatal vitamins contain fluoride.

Weight Management

Every woman needs to gain a certain amount of weight during her pregnancy. Proper weight gain helps to ensure that you and your baby are healthy at the time of delivery.

Today, recommendations for weight gain during pregnancy are higher than they were in the past; normal weight gain is 24 to 28lb (11–13kg). If you are underweight at the start of your pregnancy, you should expect to gain between 26 and 35lb (12–16kg). If you are overweight before pregnancy, you probably should not gain as much as other women during pregnancy. Acceptable weight gain for you is between 15 and 22lb (7 to 10kg). Recommendations vary, so discuss the matter with your doctor. Eat nutritious, well-balanced meals during your pregnancy. Do *not* diet now!

As an average for a normal-weight woman, some doctors suggest a weight gain of ¹/₂lb (8oz; 230g) a week until 20 weeks, then ³/₄lb (12oz; 340g) until the 40th week. This recommendation is only an average; actual suggestions vary according to the individual.

It is not unusual not to gain weight or even to lose a little weight early in pregnancy. Your doctor or midwife will keep track of changes in your weight.

Watch your weight, but don't be obsessive about it. If you are in good shape when you get pregnant, with an appropriate amount of body fat, and you exercise regularly and eat healthily, you should not have a problem with excessive weight gain.

Increasing Your Calorie Intake

During pregnancy, you may be told to increase your calorie consumption; the average recommended increase is about 300 calories a day. Some women need more calories; some women need fewer. If you are underweight when you begin pregnancy, you will probably have to eat more than 300 extra calories each day. If you are overweight, you may have less need for extra calories.

The key to good nutrition and weight management is to eat a balanced diet throughout your pregnancy. Eat the foods you need to help your baby to grow and develop. Choose wisely. For example, if you are overweight, avoid high-calorie peanut butter and other nuts as a protein source; choose water-packed tuna or low-fat cheeses instead. If you are underweight, high-calorie ice cream and milkshakes are acceptable dairy sources.

Be Prepared to Gain Weight

Getting on the scales and seeing your weight increase is hard for some women, especially those who watch their weight closely. You must acknowledge at the beginning of your pregnancy that it is all right to gain weight; it is for the health of your baby. You can control your weight gain by eating carefully and nutritiously, but you must gain enough weight to meet the needs of your pregnancy. Your doctor knows this; that is why your weight is checked at every antenatal visit.

In the past, women were allowed to gain a very small amount of weight during pregnancy, sometimes as little as 12 to 15lb (5 to 7kg) for an entire pregnancy. With the benefit of research and advances in technology, we have learned that these restrictive weight gains were not in the best interests of the mother or baby.

Where Does the Weight Go?

A weight gain of 24–28lb (11–13kg) may sound like a lot when the baby only weighs about 7lb; however, weight is distributed between you and your baby. Weight gained normally during pregnancy is distributed as shown in the following chart.

Distribution of Pregnancy Weight	
7 to 10lb (3–4.5kg)	Maternal stores (fat, protein and other nutrients)
4lb (1.8kg)	Increased fluid volume
2lb (0.9kg)	Breast enlargement
2lb (0.9kg)	Uterus
7½lb (3.4kg)	Baby
2lb (0.9kg)	Amniotic fluid
1½lb (0.7kg)	Placenta

General Weight-gain Guidelines for Pregnancy	
If You Are Currently ...	*You Should Gain Approximately ...*
Underweight	26 to 35lb (12 to 16kg)
Normal weight	24 to 28lb (11 to 13kg)
Overweight	15 to 22lb (7 to 10kg)

Obesity Brings Special Cautions

If you are overweight as you begin pregnancy, you face special challenges. Being overweight can contribute to a variety of problems, including a greater chance of developing gestational diabetes or hypertension. You may have more problems with backaches, varicose veins and fatigue. Gaining too much weight (above the normal, expected amount) may increase the chances of a caesarean section, especially for older women.

Women who are overweight may need to see their doctor more often during pregnancy. An ultrasound scan may be needed to pinpoint a due date because it is harder to determine the size and position of your baby. Abdominal fat layers make manual examination difficult.

You may be screened for gestational diabetes. Diagnostic tests may also be done on your baby as your delivery date approaches.

Gain weight very slowly. Weigh yourself weekly and watch your food intake closely. Eat nutritious, healthy foods, and eliminate those with mostly empty calories. The quality of the food you eat is more important than ever when you are pregnant.

Exercise can be beneficial, but be sure to discuss your plans with your doctor before you begin an exercise programme. If you have never exercised before, walking and swimming may be the safest for you and your baby.

When You are Eating for More Than Two

When you are eating for yourself and more than one baby, you face an even greater nutritional challenge. Taking your antenatal vitamins every day provides some assurance that you are getting the nutrients you need, but the best source of nutrients and calorics for you and your developing babies is the food you eat. Proper food choices can provide you with adequate protein, calories and calcium.

When you are expecting more than one baby, nutrition and weight gain are important. If you don't gain weight early in pregnancy, you are more likely to develop pre-eclampsia. Your babies are more likely to be significantly smaller at birth than others.

Target Weight Gain with Multiples

The target weight gain for women carrying more than one baby is significantly higher than that for women carrying one baby. The desirable weight gain for women expecting twins is about 35lb (16kg).

Usually women who gain the targeted amount of weight during their pregnancies lose it after delivery. One study showed that women who gained the suggested amount of weight during a twin pregnancy were close to their pre-pregnant weight two years after delivery. You do not have to carry the extra weight for ever, so don't worry about it now.

When you consider the average size of the babies (about 7$\frac{1}{2}$lb [3.5kg] each) and the weight of the placenta(s) (1$\frac{1}{2}$lb [700g] for each), plus the weight of the additional amniotic fluid, you can see where the extra weight gain goes. Don't be alarmed when your doctor discusses this target weight gain with you, even if it seems like a lot.

Research shows that higher weight gains (within targeted ranges) are associated with better fetal growth.

Eat the Right Foods

The food pyramid is a good place to begin when making food choices (*see* page 137). Adjust the number of portions you consume to get the extra calories you need. Eat an extra serving of a dairy product and an extra serving of a protein because you need more calcium, protein and iron when you carry multiples.

CHAPTER 13

Exercise During and After Pregnancy

Pregnant women often ask me if they can exercise safely. Experts agree that exercise during pregnancy is safe and beneficial for most pregnant women, if it is done properly. Exercise can be even more beneficial for women who are pregnant in their late 30s and 40s. It can help you to feel more energetic and help you to deal more effectively with the demands of pregnancy, career and family.

Discuss exercise with your doctor at your first antenatal visit. If you decide later to start exercising or to change your current exercise programme, to be sure to discuss this with your doctor before you begin.

Some women should not exercise during pregnancy. If you experience any of the following, do not exercise:

- a history of incompetent cervix, preterm labour or repeated miscarriages
- high blood pressure early in pregnancy
- multiple fetuses (twins, triplets, more)
- diagnosed heart disease
- pre-eclampsia
- vaginal bleeding

In the past, exercise was not always approved for a pregnant woman. Doctors were concerned about the redirection of blood flow from the fetus to the mother's muscles during exercise. We now know that this occurs to a small degree, but it is not harmful to a healthy fetus.

Any exercise that involves joint movement forces water in the tissues back into the blood and helps to pump blood back to the heart. If you experience the normal swelling of pregnancy, such as swollen ankles or legs, exercise can help with the problem. Riding an exercise bicycle is excellent for relieving these symptoms.

If You Exercise Regularly

Many women love to exercise and are willing to juggle hectic schedules to fit it into their daily routine. They believe that exercise is necessary to help them to feel fit, to control their weight and to look their best. They don't want to give up exercising and its benefits because of pregnancy.

If you exercised on a regular basis before you became pregnant, you may need to modify your exercise goals and take things a little easier during pregnancy. The goal of exercising at this time is overall good health. Exercise makes you feel better physically, and it can give you an emotional boost, but don't overdo it.

There are benefits to continuing a moderate exercise programme during your pregnancy. The box below identifies some of them.

Some doctors believe that women who exercise during pregnancy enjoy a shorter recovery time after birth. Because exercise keeps you fit, you may 'bounce back' more quickly.

You may have to change or to modify your exercise programme during pregnancy because of changes in your body. Your centre of gravity shifts, so you need to adjust your exercise for that. As your abdomen grows larger, you may not be able to do some activities very comfortably and you may have to eliminate others.

The Exercise Pay-off

Exercise during pregnancy can help you to feel more in control of your body and to relieve some of the common aches and pains of pregnancy. Exercise improves circulation. Exercise definitely helps you to adjust to carrying the extra weight you gain during pregnancy. Regular, moderate exercise can also help to:

- relieve backache
- prevent constipation and varicose veins
- strengthen muscles needed for delivery
- make you feel better about yourself
- ease labour and delivery
- leave you in better shape after delivery

It may also help to control weight gain.

During pregnancy, your heart rate is higher; you don't have to exercise as vigorously to reach your target heart rate range. Be careful not to put too much stress on your cardiovascular system. If your heart rate is too high, slow down but don't stop completely. Continue exercising at a moderate rate. If your heart rate is too low and you don't feel winded, you may pick up the pace a bit, but don't overdo it. Check your pulse rate frequently to make sure you aren't over-exerting yourself.

I am often asked by women who jog or run regularly whether they can continue this activity during pregnancy. If you are used to jogging and have been involved in regular jogging before pregnancy, you can continue to jog in moderation during pregnancy. Listen to your body when it tells you to slow down – don't get overheated, stop if you feel tired, and drink lots of water.

If You Have Never Exercised Before

I have patients who do not like to exercise or who do not exercise on a regular basis. When many of these women discover they are pregnant, they begin to think about the benefits of exercise; they want to know whether it is safe to begin an exercise programme during pregnancy. If you have never exercised before, you must discuss it with your doctor before you begin.

> Suzy never liked regular exercise, but she found that being pregnant gave her the incentive and motivation to engage in a programme specifically designed for pregnant women at a health club. It helped her to feel more in control of her health while she was pregnant – she felt she was doing something positive for her body. After she delivered her baby, she continued exercising. She found that she really missed it if she didn't.

Yes, it is possible to start exercising now; however, begin gradually. Your age may affect your ability to exercise slightly. If you have never exercised before, you may find it a little more difficult to begin because of less flexibility and tighter muscles.

If your pregnancy is uncomplicated, you should be able to exercise as long as you are comfortable doing so. The key is not to do too much, too fast. Don't be afraid that exercising might do something to hurt your developing baby; most moderate exercise is safe.

If exercise is approved for you, start with *moderate* exercise if you do not have a regular exercise routine. Walking is an excellent form of exercise. Riding an exercise bicycle can be enjoyable. Swimming and other water exercises are also good for a beginner; the water provides your body with a lot of support.

Swimming and Water Exercises

Women have told me that while they are pregnant, the only time they really feel comfortable is in the water. Being in the water has a calming effect on some women, and it can help to reduce the swelling that is related to pregnancy.

Because it supports you, you will feel much lighter in the water, and you won't have to worry about keeping your balance. Because the water also supports the weight of the fetus, your lower back is relieved of some stress. That enables you to adopt a more relaxed posture and to enjoy a greater range of motion while you are in the water.

Being in the water reduces the effect of gravity, which in turn reduces pressure on your joints – a great temporary relief for some women. In addition, exercising in the water makes it significantly easier for the heart to pump blood. That is a real benefit, especially if you have hypertension.

You can also get a good work-out in the water. Water exerts 12 times the resistance of air on limbs – you will expend more energy moving through water than you would walking down the street.

Your baby is well protected inside your body while you are in the water. There are actually three barriers that provide protection – the amniotic membrane that surrounds the baby, the cervix and the vagina. Don't be concerned about water getting to the baby. However, if your bag of waters has broken, do not exercise in the water.

Consider these suggestions if you want to work out in water or swim as part of your exercise regimen.

- Be sure that the pool water is warm enough but not hot. The ideal temperature of the water should be between 80° and 84°F (26.5° and 29°C). Avoid hot tubs and spas because the water is too hot for the fetus.
- Drink plenty of fluids before you begin exercising and during exercise. Dehydration can occur even in a pool.
- Eat easily digested foods $1/2$ to 1 hour before you work out; choose fruit or a whole-wheat product.
- To help you keep your footing when you exercise in the pool, wear

aquatic shoes, tennis shoes or jogging shoes. Be sure the shoe has a good tread so that you don't slip.

Are There Risks to Exercising during Pregnancy?

Exercise during pregnancy is not without some risks, including increased body temperature, decreased blood flow to the uterus and possible injury to you. Your age is probably not an important factor, however. Most experts recommend that you reduce your exercise to 70 to 80 per cent of your pre-pregnancy level. If you have problems with bleeding or cramping or have had problems in previous pregnancies, you must modify or eliminate your exercise with your doctor's advice.

We know the increased hormone levels of pregnancy soften connective tissues, which can make your joints more susceptible to injury. Avoid full sit-ups, double leg raises and straight-leg toe touches.

It was once believed that exercise could cause preterm labour because of a temporary increase in uterine activity following exercise. However, studies prove that this is not a problem in a normal pregnancy. The fetal heart rate increases somewhat during and immediately after exercise, but it stays within the normal fetal range of 120 to 160 beats a minute. A moderate exercise programme should not cause any problems for you or your baby.

Your Exercise Experience during Pregnancy

You may notice some changes in how your body responds to exercise during pregnancy. Your growing abdomen can put a strain on your respiratory system; you may feel out of breath sooner than usual. When you exercise, don't work to the point that you cannot talk or have trouble breathing. At that point, you are working too strenuously; cut back on your work-out.

Avoid becoming overheated during your work-out. Work out in a well-ventilated room, and drink lots of water while you exercise. *See* the fluid-intake discussion on page 147.

Which Exercises during Pregnancy?

Keep in mind a few general precautions about exercising during pregnancy that apply to most pregnant women. Your doctor may want to discuss additional precautions that apply specifically to you.

you may be able to continue, but expect to change the level at which you play. The point to remember is not to get carried away or to overwork yourself. The goal is not to win the game but to maintain fitness and have a good time! You may want to pick a less strenuous sport to participate in during pregnancy. Some are listed below; most are considered acceptable for women of any age in a normal, low risk pregnancy:

- walking
- swimming
- low-impact aerobics designed specifically for pregnancy
- water aerobics
- using an exercise bicycle
- cycling (if you are experienced)
- jogging (if you jogged regularly before pregnancy)
- tennis (played moderately)
- yoga (don't lie on your back after 16 weeks of pregnancy)

Avoid the following sports during pregnancy:

- scuba diving
- water skiing
- surfing
- horseback riding
- downhill skiing
- cross-country skiing
- any contact sport

Pregnancy Aerobics Classes

Aerobics classes designed for pregnant women are a good exercise choice. They concentrate on your unique needs, such as strengthening abdominal muscles and improving posture. When choosing a class, ensure that the instructor has proper training.

Nutritional Needs during Exercise

Because nutritional needs increase during pregnancy and because you burn extra calories during exercise, consume enough calories to ensure a balanced diet. You may need to eat more than a pregnant woman eat with your doctor. Make sure that any additional calories are nutritious and supply your body with protein, calcium and carbohydrates, not sugar and fat.

Guidelines for Exercising during Pregnancy

Always consult your doctor before you begin any exercise programme. Follow the tips below to keep you healthy and in good shape:

- Try to exercise at least three times a week for 20 to 30 minutes each time.
- Start your exercise routine with a five-minute warm-up, and end with a five-minute relaxation period.
- Wear comfortable clothes that offer support, such as a support bra and good athletic shoes.
- Drink plenty of water during exercise.
- Don't exercise strenuously for more than 15 to 20 minutes.
- Check your pulse rate frequently; keep it below 140 beats a minute.
- Don't exercise in hot, humid weather.
- After the fourth month of pregnancy, avoid exercises that require you to lie on your back.
- Never allow your body temperature to rise above 100.4°F (38°C).
- Exercise during the coolest part of the day.
- Stop immediately and consult your physician if you experience any problems.

Be aware of problems that might develop while you exercise. If you notice any unusual occurrences, report them to your doctor immediately. Be careful about the following:

- pain
- bleeding
- dizziness
- extreme shortness of breath
- palpitations
- faintness
- abnormally rapid heart rate
- back pain
- pubic pain
- difficulty walking
- breathlessness that doesn't go away

- chest pain
- loss of fetal movement

Antenatal Exercises to Do at Home or at Work

Sometimes you may find it difficult to exercise outside your home or at a health club. You can do the exercises in this section at home or at work. Try all of them, and incorporate those you like into your regular schedule.

Weightlift with Tins

Next time that you are putting away groceries, build up your arm muscles by doing a little weightlifting with each tin (water bottles also work well). As you put a tin away, flex your arm a couple of times to work your arm muscles. Alternate your arms to give yourself a good work-out.

Work-out in Line

When you're standing in line at the supermarket, post office or anywhere else, use the time to do some 'creative' exercises. Rise up and down on your toes to work your calves. Spread your feet apart slightly, and do subtle knee lunges to give your quadriceps a workout. Clench and relax your buttock muscles. Do some Kegel exercises (*see* page 168) to strengthen your vaginal muscles. Contract your stomach muscles. These exercises will help to develop and strengthen some of the muscles you will use during labour and delivery.

Standing Stretches

If you are forced to stand in one place for a long time, step forwards slightly with one foot. Place all your weight on that foot for a few minutes. If you are still waiting, do the same exercise for the other foot. Alternate the leg you begin with each time.

Reaching-Stretching

You probably have to reach for things at home or at the office. When you do, make it an exercise in controlled breathing. Before you stretch, inhale, rise up on your toes and bring both arms up at the same time.

When you are finished, drop back on your heels, and exhale while slowly returning your arms to your sides.

Sitting Quietly

Any time that you are sitting quietly – at home, at the office, in your car, on a bus or a train – do the following breathing exercise to strengthen your abdominal muscles. Breathe deeply and contract your muscles; hold for a couple of seconds, then exhale slowly. Do this whenever you get the chance.

> Cindy was concerned because it was hard to find time to exercise regularly. She discovered that she could exercise at her desk at work, doing ankle and leg exercises. This helped her to keep her legs toned and also helped her with leg cramps and swelling.

Bending to Relieve Backache

While standing at a kitchen work-top or at a work surface at work, bend your knees and lean forward from your hips. Hold the position for a few minutes. This exercise is an excellent way to relieve back stress.

Rising from a Chair

Some women find it difficult to get out of a chair gracefully during pregnancy. This exercise helps you to maintain your grace and is also beneficial to you. Use your leg muscles to lower yourself into and raise yourself out of a chair. Slide to the front edge of the seat, then push up with your legs to get out of the chair. Use your arms for balance.

Kegel Exercise

The Kegel exercise strengthens the pelvic muscles. Practising it helps you to relax your muscles for delivery. While sitting, contract the lowest muscles of your pelvis as tightly as you can. Tighten the muscles higher in the pelvis in stages until you reach the muscles at the top. Count to ten slowly as you move up the pelvis. Hold briefly, then release slowly in stages, counting to ten again. Repeat two or three times a day.

You can also do the Kegel exercise by tightening the pelvic muscles first, then tightening the anal muscle. Hold for a few seconds, then release slowly, in reverse order. To see if you are doing the exercise correctly, stop the flow of urine while you are urinating.

Your Pregnancy Work-out

Practise the exercises in the previous section, and add the following ones to your routine. You may have to set time aside to do these exercises. If you combine them with some form of aerobic exercise, such as walking, swimming or bicycling, you will get a thorough work-out.

Arm Reaches

Relieves upper backache and tension in shoulders, neck and back.
Sit on the floor in a comfortable position. Inhale as you raise your right arm over your head. Reach as high as you can, while stretching from the waist. Bend your elbow, and pull your arm back down to your side as you exhale. Repeat for your left side. Do four or five times.

Pelvic Curl

Strengthens abdominal muscles and relieves back stress.
Kneel on your hands and knees, with your back relaxed. Do not arch

Arm Reaches

your back. Inhale and relax. As you exhale, pull your buttocks under and forward until you feel your back straighten at the waist and your abdomen tighten. Hold for a count of five, then exhale and relax. Do this exercise four or five times whenever you can.

Tailor's Seat

Develops pelvic-floor strength.
Sit on the floor, bring your feet close to your body and cross your ankles. Apply gentle pressure to your knees or the inside of your thighs. Hold for a count of ten, relax and repeat. Do this exercise four or five times (*see* illustration below).

Tailor's Press

Develops pelvic-floor strength and quadriceps strength.
Sit on the floor and bring the soles of your feet together, as close to your body as you can comfortably. Place your hands under your knees, and gently press down with your knees while resisting the pressure with your hands. Count to five, then relax. Increase number of presses until you can do ten presses twice a day.

Shoulder Circles

Relieves upper backache and tension in the shoulders, neck and back.
Inhale while slowly moving your left shoulder forward and upward, to form the top half of a circle. Slowly move the shoulder to the back

Wall Push-Away

then down to complete the circle as you exhale. Repeat with your right shoulder. Do four or five times.

Wall Push-Away

Develops upper-back, chest and arm strength, and relieves lower-leg tension.

Hip-and-Back Stretch

Stand a few feet away from a wall, with your hands in front of your shoulders. Place your hands on the wall and lean forward. Bend your elbows as your body leans into the wall. Keep your heels flat on the floor. Slowly push away from wall, and straighten. Do 10 to 20 times.

Hip-and-Back Stretch

Reduces back tension and increases blood flow to the feet.
Place one hand on the back of a chair or on a wall. Lift your right knee to the side of your tummy, and put your left hand under your thigh. Round your back, and bring your head and pelvis forward. Hold the position for a count of four, straighten up, then lower your leg. Repeat with your left leg. Do two or three times.

Side Leg Lifts

Tones and strengthens hip, buttock and thigh muscles.
Lie on your left side, with your body in alignment. Support your head with your left hand, and place your right hand on the floor in front of you for balance. Inhale and relax. While exhaling, slowly raise your right leg as high as you can without bending your knee or your body. Keep your foot flexed. Inhale and slowly lower your leg. Repeat on right side. Do ten times on each side.

Your After-pregnancy Work-out

After your baby is born, continue the exercises you did during pregnancy. Add some of the following exercises to help you to focus on specific areas, especially abdominal muscles. Do these exercises when your doctor gives you permission. Start slowly and gradually work harder.

Back Bridge

Strengthens back, legs and buttocks.
Lie flat on your back on the floor. Inhale, then slowly lift buttocks and back in straight line. Hold for four seconds. Exhale and lower your back to the floor so your upper back touches the floor, then your waist touches, then your pelvis touches last. Do four or five times.

The Crunch

Strengthens abdominal muscles.
Lie on your back on the floor, with your knees bent and your feet flat.
Put your hands on your abdomen. Suck in your abdomen, pulling your
navel toward your spine. Hold for four seconds and release. When you
are able to do eight repetitions, lift your head towards your chest. Hold
for four seconds, then lower your head and hold for four seconds. Work
up to ten repetitions.

Leg and Pelvic-floor Strengthener

Strengthens legs and pelvic floor.
Lie on your back with your arms out at your sides. Cross your right ankle
over your left ankle; squeeze your legs together. Hold for five seconds
and release. Repeat for the other ankle. Do five times on each side.

Back Stretch

Strengthens buttocks, back muscles and leg muscles.
Kneel on your hands and knees, with your wrists directly beneath your
shoulders and your knees directly beneath your hips. Keep your back
straight. Contract your abdominal muscles then extend your left leg
behind you at hip height. At same time, extend your right arm at
shoulder height. Hold for five seconds and return to a kneeling
position. Repeat on the other side. Start with four exercises on each
side, and gradually work up to eight.

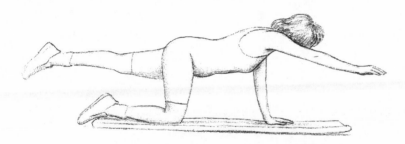

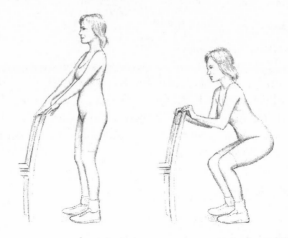

Chair Squat

Strengthens hips, thighs and buttock muscles.
Lightly grasp the back of a chair or a work-top for balance. Stand with
your feet shoulder-width apart. Keep your body weight over your heels
and your torso erect. Bend your knees, and your lower torso in a
squatting position. Don't round your back. Hold the squatting position
for five seconds, then straighten up to the starting position. Start with
five repetitions and work up to ten.

Leg Raises

Good for abdominal muscles.
Lie flat on your back. Slowly lift both legs from the hip at the same time,
using your abdominal muscles. Hold for five seconds. Slowly lower both
legs together to the floor. Start with two repetitions and work up to six.

CHAPTER 14

Current Medical Treatment and Medicines

It is a fact that the older you get, the more likely you are to develop medical conditions – some serious, most not-so-serious. Medicines you use to treat those conditions may affect your baby during your pregnancy. I will discuss some of those conditions and treatments in this chapter.

First let me comment on the subject of medication during pregnancy. Many pregnant women seem unconcerned about their use of various medicinal substances during pregnancy. They believe that if they can buy medication without a prescription, it must be safe to use. Or they believe that they can use any amount of vitamins, minerals or herbal substances without hesitation.

Beware of this type of thinking! Many substances you use *can* affect your growing baby. Some effects can be serious. Other effects may be subtle and cause minor birth defects. The effects of yet others may not be evident for years.

Researchers once believed that the placenta acted as a barrier to any agent the mother was exposed to. Today we know that is not the case. We have discovered that *almost all* drugs can cross the placenta and affect the fetus.

Teratogens

Drugs are called *environmental factors* (other things can be termed environmental factors, such as pesticides); environmental factors linked to birth defects are called *teratogens*. The first 13 weeks of development (the first trimester) are the most dangerous time in which to expose a fetus to teratogens. An embryo exposed to teratogens during the first two weeks of development may be unaffected; if the embryo is affected, the pregnancy can end in a miscarriage. The most critical period of fetal development during the first trimester is between two and eight weeks after conception that is, between four and ten weeks after the last menstrual period.

Although the first trimester is very important, your baby's systems continue to grow and to develop throughout your pregnancy. Exposure to some substances can harm a baby even after the first trimester.

Talk to Your Doctor

The best time to discuss current healthcare concerns is before you become pregnant, but this is not always possible. If you discover you are pregnant and are concerned about the medicines you use or anything else related to your health, talk to your doctor about it as soon as possible.

At your first visit with your doctor, discuss all medicines (prescription and over-the-counter) you take on a regular basis. You may have to stop taking a particular substance or adjust the dose.

Never stop taking any medication you use for a chronic health problem without first consulting your doctor! Some medication cannot and should not be stopped during pregnancy.

Some Safety Guidelines

You are an important part of your healthcare team, especially during pregnancy. You have to make many decisions about how you will take care of your body during this important time. The suggestions that follow can help you to decide what substances you use before and during your pregnancy.

- Don't use any unnecessary drugs while trying to conceive.
- Avoid all medicines during the first trimester, if possible. If you must take a medicine, consult your doctor before using it.
- Talk to your doctor openly and honestly about the medicines you use. If you have a problem that you normally treat with over-the-counter drugs, ask how to treat it during pregnancy.
- If you must use a prescription medicine, ask your doctor to prescribe it in its least potent strength.

Prescription Medicine Use during Pregnancy

Use of some prescription medicines is more common than others; the discussion below includes common substances many women must take during pregnancy. Please note – this information does *not* take the place of talking with your doctor.

Hormone Replacement Therapy

Today, the average age of menopause is 50. At menopause, you stop ovulating (necessary for conception) and stop having periods. The change is usually gradual, occurring over years, but it may be sudden. If you still have menstrual periods, you can probably still get pregnant.

In the past, women didn't start taking hormones (hormone replacement therapy or HRT) until their periods stopped, and they were certain of the menopause. Today, more women start HRT at younger ages.

If you become pregnant while taking HRT, advise your doctor immediately. Minor risks are associated with pregnancy when you have been taking female hormones. They are usually not severe enough to warrant terminating the pregnancy.

Thyroid Medication

You will need to continue taking thyroid medication throughout pregnancy. Thyroid hormone is made in the thyroid gland, which is found in the neck. It affects your entire body and is important to your metabolism. Thyroid hormone is also important in your ability to get pregnant.

Thyroxine (medication for a low-thyroid or hypothyroid condition) can be taken safely during pregnancy. Propylthiouracil (medication for a high-thyroid or hyperthyroid condition) passes to the baby; you will probably be given the lowest amount possible during pregnancy.

Fluoxetine (Prozac)

Today, many women take fluoxetine (Prozac) for depression and want to know if they can continue taking the medication during pregnancy. We have little information about its safety for a pregnant woman. Discuss taking this drug with your physician before you get pregnant or as soon as you discover that you are pregnant.

Skin-care Medications

Isotretinoin (Roaccutane) is a common acne treatment. Do *not* take it if you are pregnant! A woman taking isotretinoin during the first trimester of pregnancy is at greater risk of miscarriage and fetal malformation.

Tretinoin (Retin-A) is a medication used to help relieve minor wrinkling in the facial area. We don't know its effects on the fetus, so it is probably best to avoid tretinoin during pregnancy until we know more about its effects.

Occasionally steroid cream is prescribed for a skin condition. Before using it during pregnancy, discuss it with your doctor. You may be able to use another preparation that is considered safer during pregnancy.

Tetracycline, an antibiotic, is often prescribed for skin problems. During pregnancy, avoid all tetracyclines! Use of the drug during pregnancy can cause discoloration of your baby's permanent teeth later in life. (Tetracyclines should not be prescribed for children under age 8.)

Other Prescription Medicines

Some medications are safe to use during pregnancy but should be prescribed only if absolutely necessary. These substances include diazepam (Valium), chlordiazepoxide (Librium) and chlorazepate (Tranxene). Other substances are discussed below.

If you have a headache bad enough to be considered a migraine, call your doctor before you take anything for it. You may have heard of a relatively new medication for migraines called sumatriptan (Imigran), given by injection or in pill form. Avoid it during pregnancy; we do not know yet whether it is safe.

Common medications used for blood clots or phlebitis, called *anticoagulants*, are heparin and warfarin. Heparin does not cross the placenta, so it is safe to use during pregnancy. It is administered by injection or intravenously. Warfarin is not normally prescribed during pregnancy because it may cause significant problems in the fetus or newborn.

Many asthma medications are permissible to use during pregnancy. Inhalers can be used safely. For an asthma attack, your doctor may prescribe prednisolone; it is approved for use during pregnancy.

Medicines to treat anaemia can be important during pregnancy and are safe to use. These medicines contain iron, which may cause side-effects such as constipation, nausea or upset stomach.

Some older women may be taking hormones, including oestrogen or progesterone, when they discover they are pregnant. Most doctors recommend that you should not take hormones during pregnancy. If you are taking them when you learn that you are pregnant, contact your doctor.

In some situations, you may need pain relief during pregnancy. If you do, check with your doctor before you take anything stronger than extra-strength paracetamol. Paracetamol with codeine may be prescribed during pregnancy, but you should get your doctor's approval before you take it.

It you have a cough, you can almost always take cough drops or throat lozenges safely. Prescription cough medicine may contain codeine. Usually codeine is safe to use for a short period of time, but check with your doctor before you use it. Avoid any 'night-time' medicines that contain alcohol. Some are 25 per cent alcohol; you want to avoid alcohol use during pregnancy. Read labels before taking any preparation.

You may become constipated at some point during pregnancy and need a laxative. If you find that a laxative is necessary for more than two or three days, contact your doctor. He or she will probably advise you to make dietary changes to help with the problem.

Some medications can be taken for diarrhoea during pregnancy. Loperamide (Imodium) diarrhoea preparation is safe to use, but most doctors recommend avoiding the pink bismuth-type preparations during pregnancy. If you have bloody diarrhoea or diarrhoea that lasts longer than a few days, contact your doctor.

Pregnancy is not the time to use *any* type of diet pill. Over-the-counter diet pills contain large amounts of caffeine. Don't take prescription diet pills during pregnancy because they have not been proved safe. If you are taking diet pills when you discover that you are pregnant, stop taking them immediately!

Non-prescription/Over-the-counter Medicines

Many people, not just pregnant women, hold the false belief that medicines they can buy without a prescription (over-the-counter medicines) are harmless. Nothing could be further from the truth. Carelessness with over-the-counter preparations could cause great harm to you and your developing baby.

Take any over-the-counter medication with care during pregnancy. Ask your doctor about any medicine before you take it, whether it is prescription or non-prescription. Many over-the-counter medicines contain aspirin, caffeine or alcohol, all of which should be avoided during pregnancy. Cough syrups may contain as much as 25 per cent alcohol (that's '50 proof'!).

Use medications that contain ibuprofen with care; brand-name ibuprofen medications include Advil, Brufen, Fenbid, Novaprin and Nurofen. Avoid newer medicines, such as naproxen (Naprosyn) and ketoprofen (Orudis), until we know more about their safety during pregnancy. Read package labels, and get approval from your doctor or pharmacist before you take anything.

Some over-the-counter medicines that are safe to use while you are pregnant include:

• paracetamol (Panadol)
• antacids (Gaviscon, Gelusil, Maalox, Milk of Magnesia)
• throat lozenges
• decongestants (chlorpheniramine, Piriton)
• antidiarrhoeal preparations (kaolin mixture, Kaopectate)
• anti-itch preparations (diphenhydramine, Medinex, Nytol)
• cough medicine
• haemorrhoid preparations (Anusol)

Don't overuse any product during pregnancy. You can get 'too much of a good thing'.

Your doctor will not be angry or upset if you call the surgery with a question about a medicine. I can tell you from experience that it is much easier to answer a question and solve a potential problem about a medicine *before* a woman takes it than afterwards.

About Vitamin and Mineral Supplements

Be very cautious during pregnancy about taking vitamin and mineral supplements. Often people do not think of vitamins and minerals as harmful, but they can be, especially to your developing baby. Also see the discussion about specific vitamins and minerals beginning on page 150.

Many vitamin supplements and 'megavitamins' sold in health-food stores contain extremely large amounts of minerals, vitamins and other substances. Even some foods contain extra vitamins and minerals. Some of these 'extra' supplements could affect your developing baby.

One example is vitamin A. Studies indicate that ingesting too much of the retinol form of vitamin A during pregnancy may cause birth defects. Most people get all the vitamin A they need in the foods they eat. Supplementation is not recommended. Many vitamin supplements and megavitamins sold in health-food stores contain as much as 25,000 iu of vitamin A. That is nearly ten times the amount you need. Even some cereals contain as much as 5,000 iu per serving. Eating just two bowls a day of fortified cereal could potentially affect your developing baby! You should not eat too much liver in pregnancy. It is very rich in vitamin A and the maximum is a modest serving of liver once a week.

The more vitamin A you consume, the higher the potential danger. A women taking 20,000 iu a day has a four times greater risk of having a baby with a birth defect than a women who takes 10,000 iu.

To protect yourself and your baby, don't take any vitamins or minerals other than your antenatal vitamin and iron or folic acid supplements, unless prescribed by your doctor especially for you. Read labels on the foods you eat. Do not 'self-medicate' with other vitamins or minerals – you don't need them, and they can be dangerous if they are taken in excessive amounts.

Antenatal vitamins contain the recommended daily amounts of vitamins and minerals you need during pregnancy. They are prescribed to ensure the health of you and your baby.

Antenatal Vitamins

At your first antenatal visit, your doctor will probably advise you on antenatal vitamins. It is very important that you take these vitamins for your *entire* pregnancy.

> Kathy was a busy executive who never had time for breakfast. She might grab a diet cola and a bag of chips for lunch and often ate dinner out with clients. Her plan was to continue this regimen and take an antenatal vitamin during her pregnancy. We had a frank discussion about why her plan wouldn't work. I explained how her baby relied on her for its nourishment. I advised her that she couldn't eat that way for the entire pregnancy; she would feel terrible and not be able to work. With some help, she made a commitment to a healthy eating plan and to take her antenatal vitamins every night after dinner.

Sometimes, late in pregnancy, a woman will stop taking her antenatal vitamins; she gets tired of taking them, or she decides they aren't necessary. Studies show that nearly half of all pregnant women who are prescribed antenatal vitamins do not take them regularly. The vitamins and iron in antenatal vitamins are essential to the well-being of your baby, so be sure you take these supplements until your baby is born.

Immunizations and Vaccinations in Pregnancy

Some immunizations are not recommended for a pregnant woman because they may contain substances that are harmful to a fetus. In other cases, an immunization might be necessary for a woman's health.

Vaccines work by introducing disease components into the body in a very controlled way, which triggers the body to produce antibodies to protect it against the disease in the future. The risk of fetal exposure to various diseases is an important consideration with vaccines during pregnancy, but not all vaccines are harmful.

Don't be immunized without discussing the situation with your doctor first. If you have been exposed to a disease, or exposure is possible, your doctor will weigh the risk of the disease against the risks of the immunization, if any.

Safe Vaccines

Tetanus, diphtheria and rabies vaccines are all considered safe to have at any time during pregnancy. The flu vaccine is also considered safe to use during pregnancy. If you are in a high risk group for flu, especially if you suffer from chronic lung problems, kidney disease or cardiovascular disease, your doctor will probably tell you to go ahead and receive the vaccine.

Vaccines You Should Not Receive

Pregnant women should definitely avoid some vaccines. Live measles vaccine should never be given to a pregnant woman; this vaccine protects against measles, mumps and rubella. Don't get a primary vaccination against polio unless your risk of exposure is high – if you are travelling to a high risk area, for example. Avoid the yellow fever vaccine, which is also a live-virus vaccine. For added protection, it is wise to have a pregnancy test and be on reliable contraception before receiving measles, mumps and rubella, polio or yellow fever vaccines.

CHAPTER 15

Pregnancy Affects Your Partner, Too

Getting pregnant and having a baby involves *both* you and your partner. Although it is an exciting time for you, it may be a different experience for your baby's father – it may not be an all-encompassing experience for him.

A first time pregnancy for you may or may not be a first pregnancy for your partner. However, it will be the first pregnancy he shares with you.

Being pregnant together can teach you a lot about each other. You both will go through many changes during the pregnancy and face new challenges. Your partner may feel anxious about his ability to be a good father or to provide for you and the baby. Other challenges you both may face include making child care decisions, choosing how each of you will allot your time and delegation of responsibilities, such as who will do what chores.

While your body undergoes changes and you experience the deep wonder of a new life growing inside you, your partner will watch you change but cannot really know what you are going through. Some men become jealous of the attention their pregnant partners receive. If you notice signs of jealousy, be understanding of your partner's feelings. Offer him support and love, and include him in your pregnancy as much as you can. Help him to understand what you and the baby are going through.

Because your partner is less intimately involved with the pregnancy than you are, you may have to adjust your expectations of his enthusiasm and participation. You may need to encourage your partner to become more actively involved, such as by asking him to accompany you to antenatal visits.

Your partner can be a wonderful source of support. He can help to prepare you for labour and delivery, and support you as you labour. He can share in the joy of the delivery of your baby. He can support you emotionally during pregnancy, which can be important to you both. Involve him as much as he is willing to be involved, and make him feel that he is included in what is happening.

Discuss with him his feelings about the pregnancy. He may have fears and uncertainties he hasn't voiced. Be open and direct with each other about your feelings – it can help both of you.

Some expectant fathers manifest physical problems during their partner's pregnancy. The condition is called *couvade*, a term taken from a Caribe Indian tribe in which every expectant father engages in rituals that enable him to understand some of what his partner is experiencing. In our culture, an expectant father may experience headaches, irritability, back and muscle aches, insomnia, fatigue and depression. Many of these symptoms are the body's way of signalling that the tension level is high and something must be done to relieve the stress.

To help relieve stress, a father can discuss his feelings and fears with other men, such as those who are taking the same childbirth education classes. Exercise, reading and listening to music may also relieve stress. When a man experiences headaches and shows other stress-related symptoms during his partner's pregnancy, it is time for the couple to start taking better care of each other so they can take care of their baby when it is born.

Some Fears Men Express About Pregnancy

Your partner may feel increased anxiety as your pregnancy progresses. He may be concerned about your health, the health of the baby, sex with you, labour and delivery and his ability to be a good father. Share your own concerns with him; it may be enough to calm his anxieties.

A recent survey of about 200 men revealed common things that men are fearful of as they approach fatherhood, including:

- being able to participate in the birth
- doubts about their personal maturity
- dropping the baby
- having enough time for the baby
- in-laws and parents coming over too often
- losing the relationship they have with their partner after the baby's birth

- losing their freedom
- providing adequately for the family
- the baby's crying
- whether they will be a good father

Understanding what your partner is feeling can help you to adjust to his reactions to your pregnancy.

In my work, nearly all the phone calls I get are from women. When the answering service said they had Fred on the line, I thought they had the wrong doctor. Fred explained that his wife Silvia was a patient of mine, due in about two months. He was very upset. They had always been open and close during their ten years of marriage, but now he felt left out. They had also lost some of the intimacy they had always shared. He confessed he wasn't sure what to do or how to get involved in the pregnancy. He feared Silvia didn't need him, and they were drifting apart.

I suggested Fred come with Silvia on her next visit, and I would help him 'break the ice'. At the visit, I brought up the topic of sex and intimacy during pregnancy. It turned out they both had some misconceptions. I told him this was a normal reaction. They might need to make some changes in their lovemaking, but they could still be intimate. Silvia had felt Fred was a little aloof but she didn't know what to do about it. It took some effort from both of them, but Fred confided in me at the delivery that things were much better. Silvia really did need him after all.

Your Partner Can Help You

Let your partner know that there are things he can do for you during pregnancy. Tell him how important he is to you. Be specific about what you want, so he can help you effectively. Some helpful things your partner can do are listed below:

- keep stress to a minimum
- communicate with you about everything
- be patient and supportive
- promote good nutrition
- encourage exercise, and exercise with you
- help around the house when possible, and do the strenuous chores
- attend antenatal check-ups when possible
- plan for the baby's arrival

- learn about the birth process
- read, study and prepare with you

Ways to Reassure Your Partner

You can reassure your partner and help him to grow more comfortable with your pregnancy and the idea of fatherhood. Suggestions my patients have shared with me include the following:

- Reassure your partner about the impending birth. Let him know that you are comfortable with whatever level of participation he is willing to give.
- Appreciate his help. He will probably be more willing to offer his help if he knows that it means something to you.
- Listen when he talks. Encourage him to express his hopes, fears and expectations about the baby's birth and being a father.
- Be as supportive of him as you can be. Let him know that you have faith in his abilities.
- Talk about how you will divide responsibilities. List what you can do and what your partner can do. If possible, practise before the baby's birth!
- Help to inform your partner about the birth and living with a new baby. Together, take childbirth education classes and other classes that are offered. Share this and other books with him. Tour the hospital, and discuss any questions and concerns you have.
- Encourage your partner to be as involved with the baby as he wants to be. If he wants to take paternity leave from work, encourage it. Help him to learn about changing nappies, feeding and bathing, and living with a new baby.

Jeannie thought her pregnancy couldn't have come at a worse time. She had just been promoted, with more pay and greater responsibilities. She came to her first visit feeling unhappy and discouraged. She wanted a baby but not right now. I told her that her reaction was not unusual; many of my patients have 'accidents' or unplanned pregnancies. I encouraged her to look at the positive things about her pregnancy. She admitted that her husband was thrilled; he had assured her that things would be fine. Later in the pregnancy, Jeannie expressed amazement about how she felt early on and about how well things were working out. I think she felt guilty about her feelings earlier and the time she lost feeling down about her pregnancy.

How a Father's Health Can Affect Pregnancy

It was once believed that a man had little to do with a pregnancy, other than contributing sperm to fertilize an egg. Today, we know that a father-to-be can affect his baby even before it is born. Research has proved that reproduction and fetal development may be affected if a man is exposed to various chemical hazards before conception. Exposure to alcohol, cigarettes, certain drugs and some environmental hazards by the father can harm an unborn baby. Usually male exposure is most harmful it if occurs just before or at the time of conception (rather than months or years before).

The age and health of your baby's father is also important. If he is over 50, doctors suspect that there is an increased risk of Down's syndrome, although we do not have a great deal of evidence to support this theory.

Some researchers believe that heavy alcohol consumption by the baby's father may produce fetal alcohol syndrome in the baby. Chapter 6 has more information on this syndrome. Alcohol intake by the father has also been linked to intra-uterine-growth retardation.

A non-smoking pregnant woman and her unborn baby who are exposed to secondary smoke are exposed to chemicals that can harm them both. If your partner smokes, ask him to stop during your pregnancy or at least to smoke outside your home.

Even substances on your partner's work clothes could be harmful to you or your developing baby. If you think you may be exposed to hazardous substances in this manner, be sure to discuss it with your doctor.

A Father Can Bond with Baby

Bonding between parent and child is very important. It is easy for a mother to bond with her baby because they are linked in a number of physical ways. It is more difficult for a man to bond with the baby, but you can help your partner to do this. He can begin bonding with the baby before birth and continue after the baby is born. Encourage your partner to do the following:

- Talk to the baby while it is in the uterus.
- Talk to the baby soon after birth. Babies bond to sound very quickly.
- Hold the baby close and make eye contact; a baby makes associations based on sight and smell.

- Feed the baby. It is easy if you bottle-feed. If you breast-feed, let him give the baby a bottle of expressed breast milk or water.
- Help with daily chores, such as changing nappies, holding the baby when it is restless, bathing and dressing the baby.

Steve came with Liz for an ultrasound examination, and he couldn't wait to tell me that he thought he had a new 'medical breakthrough'. He said that he had been a little nervous about the pregnancy, afraid to touch Liz or her tummy. But one night, while they were lying in bed, he saw Liz's belly-button move. He decided to feel it gently. He felt a foot or an arm, and when he pushed it, it pushed back! For the next 20 minutes, he continued the gentle pushing and feeling. This had become a regular activity that he looked forward to. He felt he was getting to know his baby's personality. Some nights it would want to 'play' for ten minutes, sometimes longer. Steve wanted to know if this was all right or harmful. I reassured him that it was fine, and that many couples bond with their baby in this way before it is born.

Sex during Pregnancy

Most couples are concerned about sexual activity during pregnancy; however, men are more often concerned with this aspect of a relationship. It is an important topic, so discuss it with your doctor. You will need to rule out any complications and ask for individual advice. Most doctors agree that sex can be a part of a normal, low risk pregnancy.

Sex doesn't just mean sexual intercourse. There are many ways for couples to be sensual together, including giving each other a massage, bathing together and talking about sex. Whatever you do, be honest with your partner about how you are feeling – and keep a sense of humour!

Can Sex during Pregnancy Hurt the Baby?

Sexual activity does not harm a growing baby. Neither intercourse nor orgasm should be a problem if you have a low risk pregnancy.

The baby is well protected by the amniotic sac and amniotic fluid. Uterine muscles are strong, and they also help to protect the baby. A thick mucus plug seals the cervix, which helps to protect against infection. Discuss sexual activity with your doctor, if your partner goes with you to your appointments. If he doesn't, assure him that there should be no problems, if your doctor gives you the go-ahead

Frequent sexual activity should not be harmful to a healthy pregnancy. Usually a couple can continue the level of sexual activity they are used to. If you are concerned, discuss it with your doctor.

How Pregnancy Affects You Sexually

Generally, women experience one of two sex-drive patterns during pregnancy. One is a lessening of desire in the first and third trimesters, with an increase in the second trimester. The second is a gradual decrease in desire for sex as pregnancy progresses.

During the first trimester, you may experience fatigue and nausea. During the third trimester, your weight gain, enlarging abdomen, tender breasts and other problems may make you desire sex less. This is normal. Tell your partner how you feel and try to work out a solution that is satisfactory to you both.

Pregnancy actually enhances the sex drive for some women. In some cases, a woman may experience orgasms or multiple orgasms for the first time during pregnancy. This is due to heightened hormone activity and increased blood flow to the pelvic area.

Some women feel less attractive during pregnancy because of their size and the changes in their bodies. Discuss your feelings with your partner. Tenderness and understanding can help you both.

You may find that new positions for lovemaking are necessary as pregnancy progresses. Your abdomen may make some positions more uncomfortable than others. In addition, physicians advise you not to lie flat on your back after 16 weeks until the baby's birth because the weight of the uterus restricts circulation. You might try lying on your side or in a position that puts you on top.

When to Avoid Sexual Activity

Some situations should alert you to abstain from sex during pregnancy. If you have a history of early labour, your doctor may warn against intercourse and orgasm; orgasm causes mild uterine contractions. Chemicals in semen may also stimulate contractions, so it may not be advisable for a woman's partner to ejaculate inside her. *See* the list below for other times to avoid sexual activity.

If you have a history of miscarriage, your doctor may caution you against sex and orgasm. However, no data actually links the two. Avoid sexual activity if you have any of the following problems or conditions:

- placenta praevia or a low-lying placenta
- incompetent cervix
- premature labour
- multiple fetuses
- ruptured bag of waters
- pain with intercourse
- unexplained vaginal bleeding or discharge
- inability to find a comfortable position
- either partner has an unhealed herpes lesion
- you believe that labour has begun

Sexual Practices to Avoid

Some practices should be avoided during sex when you are pregnant. Don't insert any object into the vagina that could cause injury or infection. Blowing air into the vagina is dangerous because it can force a potentially fatal air bubble into a woman's bloodstream. (This can occur whether or not you are pregnant.) Nipple stimulation releases oxytocin, which causes uterine contractions; you might want to discuss this practice with your doctor.

Bed Rest and Your Partner

In some situations, a woman may be ordered to bed for part of her pregnancy. (*See* the discussion of bed rest starting on page 194.) She may also have to abstain from sex. Bed rest can be tedious for the woman; however, it may be just as difficult for her partner.

Partners of women with pregnancy complications carry a heavy load. In addition to worrying about their partner and the growing baby, they may also have to handle housework, cooking, child care and care of their partner. It can be difficult for a man to handle his work and the added responsibility at home. Resentment is common.

If you are ordered to bed, make sure that you consider your partner's feelings about it. Let him know how valuable he is to you. Be supportive (this can be tough when you are the one in bed!), and try not to ask for too much. Arrange for others to help out when possible.

For all the inconveniences and disruptions in your life that bed confinement causes, the experience may strengthen your relationship. When he gives his time and attention to this demanding task, your partner is really offering you support and love. Let him know how much you appreciate it.

PART FOUR

If You Have a Problem

CHAPTER 16

Pregnancy Problems and Warning Signs

Pregnancy is usually a happy time, but you may experience situations that cause you some concern. Some diagnoses, such as for diabetes and hypertension, are not unusual and cause no noticeable discomfort but are always serious and must be treated for your health and that of your baby.

If you feel uncomfortable or have questions, don't be afraid to ask for help. Call your doctor to discuss your concerns. This part of the book can help you to formulate the questions you may want to ask.

Although you may believe that it is easier to get advice or information from family members or friends, *don't* rely on them for medical advice. Your doctor has probably dealt with the same situation many times. The answers he or she gives you will be right for your particular pregnancy.

If you experience any of the following signs or symptoms, call your doctor immediately. General warning signs include:

- vaginal bleeding
- severe swelling of the face or fingers
- severe abdominal pain
- loss of fluid from the vagina (usually a gushing of fluid but sometimes a trickle or a continual wetness)
- a big change in the movement of the baby or a lack of fetal movement
- high fever – more than 101.6°F (38.7°C)
- chills
- severe vomiting or an inability to keep food or liquids down
- blurring of vision

- painful urination
- a headache that won't go away or a severe headache
- an injury or accident that hurts you or gives you concern about the well-being of your pregnancy, such as a fall or a car accident

If You Fall

A fall is the most frequent cause of minor injury during pregnancy. Fortunately, a fall usually doesn't cause serious injury to the fetus or to the mother. Movement of the baby after a fall is reassuring. A possible problem after a fall may be indicated by any of the following:

- bleeding from the vagina
- a gush of fluid from the vagina, indicating rupture of membranes
- severe abdominal pain

If you fall, contact your doctor; you may require attention. If you have had a very bad fall, your doctor may advise monitoring the baby's heartbeat or order an ultrasound scan for further evaluation.

It was a late-night call, and Jan apologized for bothering me. She was 34 weeks pregnant and had fallen in her driveway bringing in groceries. She had landed squarely on her bottom. She felt well but was concerned about the baby. The baby hadn't moved since the fall and that scared her. She said that she wasn't bleeding or leaking any fluid, but her uterus was tightening. She didn't know if it was contractions, but it was uncomfortable. I reassured her that her baby was cushioned very well, better than she was, but it was something to be concerned about.

Even though it was late and cold outside, I asked her to go to hospital for a check-up. We all felt better after Jan had a cardiotocogram, and the baby was fine. The contractions stopped, and Jane was able to take some paracetamol for her bumps and bruises. At her next visit, I told Jan not to apologize for calls like that – it was the right thing to do.

Bed Rest

Bed rest is ordered for a woman to improve her chances of giving birth to a healthy baby. Today, one in five women spends at least one week in bed during pregnancy. If the condition is severe, hospital admission may be advised.

When a woman has to rest in bed, it can disrupt the normal routines of her family, especially when it lasts more than a short time. Adjusting to around-the-clock bed rest can be difficult.

A woman may be advised to rest in bed when certain conditions threaten the baby's or mother's health. These conditions include:

- a history of premature labour
- early rupture of the membranes
- pre-eclampsia
- high blood pressure
- multiple fetuses, especially triplets or more
- incompetent cervix
- premature labour
- risk of miscarriage
- intra-uterine-growth retardation
- chronic heart condition
- diabetes, with complications

How Bed Rest Works

Resting in bed works two ways. First, resting on your side maximizes the blood flow to your uterus, which brings more oxygen and nutrients to the baby. Second, lying down takes the pressure of the baby's weight off the cervix, which can help when a woman experiences premature labour.

If You Are Ordered to Bed

Bed rest can seriously disrupt your routine. You may not be able to work, and you may have to curtail other activities. Bed rest can be difficult when you have young children. Changing your routine can be stressful for people around you, including family members and co-workers. Staying in bed may be hard, but it is better to do it at home than in hospital!

Ask your doctor what you can and cannot do while you are on bed rest. Sometimes you aren't allowed to get out of bed except to eat, go to the toilet and go to antenatal appointments. At other times, bed rest may be less strict. You may be able to sit up or be a little more active for part of the day. You may have to take medicine and limit your activities.

You may be advised to lie only on your left side to increase blood flow to the uterus. This position relieves pressure on the vena cava and increases blood flow to the legs and uterus. You may be allowed to alternate between sides. However, you may *not* lie on your back. Lying on your back puts too much pressure from your uterus on the vena cava.

Surviving Bed Rest

Staying in bed isn't fun, especially if you haven't yet prepared for your baby's arrival. You may feel resentful. You may have to abstain from sex, which can add stress to an already difficult situation. You can make the experience more bearable if you plan for your time of confinement. If you work, ask your doctor if you can read or work on projects at home. The following suggestions may help you get through your time in bed:

- Spend the day in a room other than your bedroom. Use the living room for daytime activities.
- Use foam-mattress pads and extra pillows for comfort.
- Keep reading material, the television remote control, a radio and other essentials near by.
- Establish a daily routine. When you get up, change into daytime clothes. Shower or bathe every day. Comb your hair and put on lipstick. Take a nap if you need it. Go to bed when you normally do.
- Keep food and drinks close at hand. Use a cool-bag to keep food and drinks cold. Use an insulated container for hot soup or coffee.

For support, contact other women who have been on bed rest.

If You Have Children

Bed rest can be especially hard for a pregnant woman with young children at home. Try some of the following suggestions to help you to make the experience more tolerable:

- Have someone come to your home to help during the day.
- If you can't find someone to come to your home, see if a friend or neighbour can take your children for all or part of the day.
- Keep books and toys near by to help to entertain the children when they are with you.
- Ask your children to help you. A child can put toys away or get

something for you. Children love to feel important, and asking a child to help you can make him or her feel very grown up.

• Do some quiet activities with your child; look at photograph albums or read books together.

If you must rest in bed, stay positive! No matter how long you have to rest in bed – a few days or weeks – the goal is a healthy baby and a healthy mother. You may be upset or feel anxious. Keep in mind that you are doing this for you and your baby, and give yourself a pat on the back.

Bleeding during Pregnancy

Bleeding during pregnancy is not unusual and does not always indicate a problem; about one woman in five bleeds some time in early pregnancy. Most of the time we cannot say what causes bleeding, but we do know that it is not usually serious. Always tell your doctor about any bleeding; he or she may want you to have an ultrasound scan.

Bleeding later in pregnancy raises concerns regarding premature labour, premature rupture of the membranes, placenta praevia or placental abruption. If you bleed late in pregnancy, call your doctor *immediately*. Your problem may not be serious, but it must be evaluated by your doctor.

Most women who experience bleeding during pregnancy want to know if they can take medicine or do something to stop the bleeding. Bed rest may help. Unfortunately, no surgery or medicine will help. You may be scheduled for an ultrasound scan. A scan won't stop the bleeding, but it may provide reassurance. Your doctor will make treatment decisions based on your individual history. Follow his or her instructions.

Blood Clots

Some women develop blood clots, usually in their legs, during pregnancy. These clots may break loose, travel through the blood system and lodge elsewhere in the body, such as the lungs. Blood clots are an uncommon problem and occur only once in every 3,000 to 7,000 pregnancies. However, it is a serious complication and can affect you and your baby.

Clots occur in pregnancy because of changes in blood circulation. The most likely cause of a blood clot in the legs is decreased blood flow, called *stasis*. Blood flow slows because of pressure from the uterus on blood vessels and changes in the blood and its clotting mechanisms.

A blood clot in the legs is not always a serious problem. Unlike deep vein clots, clots created in the superficial veins of the leg are treated with mild pain relievers, heat, elevation of the leg and support of the leg with surgical stockings or support tights.

Conditions that refer to blood-clotting problems are also called *venous thrombosis, thromboembolic disease, thrombophlebitis* and *lower deep vein thrombosis*.

Deep Vein Thrombosis

Clotting in the deep veins of the legs, called *deep vein thrombosis* or *phlebo-thrombosis*, is serious. A blood clot that forms deep in the leg is more likely to break loose and travel to another part of the body, such as the lungs, heart or brain, where it can indirectly damage those tissues. Signs and symptoms of deep-vein thrombosis vary widely and include:

- abrupt onset
- paleness of the leg
- leg is cool to the touch
- a portion of the leg may be tender, hot and swollen
- there may be red streaks over the veins of the leg
- squeezing the calf or walking may be very painful

In a pregnant woman, an ultrasound scan of the legs is the only test, other than a physical examination, with which a doctor diagnoses phlebo-thrombosis. At other times, X-ray or ultrasound is used.

Treating Deep Vein Thrombosis

Deep vein thrombosis is usually treated by hospital admission and the administration of heparin, a blood thinner. While heparin is given, the woman is required to stay in bed. Heat is applied to the elevated leg.

Heparin is safe to use during pregnancy. It is administered by injections you give yourself two or three times a day, by an intra-venous drip attached to your arm or by a device called a *heparin pump*.

Warfarin is not usually given during pregnancy because it crosses the placenta and is not safe for the baby. After you give birth, you may be given warfarin for a few weeks, depending on the severity of the blood clot.

If you have had a blood clot with a previous pregnancy or at any other time, such as after surgery, be sure that you share the information with your doctor as soon as you know that you are pregnant. You may need heparin during this pregnancy.

Breast Lumps

Sometimes a woman develops lumps in her breasts during pregnancy. Because your breasts go through so many changes in pregnancy, it may be harder for you to discover a lump. It is a good idea to examine your breasts every four or five weeks throughout your pregnancy.

If you discover a lump, tell your doctor immediately. It is normal for breasts to change and to grow larger during pregnancy, but don't ignore a breast lump and hope that it will go away. Lumps need to be checked out.

After examination by your doctor, you may undergo a mammogram or an ultrasound scan. If you are supposed to have a mammogram, tell the technician that you are pregnant, so your abdomen is shielded properly with a lead apron.

A lump in the breast usually can be drained or aspirated. If not, a doctor may have to perform a biopsy (take a sample of the tissue involved). Depending on those findings, surgery or other treatment may be needed.

There is controversy about whether pregnancy causes breast cancer to grow faster. Most researchers do not believe that pregnancy accelerates the course or growth of a breast cancer.

Diabetes

Diabetes was once a very serious medical problem during pregnancy for a woman of any age. It continues to be an important complication of pregnancy, but today many diabetic women can go through pregnancy safely if they have proper medical care, watch their diet and follow their doctor's instructions. If you know that you are diabetic, inform your doctor of the fact as soon as you become pregnant – or before, if possible.

We believe that diabetes can appear during pregnancy for two reasons – the mother's body decreases its production of insulin for some reason, or the mother is unable to use insulin appropriately. (Insulin is used to break down blood sugar.) In either case, the mother's blood sugar levels rise unacceptably.

Pregnancy problems are more likely for diabetic women. If diabetes is not controlled very well at conception and through the first few weeks of pregnancy, there is a 3 to 6 per cent increase in the risk of major fetal abnormalities, including heart, genito-urinary and gastrointestinal problems. Miscarriages occur more often. Symptoms of diabetes include:

- an increase in urination
- blurred vision
- weight loss
- dizziness
- increased hunger

Diabetes is diagnosed with a blood test, sometimes called a *fasting blood sugar* or *glucose tolerance test*. If your doctor finds sugar in your urine during routine tests at his or her clinic, it does not always mean that you have diabetes. Pregnant, non-diabetic women commonly have a small amount of sugar in their urine, called *glycosuria*, because of the way that sugar is handled in the kidneys during pregnancy.

Pregnancy-induced Diabetes

Some women develop diabetes only during pregnancy, called *gestational diabetes*. Diabetes that occurs during pregnancy can be a greater problem for older women.

Gestational diabetes affects about 10 per cent of all pregnancies. After pregnancy, nearly all women with gestational diabetes return to normal, and the problem disappears. However, more than half of all women who experience diabetes during pregnancy become diabetic later in life. A woman who develops gestational diabetes in one pregnancy has a good chance of developing it in a subsequent pregnancy.

Women at greater risk of developing gestational diabetes are overweight, with family members who have insulin-dependent or diet-controlled diabetes. Occasionally a woman with no known personal or family risk factors develops the problem. Gestational diabetes is triggered when the usual hormone changes of pregnancy, combined with dietary factors, result in higher blood sugar levels.

Children of diabetic women are more likely to develop diabetes themselves. Daughters of women who developed gestational diabetes are likely to become diabetic during their own pregnancies. If your mother developed gestational diabetes, be sure that you give this information to your doctor.

How Gestational Diabetes Affects You

During pregnancy, diabetes can cause several medical complications, including kidney, eye, blood and vascular problems. Any of these can be serious for you and for your baby. If diabetes goes untreated, you and your baby will be exposed to a high concentration of sugar in the blood, a condition called *hyperglycaemia*. This is not healthy for the baby.

Gestational diabetes sometimes causes *hydramnios* (production of excessive amounts of amniotic fluid), which can develop at any time during pregnancy. The condition may cause premature labour because the uterus becomes overdistended.

A woman may experience a very long labour because the baby is large. Sometimes a baby cannot fit through the birth canal, and a caesarean section delivery is required.

If your blood sugar level is elevated, you may experience more infection during pregnancy. The most common infections involve the kidneys, the bladder, the cervix and the uterus.

How Gestational Diabetes Affects Your Baby

All of a baby's nutrition comes from its mother. If an expectant mother's blood sugar levels are high, the baby's insulin output increases to try to process the excess and re-establish a balance. However, the baby's insulin can't cross the placenta back to the mother, so the effort doesn't help to balance their shared blood chemistry. The extra insulin remains in the amniotic sac and the baby's growth may be exaggerated because of it. In some cases, the baby grows so large that it cannot be delivered safely by vaginal birth.

After birth, a baby may also have very low blood sugar, called *hypoglycaemia*, because the baby's body now controls its own blood sugar. Every baby should be checked for the condition immediately after delivery. If the blood-sugar level is low, the baby may be given some sugar.

The baby may be born with hyperbilirubinaemia (severe jaundice). Some babies have weak or high-pitched cries, appear shaky and tire quickly. A baby may be unable to nurse well or for long enough to get adequate nutrition, which can affect its growth.

Treating Gestational Diabetes

The best way to treat diabetes during pregnancy is to eat properly. If you are diabetic, your doctor will probably recommend a six-meal, 2,000- to 2,500-calorie per day eating plan and may ask you to see a dietitian.

Under a typical plan, you eat six small meals a day of low-fat, sugar-free, high-fibre foods. Eating this way enables your body to keep sugar production at a more constant level.

Getting regular exercise and drinking lots of water every day are also very important in this plan. If you have gestational diabetes, your blood-sugar level may be tested at antenatal clinic visits and by you at home.

Ectopic Pregnancy

Ectopic pregnancy, sometimes called a *tubal pregnancy*, is not common; it occurs only about once in every 100 pregnancies. An ectopic pregnancy occurs when the fertilized egg implants outside the uterine cavity, usually in the fallopian tube. One of the most common signs of an ectopic pregnancy is pain. It isn't unusual to have mild pain early in pregnancy from a cyst on the ovary or stretching of the uterus or ligaments. However, if the pain is severe and causes you concern, call your doctor.

Factors that Increase the Risks of an Ectopic Pregnancy

You cannot prevent an ectopic pregnancy. However, some factors increase its likelihood, including:

- pelvic infections (PID; pelvic inflammatory disease)
- previous ruptured appendix
- previous ectopic pregnancy
- surgery on your fallopian tubes (such as the reversal of a tubal ligation or infertility surgery)
- use of an intra-uterine device (coil) for contraception

Diagnosing an Ectopic Pregnancy

Diagnosis of an ectopic pregnancy can be very difficult. It may require several tests and some waiting; tests used include ultrasound, quantitative HCG and laparoscopy (a type of minor surgery). It may take a few days to make a definitive diagnosis.

Sometimes a doctor orders a couple of quantitative HCG tests a few days apart. A quantitative HCG (human chorionic gonadotropin) test is a special pregnancy blood test. HCG is produced when you are pregnant; it increases rapidly early in pregnancy. A quantitative HCG tells how far along in pregnancy you are. The values aren't exact, but they increase in a way that can help your doctor to decide if it is a normal or abnormal pregnancy. The HCG test is not used in normal pregnancies but it can be very helpful when there is concern about an ectopic pregnancy.

Treatment of an Ectopic Pregnancy

An ectopic pregnancy cannot normally be carried to full term. Surgery is almost always required to correct the problem, which results in the loss of the pregnancy.

Hypertension

Hypertension is the most common chronic illness in older pregnant women. About one pregnant woman in ten experiences the condition during pregnancy; however, women in their 30s and 40s have a higher incidence of pregnancy-induced hypertension than younger women. (Hypertension is also called *high blood pressure*.) Most women who are hypertensive during pregnancy do not have high blood pressure when they are not pregnant. Other women enter pregnancy with the problem.

How Hypertension Affects You and Your Baby

Blood vessels in the uterus supply the developing baby with nutrients and oxygen. High blood pressure constricts uterine blood vessels, which can slow the passage of nutrients and oxygen from the mother to the baby, which in turn slows fetal development. Hypertension increases the risk of placental abruption (separation of the placenta from the wall of the uterus before delivery). This situation can cause heavy bleeding and shock, which are dangerous conditions for you and your baby.

Hypertension has other effects. About 20 per cent of all women who experience chronic hypertension (high blood pressure before pregnancy) develop pre-eclampsia. About 25 per cent of those women who develop pregnancy-induced hypertension also develop pre-eclampsia. (By comparison, 6 per cent of women who begin pregnancy without hypertension develop pre-eclampsia.) A discussion of pre-eclampsia begins on page 208.

Pregnancy-induced hypertension occurs only during pregnancy and disappears after the baby is born. The condition is treated with bed rest, and sometimes sedation. Medicines to lower blood pressure may be prescribed if rest is not effective. Women who do not respond to these measures may be admitted to hospital.

Miscarriage

A *miscarriage* is a loss of a pregnancy before 20 weeks of pregnancy. An embryo or a fetus is delivered before it can survive outside the womb. At some time during pregnancy, nearly every woman thinks about the possibility of miscarriage.

Having a miscarriage is an emotional experience for any woman. It may also be an emotional loss for your partner. Many women mistakenly blame themselves when a miscarriage occurs. It isn't your fault, so don't blame yourself.

Causes of Miscarriage

When a miscarriage occurs with one of my patients, one of the first questions I am asked is, 'Did I cause it?' Patients also want to know, 'What could I have done to prevent it?'

Most of the time we don't know why a miscarriage occurs; it can happen for many different reasons. The most common finding of studies done of early miscarriages is abnormal development of the embryo. Research indicates that more than half of these miscarriages have chromosome abnormalities.

Outside factors, such as radiation and some chemicals (drugs or medications), may cause a miscarriage. Maternal factors may also result in a miscarriage. Several maternal factors that have been identified include:

- unusual infections
- genital infections
- antibodies produced in the body that attack the fetus or disrupt the function of the placenta
- smoking

- alcohol or drug use (especially cocaine)

In some cases, the uniting of the couple's sperm and egg results in a miscarriage. Let me explain. When the couple's genes unite at fertilization, the union can produce genetic abnormalities that cause a miscarriage. Genetic screening can reveal this problem; a discussion of genetic counselling begins on page 215.

Types of Miscarriage

Different medical descriptions of miscarriages actually describe different types of miscarriage. Medically speaking, there are five basic types.

A *threatened miscarriage* occurs when there is a bloody discharge from the vagina during the first half of pregnancy. Bleeding may last days or weeks. A woman may or may not experience cramping and pain. The pain may feel like a menstrual cramp or mild backache. Resting in bed is about all a woman can do, although being active does not cause miscarriage. (In most instances early in pregnancy, the bleeding or spotting stops and everything is fine.)

An *inevitable miscarriage* occurs with rupture of membranes, dilatation of the cervix and passage of blood clots and tissue. Loss of the pregnancy is almost certain in these circumstances. The uterus usually contracts, expelling the embryo or products of conception.

With an *incomplete miscarriage*, the entire pregnancy may not be expelled. Part of the pregnancy may be passed while the rest remains inside the uterus. Bleeding may be heavy and continues until the uterus is empty.

A *missed abortion* can occur when an embryo that has died earlier is retained in the uterus. A woman may not bleed or have any other symptoms. The period between the failure of the pregnancy until the time the miscarriage is discovered is usually weeks.

Habitual miscarriage usually refers to three or more consecutive miscarriages.

Warning Signs

The first warning sign of a miscarriage is bleeding from the vagina, followed by cramping. Call your doctor if you experience this! Unfortunately, in nearly all instances, there is little you or your doctor can do to stop a miscarriage from happening. No surgical technique or medicine can stop a miscarriage.

Most physicians recommend bed rest and decreased activity. (*See* the discussion of bed rest that begins on page 194.) An ultrasound scan and blood tests may help your doctor to determine whether you are going to miscarry, but you may have to wait and see.

If you pass all of the pregnancy, bleeding stops and cramping goes away, you may be done with it. If everything is not expelled, it is necessary to perform a D&C (dilatation and curettage), which is minor surgery to empty the uterus. A D&C is recommended so that you won't bleed for a long period of time, risking anaemia and infection.

If you are Rhesus-negative and have a miscarriage, you will need to receive an injection of anti-D immunoglobulin. This applies *only* if you are Rhesus-negative.

The Placenta

The placenta is very important during pregnancy. It carries nourishment and oxygen from you to your developing baby and carries away the baby's waste products. More information on the placenta and its function begins on page 90. Problems occasionally develop with the placenta, especially for older women, including *placenta praevia*, *placental abruption* and *retained placenta*.

Placenta Praevia

When a woman has placenta praevia, the placenta covers part or all of the cervix. The placenta may separate from the uterus as the cervix begins to dilate (open) during labour. This causes heavy bleeding, which can be dangerous for the mother and the baby. Placenta praevia affects about 2 to 3 per cent of all women in the last trimester of pregnancy.

Signs and symptoms of placenta praevia vary, but the most characteristic symptom is painless bleeding. If you experience painless bleeding, your doctor may order an ultrasound scan to determine the location of the placenta, if he or she is concerned about placenta praevia. Your physician will not perform a pelvic examination because it may cause heavier bleeding. If you see another doctor or when you go to the hospital, tell whomever you see that you have placenta praevia and that you should not have a pelvic examination.

If your doctor determines that you have placenta praevia, you will have to curtail certain activities. Most physicians recommend avoiding intercourse and not travelling in addition to avoiding pelvic examinations.

With placenta praevia, the baby is more likely to be in a breech position. For this reason and to avoid bleeding, a physician will almost always perform a caesarean section delivery.

Placental Abruption

Placental abruption occurs when the placenta separates from the wall of the uterus before birth. Normally the placenta does not separate until after delivery of the baby. Separation of the placenta before birth can be dangerous for mother and baby.

Placental abruption occurs about once in every 80 deliveries. Its cause is unknown; however, certain conditions may make it more likely to occur. These include:

- trauma to the mother, such as from a fall or a car accident
- an umbilical cord that is too short
- very sudden change in the size of the uterus, as with the rupture of membranes
- hypertension
- dietary deficiency in the mother
- an abnormality of the uterus, such as a band of tissue in the uterus called a *uterine septum*

The symptoms of placental abruption include the following signs, not all of which may be present:

- heavy bleeding from the vagina
- uterine tenderness
- uterine contractions
- premature labour
- lower back pain

An ultrasound scan may help to establish the diagnosis of placental abruption in some cases. If bleeding is severe, a woman experiencing placental abruption may bleed internally because her blood doesn't clot properly.

The most common treatment of placental abruption is delivery of the baby. However, the decision of when to deliver the baby varies, based on the problem's severity. Sometimes a Caesarean section is necessary, but each case is handled individually.

Maternal smoking and alcohol use may increase the risk of placental abruption. If you smoke cigarettes or drink alcohol, you will be advised to stop both activities (it is also advisable for many other reasons). Cocaine use also causes placental abruption.

Retained Placenta

Some women have problems with the placenta after their baby is born. Usually the placenta separates with contraction of the uterus from the implantation site on the uterus a few minutes after delivery. When the placenta does not deliver following the birth of the baby, we call it a *retained placenta.*

In some cases, the placenta doesn't separate because it is attached to the wall of the uterus. This can be very serious and cause heavy blood loss. In other cases, part of the placenta may deliver while part is retained. Your doctor will check the placenta after delivery to be sure that it has all been delivered.

The most significant problem with a retained placenta is heavy bleeding after delivery, which can be severe. If the placenta cannot be delivered, your doctor may attempt to remove the placenta manually. If the placenta is attached through the wall of the uterus, it may be necessary to remove the uterus by performing a hysterectomy; this is rare.

Reasons for a retained placenta include a placenta attaching over a previous caesarean section scar or other incision scar on the uterus, attaching in a place that has been previously curetted, such as for a D&C or abortion, or attaching over an area of the uterus that was infected.

Pre-eclampsia

Pre-eclampsia, also called *toxaemia of pregnancy*, can be a serious complication of pregnancy. Pre-eclampsia occurs *only* during pregnancy; left untreated, it poses a serious threat to you and your baby. Older women are more likely to develop pre-eclampsia.

Most cases are mild and treatable. With mild pre-eclampsia, your blood pressure is slightly elevated. (Hypertension is discussed on page 203.) The only other obvious symptom of mild pre-eclampsia might be swelling of the legs, hands and face.

If pre-eclampsia worsens, it can quickly progress to a serious condition called *eclampsia*, which is accompanied by seizures or convulsions. A woman can also go into a coma. A *seizure* is a loss of body control, such as passing out, and often includes twitching or shaking. (A *convulsion* is a severe seizure.) If you think that you have had a seizure, contact your doctor immediately.

Causes

We don't really know what causes pre-eclampsia. When a woman suffers from pre-eclampsia, her body may be producing too much thromboxane A and too little prostacyclin, both blood chemicals. Thromboxane A constricts blood vessels; prostacyclin dilates them. A diet that is too low in protein may increase your risk of developing pre-eclampsia.

Women at Risk

Some women are at greater risk of developing pre-eclampsia than others. Your chance of getting the problem increases if any of the following applies to you:

- 35 or older
- family history of pre-eclampsia
- first pregnancy
- kidney disease
- lupus erythematosus
- diabetes
- a multiple pregnancy
- overweight
- personal history of pre-eclampsia, combined with high blood pressure before pregnancy

The best way to reduce the risk of developing pre-eclampsia or eclampsia is to keep all your antenatal appointments. Your doctor will follow changes in your blood pressure throughout your pregnancy. With your help and co-operation, your doctor can usually treat pre-eclampsia before it becomes a serious problem.

Warning Signs of Pre-eclampsia

Pre-eclampsia may develop after 20 weeks of pregnancy, although most cases occur after 30 weeks. Symptoms include:

- hypertension
- protein in the urine
- sudden weight gain
- swelling
- changes in muscle reflexes

Certain signs indicate a worsening condition. Contact your doctor immediately if you have pre-eclampsia and develop any of these signs:

- pain under the ribs on the right side
- headache
- spots before the eyes or other vision changes

If your legs or feet are swollen, it does *not* mean that you have pre-eclampsia. Most pregnant women experience some swelling, but a diagnosis of pre-eclampsia includes the other symptoms described.

Treating Pre-eclampsia

For a mild case of pre-eclampsia, your doctor will probably order bed rest until your blood pressure stabilizes.

You will need to visit your antenatal clinic more frequently if you are diagnosed as having pre-eclampsia. In some cases, you are given medication to lower your blood pressure. You may be given medication to protect against seizures, or you may be prescribed anti-seizure medicines, such as phenobarbitone.

If pre-eclampsia worsens, you may be admitted to the hospital for observation. Your blood pressure is measured several times a day, and your weight and the level of protein in your urine are recorded. Your developing baby is also monitored. Fetal movements are recorded every day, and a cardiotocogram is done.

If your blood pressure continues to rise and other symptoms worsen, the baby may need to be delivered to protect you from serious complications, including convulsions, stroke, liver damage and kidney damage. Before delivery, you may receive magnesium sulphate intravenously to prevent convulsions during labour and the baby's birth.

Emergency Surgery during Pregnancy

Emergencies occur, even during pregnancy. When you are pregnant, a medical emergency must be dealt with in a way that is best for you and your developing fetus. Sometimes surgical procedures are necessary. Some common reasons for surgery during pregnancy are ovarian cysts, appendicitis, gall-bladder removal, broken bones and dental emergency.

Ovarian Cysts

Ovarian cysts can be a serious complication during pregnancy. A *cyst* is a sac that develops in the ovary and consists of one or more fluid-containing chambers. It may have to be surgically removed because of pressure, twisting, bleeding or blockage of the birth canal. Ovarian cysts that develop in pregnancy are almost always benign.

Ovarian cysts can cause pain, bloating and abdominal swelling. A physical examination and ultrasound scan are used to diagnose the problem. Treatment is usually pain medication and observation; surgery is usually avoided unless it is absolutely necessary.

If surgery is necessary, the cyst may be drained or removed. In some cases, the doctors must remove the entire ovary. If surgery can be postponed, the safest time to do it is after the first trimester has ended.

Risks to the fetus vary, depending on when surgery is performed. In early pregnancy, loss of an ovary could mean loss of hormones that are necessary to support the pregnancy. Late in pregnancy, a cyst could block the birth canal, requiring a caesarean section delivery. Other risks include those associated with general anaesthesia, infection and premature delivery.

Appendicitis

The incidence of appendicitis in pregnancy is about 1 in every 2,000 pregnancies. Diagnosis of appendicitis is more difficult during pregnancy because some of the symptoms, including nausea, vomiting and a high white-blood cell count, are the same as those for normal pregnancy or other problems. Pregnancy can also make diagnosis difficult because as the uterus grows larger, the appendix moves upward

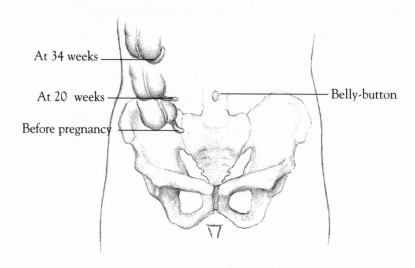

Location of the appendix during pregnancy

and outward, so pain and tenderness are in a different location than usual (*see* the illustration above). Diagnosis of appendicitis during pregnancy requires a physical examination, blood tests and sometimes ultrasound scanning.

Surgery is performed immediately. It is major abdominal surgery and often requires a few days in hospital. Laparoscopy is used in some situations, but it may be more difficult to perform during pregnancy because of the enlarged uterus.

Risks to the developing fetus with appendicitis include the risks associated with general anesthesia, infection and premature labour.

Gall-bladder Problems

Inflammation of the gall bladder, also called *cholecystitis*, occurs most often in women in their 30s and 40s. Treatment consists of pain medication and surgery. If you are pregnant, your doctor will try to avoid surgery until after the baby is born, when possible. However, if your pain is severe and does not improve with pain medication, surgery may be necessary.

The ideal time to perform gall-bladder surgery during pregnancy is the second trimester. The risk of miscarriage or premature delivery is lower.

The surgical procedure for gall-bladder removal requires general anaesthesia and an incision, with a hospital stay of up to three or five days. If laparoscopy is used to remove the gall bladder, the surgeon makes three or four small incisions, and the gall bladder is examined and removed. The hospital stay is one to three days. In most cases, laparoscopy is not recommended after 20 weeks of pregnancy.

Risks to the fetus from gall-bladder surgery include premature labour, infection and risks associated with anaesthesia. If surgery is required, you will be monitored very closely to watch for and prevent premature labour.

Broken Bones

A fall or accident can break a bone, which may require X-rays or surgery. Treatment cannot be delayed until after pregnancy; the problem must be dealt with immediately. If you break a bone, insist that your obstetrician be contacted before any test or treatment is done.

If X-rays are required, technicians should shield your pelvis and abdomen. If the pelvis and abdomen cannot be shielded, the need for the X-ray must be weighed against the very small risks it poses potentially to the fetus.

Anaesthesia or pain medication may be necessary for a simple break that requires setting or pinning. Keep its use to a minimum. It is best for you and the baby to avoid general anaesthesia if possible. If general anaesthesia is required, doctors will monitor the baby closely throughout surgery.

Dental Emergencies

Dental emergencies can occur during pregnancy. Some emergencies you might face include root canal, tooth extraction, a large cavity, an abscessed tooth or problems resulting from an accident or injury. Any of these emergencies can occur during pregnancy; it might be unwise to postpone treatment until after your baby is born.

If you have a dental problem, contact your dentist and your doctor before you do anything else. Your dentist and your doctor may find it helpful to talk before any decisions are made.

Dental X-rays may be necessary and can be done during pregnancy. Be sure your abdomen is shielded with a lead apron before X-rays are taken. If possible, wait until after the end of the first trimester to have dental work done.

Avoid gas or general anaesthesia for a dental procedure. Local anaesthetics are fine, as are many antibiotics and pain medications. Be sure that you consult your doctor before you take any medicines.

If you have a serious dental problem, such as an abscess, get it treated. Problems, such as infection, that could result from not treating it are more serious than the normal risks associated with treatment.

CHAPTER 17

Special Concerns of the Older Pregnant Woman

Most women over 30 have problem-free, healthy pregnancies and deliver healthy babies. However, for women who are 30 or older, age can be a factor in pregnancy. If you experience any of the situations covered in this chapter, discuss it with your doctor.

Chromosome Abnormalities Discovered by Genetic Counselling

Genetic counselling can identify some chromosome abnormalities. Chromosome abnormalities can occur in any cell, and they can occur as an abnormal chromosome number or as an abnormality in the structure of the chromosome itself. With Down's syndrome, an individual has 47 chromosomes instead of the normal 46. With Turner's syndrome, one chromosome is missing; the individual has 45 chromosomes. For more information about Down's and Turner's syndromes, *see* pages 216 and 220.

A loss, a gain or a repositioning of the chromosome material identifies a structural abnormality. Terms used to describe these various conditions include *additions, duplications, deletions, inversions* and *translocations*.

Causes of Chromosome Abnormalities

Chromosome abnormalities are usually attributed to one of three conditions: advanced parental age; radiation exposure of the mother, father or fetus; or gene regulation problems.

'Advanced parental age' usually refers to the mother's age, but some research has also implicated the father's age. Age is a factor for the mother because females are born with all the eggs they will ever have. They are exposed to radiation and other teratogens in the environment throughout life. The exposures have an additive effect – the more teratogens a woman is exposed to, the greater her chance of damaging the eggs.

Radiation exposure, such as X-rays, can damage genetic material and affect gene function and regulation. This is serious because genes control development of the fetus, its organs and growth. Three of the most common examples of chromosomal abnormalities are discussed below:

- *Down's syndrome* is the most common chromosome abnormality; it occurs in about 1 in 600 births. The syndrome is caused by an extra chromosome. Those born with Down's syndrome can live fairly long lives and may be moderately to severely mentally retarded. About half have congenital heart disease; particular physical abnormalities are common to the syndrome. A more complete discussion begins on page 217.
- *Trisomy 18 (Edwards' syndrome)* is a severe chromosome abnormality occurring in approximately 1 in 6,000 births. Babies with trisomy 18 have multiple abnormalities of major organs, including mental retardation, microcephaly (small head), heart problems, kidney problems and gastro-intestinal problems. The syndrome is caused by an abnormal chromosome 18. Most babies born with the problem die within the first year of life.
- *Trisomy 13 (Patau's syndrome)* occurs about once in 5,000 births. The syndrome is caused by an extra chromosome 13. Babies born with trisomy 13 may have multiple abnormalities, including mental retardation, microcephaly, cleft palate, cleft lip, heart problems and gastro-intestinal problems. The prognosis for these infants is poor; most die by the age of 3.

Sex-chromosome Abnormalities

Abnormalities of the sex chromosomes are relatively common and are seen in 1 of every 500 live births. It is believed that this type of abnormality causes about 25 per cent of all miscarriages. The two most common sex-chromosome abnormalities are Turner's syndrome and Klinefelter's syndrome.

Turner's syndrome occurs about once in 10,000 female births. It is the most common chromosome abnormality identified in miscarriages. Instead of having two X chromosomes, a baby girl born with Turner's syndrome has only one X chromosome, a situation called 45X. A mature girl with Turner's syndrome is short and has a webbed neck, very small ovaries, is underdeveloped sexually, and often has heart and kidney problems. The condition may not be identified until she reaches puberty.

Klinefelter's syndrome is found in approximately 1 in every 1,000 newborn males. The most common characteristic is very tall stature when the boy reaches maturity. These boys are born with an extra sex chromosome, thus the 47XXY label. A boy is very tall, underdeveloped sexually and has small testes.

Fragile-X syndrome (also called *X-linked*) is one of the most common causes of mental retardation in males. Major physical characteristics include large ears, large hands and language-development delays.

Environmental Causes of Malformations

A birth defect (congenital malformation) results from abnormal tissue differentiation during early development stages or abnormal interaction of developing cells during fetal development of the organs and organ systems. Less than 3 per cent of all birth defects are caused by environmental factors, called *teratogens*. These include drugs, chemicals, radiation, congenital infection and the pregnant woman's environment. *See* teratogens, page 175.

Congenital Infections

Rubella was one of the first maternal infections researchers identified as a cause of fetal malformations. Other infections that have been identified that can cause malformations include cytomegalovirus (CMV), toxoplasmosis, herpes simplex, parvo-virus 19 and syphilis.

Congenital infections can cause a wide spectrum of problems in a baby. These range from major malformations, such as heart defects, to newborn infection at birth.

Down's Syndrome

Nearly every woman who experiences pregnancy receives information on Down's syndrome. When you are older, you are offered various tests to determine whether the fetus you carry is affected by the condition.

If tests determine that a woman is carrying a child with Down's syndrome, she will be offered counselling.

Down's syndrome was given its name by British physician J. Langdon Down in the 19th century. He discovered that babies born with the syndrome have an extra chromosome 21. Symptoms of the condition are present to some degree in all babies born with the syndrome. These symptoms include mental retardation, a sloping forehead, short, broad hands with a single palm crease, a flat nose or absent nose bridge, low-set ears and a generally dwarfed physique. The syndrome was formerly known as 'mongolism'.

Through medical research, we know that some women are at higher risk of giving birth to a child with Down's syndrome than others. Women with increased risk include older women, those who have given birth previously to a child with Down's syndrome and those who have Down's syndrome themselves.

The statistical risk of delivering a baby with Down's syndrome increases with age. If you are 45, you have a 97 per cent chance of *not* having a baby with Down's syndrome. If you are 49, you have a 92 per cent chance of delivering a child *without* Down's syndrome. The risk of delivering a child with Down's syndrome, depending on your age, is as follows:

- at age 25 the risk is 1 in 1,300 births
- at 30 it is 1 in 965 births
- at 35 it is 1 in 365 births
- at 40 it is 1 in 109 births
- at 45 it is 1 in 32 births
- at 49 it is 1 in 12 births

Diagnosing Down's Syndrome before Birth

Many tests are available that can help to diagnose Down's syndrome in a developing fetus. They are not offered to every woman; they are usually offered only to women at high risk or those over 35. Some women with higher risk choose not to take the tests because they would not terminate their pregnancy even if the child had Down's syndrome.

Tests performed for Down's syndrome include:

- maternal serum alpha-fetoprotein test (*see* page 107)
- amniocentesis (*see* page 107)

- chorionic villus sampling (CVS) (*see* page 108)
- triple-screen test (assessment of HCG, unconjugated oestriol and alpha-fetoprotein) (*see* page 108)
- quad-screen test (assessment of HCG, unconjugated oestriol alpha-fetoprotein and inhibin-A) (*see* page 108)
- ultrasound scanning (*see* page 101)

If you are concerned about Down's syndrome and you believe that you would choose to terminate a pregnancy if the fetus were afflicted, I suggest that you have one or more of these tests. Testing might be indicated even if you would not terminate the pregnancy; you might have the test if you and your partner (and the rest of the family) wanted to be mentally and emotionally prepared for this special child.

Some patients have told me they would welcome any child into their lives, no matter what. If this is your attitude, enjoy your pregnancy and don't worry about it.

Down's Syndrome Children Are Special

People often ask me if there are any positive aspects of giving birth to a child with Down's syndrome. I always answer 'Yes!' to anyone who asks.

As a society, we have come to realize that those born with Down's syndrome bring a special, valuable quality of life into our world. Down's children are well known for the love and the joy they bring to their families and friends. They remind us of the pleasure in accomplishing simple tasks when they learn new skills. They embody the concept of unconditional love, and we can often learn how to cope and to grow as we interact with them.

Rearing a child with Down's syndrome can be challenging, but some of my patients and others I know who have faced this challenge are positive about the impact these special children have on their lives. If you have a child with Down's syndrome, you may work harder for every small advancement in your child's life. You may experience frustration and feelings of helplessness at times, but every parent has these feelings at some time.

Many physicians present only the negative side of Down's syndrome. They describe the worst-case scenario and never look at another side of the issue. All women carrying a child with Down's syndrome need to know the following facts:

- The average intelligence quotient (IQ) for a child with Down's syndrome is between 60 and 70 (average normal is 100). Most are in the low, mildly retarded range.
- Some children with Down's syndrome have normal IQs.
- IQ scores for those with Down's syndrome have risen steadily in the last 100 years.
- Less than 5 per cent of those with Down's syndrome are severely to profoundly retarded.
- Nearly 90 per cent of all those with Down's syndrome are employable as adults.
- Most adults with Down's syndrome are capable of living independently or in group homes.
- A person with Down's syndrome has a life expectancy of 55 years, if he or she survives infancy.
- Many families are on waiting lists to adopt children with Down's syndrome.
- A child with Down's syndrome usually makes a positive impact on a family.

A few years ago, I delivered a Down's syndrome child for a patient of mine in her early 40s. We did an amniocentesis early in the pregnancy and she knew that she was expecting a Down's syndrome child. A year later she reported to me the joy and love this special child had brought the entire family. She told me, 'I don't know what our family would have been like without the blessing of this very special child. We cherish her.'

It's Your Decision

After testing, if you are advised that you are carrying a child with Down's syndrome, you and your partner have many aspects of the situation to consider. Some couples elect to terminate the pregnancy. Many others welcome the birth of this special child into their families.

Whatever decision you make, it must be *your* decision. Do not allow yourself or your partner to be pressured into making any decision without your full understanding of the situation. Seek information. Talk to parents of children with Down's syndrome. Make your decision based on the feelings that you and your partner share. There are positive and negative aspects to consider, as there are with any child. Whatever decision you make may be difficult for you. Involve your physician and your partner in the process.

Cancer during Pregnancy

Most women don't need to be concerned about contracting cancer during pregnancy; it is rare. However, because many women today wait until they are older to have babies, and cancer strikes more older women, it is good to have this information available so that you can discuss the situation with your doctor if you are concerned about it.

Cancer at any time is stressful; during pregnancy, it can be devastating. Many issues must be considered before a course of treatment is decided upon, including the following:

- Must the pregnancy be terminated?
- Can the malignancy affect the developing baby?
- Can treatment be delayed until after the baby is developed or delivered?
- How do medicines, chemotherapy or radiation used to treat the cancer affect the fetus?

The most common cancer discovered during pregnancy is breast cancer. Gynaecological cancers, leukaemia, lymphoma, melanoma and bone tumours have also been found.

Cancers may appear during pregnancy for several reasons. Some cancers arise from tissues or organs that are influenced by the increase in hormone levels caused by the pregnancy. In others, increased blood flow and changes in the lymphatic system in pregnancy are thought to contribute to the transfer of cancer to other parts of the body.

Breast Cancer

Breast cancer is the type of cancer discovered most often during pregnancy. Unfortunately, it is harder to find breast cancer at this time because of changes in the breasts, including tenderness, increased size and even lumpiness. About 2 per cent of all women who have breast cancer are pregnant when it is diagnosed, statistics suggest that 10 to 30 women per 100,000 pregnancies are diagnosed with breast cancer.

Breast cancer can be treated during pregnancy. Treatment varies, depending on the woman; surgery, chemotherapy or radiation, or all three, may be required.

Gynaecological Cancers

Various cancers of the female organs, including the cervix, the uterus, the vagina, the ovaries, the bladder and the Fallopian tubes, have been reported during pregnancy. Let me reassure you that these cancers are very rare during pregnancy, no matter what your age.

Cervical cancer occurs only about once in 10,000 pregnancies. However, about 1 per cent of the women who have cancer of the cervix are pregnant when the cancer is diagnosed. Cancer of the cervix is extremely curable, especially when it is discovered early. That is one reason your cervical smear is important before and during pregnancy.

Cancer Treatments

Treating cancer during pregnancy can be difficult because of the effects that various substances and procedures have on the mother and the fetus. Treatment can cause a variety of problems, including miscarriage, fetal death, fetal malformations and fetal growth retardation. A pregnant woman may also experience side-effects.

Discuss any questions about cancer treatment during pregnancy with your doctor. He or she can give you the best answers and help to reassure you.

Other Cancers in Pregnancy

Other types of cancer, such as Hodgkin's disease, leukaemia or melanoma, may or may not complicate pregnancy. If you are diagnosed with *any* form of cancer, your doctor will discuss ways of treating it.

PART FIVE

Labouring and Delivering Your Baby

CHAPTER 18

Labour and Delivery

Many of my patients in their 30s and 40s want to know if labour and delivery will be different for them than for younger women. Labour may be longer for a woman in her 30s or 40s than for a woman under 30 because the cervix does not dilate as easily as it does in a woman under 30. We also know that more older women need a caesarean section delivery.

Just as your uterus may not contract as readily during labour, so it may not contract as quickly as it would for a younger woman after delivery. Postpartum bleeding may last longer and be heavier.

However, your labour and delivery will be unique to you, no matter what your age. Every woman labours differently, and there is often a difference in the way a woman labours from one birth to another.

You don't have a lot of control over the kind of labour you will have. But you *do* have control over other areas related to your delivery. You can prepare for delivery in advance and be ready to go. Have your bag packed and ready. Have your case record card available. At best, your antenatal classes will be over, and you will have visited the labour and delivery area of the hospital you have chosen. You will have made arrangements for your older children to be cared for by someone you trust. You will have everything at work organized so that you can leave with a clear conscience. Doing these tasks will help to reassure you and put you in the best possible frame of mind. This chapter can also help you to prepare for you baby's birth.

Before Labour Begins

By now, you may be impatient for your baby's birth. When the day finally comes, you will experience new sensations as your body prepares to labour and to deliver your baby. Signs you may notice include:

- increase of Braxton-Hicks contractions (described below)
- feeling the baby 'drop' lower into your pelvis
- weight loss or a break in weight gain
- increased pressure in the pelvis and rectum
- changes in vaginal discharge
- diarrhoea

Braxton-Hicks contractions are painless, non-rhythmical contractions you may feel when you place your hand on your abdomen. They can begin early in pregnancy and continue until your baby is born. They occur at irregular intervals and may increase in number and strength when your uterus is massaged.

The feeling of having your baby drop, also called *lightening*, means that the baby's head has moved deep into your pelvis. It is a natural part of the birthing process and can happen a few weeks or a few hours before labour begins or during labour. Often a woman feels that she has more room to breathe when the baby descends into the pelvis, but this relief may be accompanied by more pelvic pressure and discomfort.

When Your Water Breaks

Your baby is surrounded by amniotic fluid in the uterus. As labour begins, the membranes that surround the baby and hold the fluid ('waters') may break, and fluid leaks from your vagina. You may feel a gush of fluid, followed by slow leaking, or you may just feel a slow leaking, without the gush of fluid. A sanitary pad helps to absorb the fluid.

Not every woman's water breaks before she goes into labour. Usually, the doctor or midwife will rupture the membranes. Occasionally the bag of waters breaks before a baby is ready to be born. There are several ways a doctor can confirm if your membranes have ruptured:

- *By your description of what happened.* For example, if you describe a large gush of fluid from your vagina.
- *With nitrazine paper.* Fluid is placed on the paper; if membranes have ruptured, the paper changes colour.
- *With a ferning test.* Fluid is placed on a glass slide, allowed to dry, then examined under a microscope. A fern-like appearance indicates that it is amniotic fluid.

If you believe that your water has broken, contact the hospital immediately. You may be advised to go to the hospital.

If you are not near term, the hospital may ask you to come for an examination. You may not be ready to deliver your baby yet, and your doctor will want to confirm that your water has broken and to prevent any infection. The risk of infection increases when your water breaks.

Preterm Birth

Preterm birth refers to a baby born prematurely (more than 3 weeks early); it is also called *premature birth*. About 10 per cent of all babies are born prematurely. Some preterm births are linked to the mother's health, such as when a mother suffers from high blood pressure or has an injection. Usually we do not know the reason a baby is born early.

Preterm delivery of a baby can be dangerous because a baby's lungs and other systems may not be ready to function on their own. Your doctor may take steps to halt contractions if you go into labour too early. Most doctors start with bed rest and sedatives to stop labour. Some medicines given orally, by injection or intravenously, also help to stop labour.

Causes of Premature Labour

While the cause of premature labour is unknown in most cases, we do know that premature labour can start for the following reasons:

- a uterus with an abnormal shape
- a large uterus
- hydramnios (excess amniotic fluid)
- an abnormal placenta
- premature rupture of the membranes
- incompetent cervix
- multiple fetuses
- abnormalities of the fetus
- fetal death
- retained intra-uterine device (coil)
- serious maternal illness
- vaginal infections

Treating Premature Labour

Your baby needs to remain inside your uterus until it is ready to be born. The goal in treating premature labour is to reduce the risks of problems related to premature delivery.

The treatment most often prescribed for premature labour is bed rest, which means lying on your side in bed. Either side is all right, but the left side is better. *See* the bed rest discussion beginning on page 194.

Doctors advise bed rest because it works in many cases. However, bed rest means that you may have to stop or to modify activities. Bed rest was once the only treatment for premature labour; now, even if you have the drugs, you will probably be advised to rest in bed. Three types of drug relax the uterus and decrease contractions: beta-adrenergics given intravenously, indomethacin given rectally, and glyceryl trinitrate given in skin patches.

Packing for the Hospital

Packing for the hospital can be unnerving. You don't want to pack too early and have your suitcase staring at you. But you don't want to wait until the last minute, throw your things together and take the chance of forgetting something important.

It is probably a good idea to pack about three weeks before your due date. Pack things that you will need during labour for you and your labour companion and items that you and the baby will need after delivery, as well as for the hospital stay.

One advantage to packing early for your trip to the hospital is that you will have the time to really think about what you want to take with you. You will avoid 'panic packing' and perhaps including items that you don't need while forgetting the more important ones.

There are many things to consider, but the list below should cover nearly all of what you might need:

- antenatal record card
- thick socks to wear in the delivery room
- an item to use as a focal point
- a cotton nightgown or T-shirt for labour
- a light diversion, such as books or magazines, to use during labour
- one or two nightdresses to wear after labour
- slippers with rubber soles
- a dressing-gown for walking in the corridors

- two bras (nursing bras and pads if you breast-feed)
- three pairs of panties
- toiletries, including brush, comb, toothbrush, toothpaste, soap, shampoo, conditioner
- hairband or ponytail holder, if you have long hair
- loose-fitting clothes for going home
- sanitary pads, if the hospital doesn't supply them

You may also want to bring a few pieces of fruit to eat after the delivery. Don't pack them too early!

It is also a good idea to include a few items in your hospital kit for your partner or labour companion to help you both during the birth. You might bring the following:

- a watch with a second hand
- talcum powder for massaging you during labour
- a paint roller or tennis ball for a low-back massage during labour
- tapes or CDs and a player, or a radio to play during labour
- camera and film
- a list of telephone numbers
- phonecard and change for telephones and vending machines
- snacks for your partner or labour companion

The hospital will probably supply most of what you need for your baby, but you should also have a few items:

- clothes for the trip home, including a vest, sleepsuit, outer clothes (a hat if it is cold outside)
- a couple of baby blankets
- nappies, if your hospital doesn't supply them

Be sure that you have an approved infant car seat in which to take your baby home. It is important to use a car seat from the very first time that he or she rides in a car. Some hospitals will not let you take your baby home without one.

Going to Hospital

Ask your doctor or midwife how you should prepare to go to the hospital; he or she may have specific instructions for you. You might want to ask the following questions:

- At what point should I go to the hospital once I am in labour?
- Should I call you before I leave for the hospital?
- How can I reach you outside normal surgery hours?
- Are there any particular instructions to follow during early labour?

Going to the hospital to have a baby can make anyone a little nervous, even an experienced mother. Make some plans before you go so that you will have less to worry about – for example:

- Tour the labour and delivery area of your hospital.
- Talk to your doctor about what will happen during your labour.
- Plan the route, and have your partner drive it a few times.
- Make alternative plans in case your partner cannot be with you.
- Know how to get in touch with your partner 24 hours a day.
- Pack your bag with items for you, your labour companion or partner, and the baby.

After You Are Admitted to Hospital

After you are admitted to hospital, you will probably be settled into a labour room. You are checked to see how much your cervix has dilated. A brief history of your pregnancy is taken. Vital signs, including blood pressure, pulse, temperature and your baby's heart rate are noted. You may receive an enema, or an intravenous drip may be started; blood will probably be drawn. You may have an epidural anaesthetic put in place, if you request one.

You may have your pubic hair shaved, although this is not always necessary. Patients who chose not to have their pubic hair shaved have told me later that they experienced discomfort when their pubic hair became entangled in their underwear because of the normal vaginal discharge after the birth of their baby. It may be something to consider.

Intravenous drip (IV). Some women are concerned about having an intravenous drip started in their arm. An IV is necessary with an epidural painkiller; however, if you have chosen not to have an epidural, an IV is not always required. Most physicians agree that an IV is helpful if a woman needs medications or fluids during labour. It is also a good safety precaution for problems, such as bleeding; if a woman bleeds heavily before or during labour, medications or blood can be administered quickly. If you are concerned about having an IV, discuss it at your antenatal clinic before the birth of your baby.

Enemas. Many of my patients also want to know if they will have to have an enema to empty their bowels. Not every woman is required to have one; usually it is a choice.

There are benefits to having an enema in labour. It decreases the amount of faecal contamination during labour and at the time of delivery. It may also help you after delivery if you have an episiotomy (*see* page 245) because having a bowel movement very soon after delivery can be painful. Discuss any concerns you have about enemas with the doctor at one of your antenatal appointments.

When you get to hospital, you may learn that the doctor or midwife you have seen in the antenatal clinic is not available and someone else will deliver your baby. Although the doctor or midwife you know might like to be present at the birth of your baby, this is often not possible.

Labour

Nearly every woman wants to know if labour will be painful. The only fact I can give you, which is true for every labour, is that no two labours are alike, not even for the same woman. Because labour is different for every woman, no one can predict what your labour will be like before it begins.

Labour is defined as the dilatation (stretching and expanding) of your cervix. The cervix opens while your uterus, a muscle, contracts to push out your baby.

Some women experience long, intense labours; others have short, relatively pain-free labours. I have found that if a woman understands the labour process and what causes childbirth pain, she has a better chance of reducing it.

Your uterus is a muscular sac shaped like an upside-down pear. This muscle tightens and relaxes during labour (contractions) to expel the baby. During labour, your bladder, rectum, spine and pubic bone receive strong pressure from the uterus as it tightens and hardens with each contraction. The weight of the baby's head as it moves down the birth canal also causes pressure.

The Stages of Labour

Labour is divided into three stages – each stage feels distinctly different and has a specific purpose. *See* the chart on pages 235 to 237 to see what you might expect during labour and delivery.

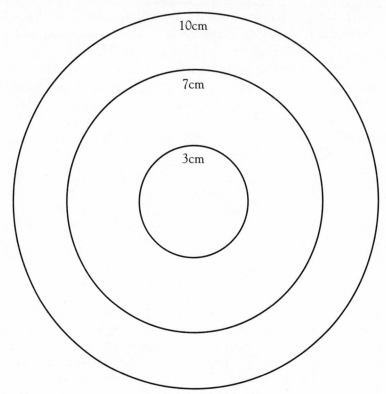

Dilatation of the cervix from 3 to 10cm (shown actual size)

Signs that Labour Is About to Begin

You may bleed a small amount following a vaginal examination late in pregnancy or at the beginning of labour. This *bloody show* occurs as the cervix stretches and dilates. If it causes you concern or appears to be a large amount of blood, contact your doctor or midwife immediately.

Along with light bleeding, you may pass some mucus, sometimes called a *mucus plug*. Passing mucus doesn't always mean that you will have your baby soon or that labour is beginning.

Timing Contractions

It is important for your doctor or midwife to know how often contractions occur and how long each one lasts. Knowing this, he or she can help you to decide if it is time to go to hospital. Contractions are timed to see how long a contraction lasts and how often contractions occur.

True Labour or False Labour?		
Considerations	*True Labour*	*False Labour*
Contractions	Regular	Irregular
Time between contractions	Come closer together	Do not get closer together
Contraction intensity	Increases	Doesn't change
Location of contractions	Entire abdomen or back	Various locations
Effect of anaesthetic or pain relievers	Will not stop labour	Sedation may alter frequency or stop contractions
Cervical change	Progressive cervical change (effacement and dilatation)	No cervical change

Ask your doctor how he or she prefers you to time your contractions. There are two ways to do it:

Method 1. Start timing when the contraction starts, and time it until the next contraction starts. This is the most common method.
Method 2. Start timing when the contraction ends, and note how long it is until the next contraction starts.

Your Partner's Involvement

Well before your delivery date, sit down and talk with your partner about how you will stay in touch as your due date approaches. Some of my patients' partners hire personal pagers for the last few weeks. Arrange for a back-up support person, in case your partner cannot be with you or you need someone else to take you to hospital.

Your partner can be a big help now. He can help to prepare you for labour and delivery and support you as you labour. He can share the joy of your baby's delivery. He can support you emotionally, which is very important to you both.

Your partner may choose to be your labour companion. A labour companion can do a lot to help you through labour. He or she can:

- time your contractions so that you are aware of the progress of your labour
- encourage and reassure you during labour
- help to create a mood in the labour room
- keep a watch on the door, to protect your privacy
- report symptoms or pain to the nurse or doctor
- help you to deal with physical discomfort

Maria was upset at her 32-week visit. Her husband's reserve unit has been activated, and he would be gone for at least six months. Maria was sure that she would not be able to deliver without her husband as her labour companion. We talked about other possible companions. Maria didn't know that someone else could act as her companion. When she came in two weeks later, Maria was happy to report that her sister (who had delivered a year earlier) was thrilled and honoured to help. They had even been to an antenatal class together to get ready.

Eating and Drinking during Labour

During labour, you are not allowed to eat or drink anything. Women often get nauseated during labour, which could cause vomiting. For your safety, keep your stomach empty. You may be able to sip water or to suck on ice cubes.

Tests during Labour

Tests done on your baby during labour give your doctor a great deal of information. These tests include fetal blood sampling, external fetal monitoring and internal fetal monitoring. These tests are discussed on page 114.

Coping with the Pain of Labour and Childbirth

Today, doctors encourage frank discussions about the pain of labour and delivery. Childbirth is usually accompanied by pain, and pain varies among women, from very little to a great deal. Research shows that the *expectation* of pain can, in itself, evoke fear and anxiety. The best way to deal with pain is to become informed about it.

Many women believe that they will feel guilty after their baby is born if they ask for pain relief during labour. Sometimes they think the baby will be harmed by the medication they take. Some women

Stages of Labour

Stage 1 – Early Phase

What is happening	• Cervix opens and thins out due to uterine contractions. • Cervix dilates to about 2cm. • This phase can last 1 to 10 hours.
What mother is experiencing	• Membranes may rupture, accompanied by a gush or trickle of amniotic fluid from vagina. • Pinkish discharge may appear ('bloody show'). • Mild contractions begin at 15- to 20-minute intervals; they last about 1 minute. • Contractions become closer together and more regular.
What mother or partner can do	• Mother should not eat or drink anything once labour begins. • Mother may be able to stay at home if she is at term. • Begin using relaxation and breathing techniques learned in childbirth classes. • If water has broken, if labour is preterm, if there is intense pain, if pain is constant or there is bright-red blood, contact doctor or maternity hospital immediately!

Stage 1 – Active Phase

What is happening	• Cervix dilates from about 2cm to 10cm. • Cervix continues to thin out. • This phase can last 20 minutes to 8 hours.
What mother is experiencing	• Contractions become more intense. • Contractions come closer together. • Contractions are about 3 minutes apart and last about 45 seconds to 1 minute.
What mother or partner can do	• Keep practising relaxation and breathing techniques. • An epidural can be administered during this phase.

	Stage 1 – Transition Phase
What is happening	• Stage 1 begins to change to Stage 2. • Cervix is dilated to 10cm. • Cervix continues to thin out. • This phase can last a few minutes to 2 hours.
What mother is experiencing	• Contractions are 2 to 3 minutes apart and last about 1 minute. • Mother may feel strong urge to push; she should not push until cervix is completely dilated. • Mother may be moved to delivery room, if she is not in one.
What mother or partner can do	• Relaxation and breathing techniques help to counteract mother's urge to push.
	Stage 2
What is happening	• Cervix is completely dilated. • Baby continues to descend into the birth canal. • As mother pushes, baby is delivered. • Doctor or nurse suctions baby's nose and mouth, and clamps umbilical cord. • This stage can last a few minutes to 1–3 hours (pushing the baby can last a long time).
What mother is experiencing	• Contractions occur at 2- to 5-minute intervals and last from 60 to 90 seconds. • With an epidural, mother may find it harder to push. • An episiotomy may be done to prevent tearing vaginal tissues as baby is born.
What mother or partner can do	• Mother will begin to push with each contraction after cervix dilates completely. • Mother may be given analgesic or local anaesthetic. • Mother must listen to doctor or nurse when baby is being delivered; doctor or nurse will tell mother when to push. • As mother pushes, she may be able to watch baby being born, if a mirror is available.

	Stage 3
What is happening	• Placenta is delivered. • Doctor examines placenta to make sure that all of it has been delivered. • This stage can last a few minutes to an hour.
What mother is experiencing	• Contractions may occur closer together, but be less painful. • Doctor repairs episiotomy.
What mother or partner can do	• You will meet and hold your baby. • You may need to push to expel the placenta. • You may be able to hold your baby while the doctor repairs your episiotomy. • A nurse will rub or massage the uterus through the abdomen to help it contract to control bleeding.
	After Delivery
What is happening	• Placenta has been delivered. • Uterus continues to contract, which is important to control bleeding. • This stage usually lasts a couple of days.

believe that they will deprive themselves of the 'complete' birth experience.

You learn about pain and pain relief through several channels. Childbirth education classes are good sources of information. You can learn about pain-relief methods that don't require medication, such as breathing methods and relaxation techniques.

Talk to your doctor about pain relief. I have found that using medication for pain relief is usually a personal choice, not a medical decision.

Keep an open mind about using medication for pain relief during labour. Your labour may be harder (or easier) than you expect. You may have a greater or lesser need for pain relief than you think. You can always change your mind if you need to or want to.

Martha was certain that she would not need an epidural. At one of her visits late in the pregnancy, she tried to make me promise that I would not make her have one. I explained that an epidural was an option, not a requirement, and that no one would make her have one. I knew she thought that I was trying to talk her into it, but I wasn't. Experience has taught me that no matter how much a woman prepares, no mother-to-be knows what labour will be like for her. I try to help them keep an open mind about the experience. Among her other requests, Martha didn't want an intravenous infusion or an enema and certainly not an episiotomy. Martha's labour turned out to be an adventure – a long one. At 3cm, she was screaming for relief. She got to 5cm and stayed there for quite a while. In the end, I had to do a caesarean section for her 9lb 4oz (4.2kg) healthy baby boy.

I wasn't sure what her reaction was going to be after the birth. When I saw her the next day, Martha was in good spirits and very happy. She felt her expectations before delivery had been misdirected. She jokingly said to me, 'The only thing on my list that didn't happen was an episiotomy.'

Pain Relief without Drugs

Some women do not want drugs during labour to relieve pain. They prefer to use different labouring positions, massage, breathing patterns, relaxation techniques or hypnotherapy to relieve their pain.

Breathing patterns and relaxation techniques are usually learned in a childbirth-education class. *See* page 37 for a discussion of the various options.

Different labouring positions and massage enable a woman and her partner (or labour companion) to work together during labour to find relief. This interaction can help them to feel closer, and it lets them share the experience. Some patients have told me that using these methods brought them closer to their partner and made the birth experience a more joyful one.

Labouring Positions

Most women in North America and Europe give birth on their backs, in bed. However, some women are trying different positions to find relief from pain and to make the birth of their baby easier.

In the past, women often laboured and gave birth in an upright position that kept the pelvis vertical, such as kneeling, squatting, sitting or standing up. Labouring in this position enables the abdominal wall to relax and the baby to descend more rapidly. Because contractions are stronger and more regular, labour is often shorter.

Today, many women are asking to choose the birth position that is most comfortable for them. Freedom to choose the birth position can make the woman feel more confident about managing birth and labour. Women who choose their own methods may feel more satisfied with the entire experience.

If this is important to you, discuss the matter with your doctor or midwife. Ask about the facilities at the hospital you will use; some have special equipment, such as birthing chairs, squatting bars or birthing beds, to help you feel more comfortable. Positions you might consider for your labour are described below:

- *Walking and standing* are good positions to use during early labour. Walking may help you to breathe more easily and to relax more. Standing in a warm shower may provide relief. When walking, be sure that someone is with you to offer support (both physical and emotional).
- *Sitting* can decrease the strength and frequency of contractions and can slow labour. Sitting to rest after walking or standing is acceptable; however, sitting can be uncomfortable during a contraction.
- *Kneeling on hands and knees* is a good way to relieve the backache of labour.
- *Kneeling against a support*, such as a chair or your partner, stretches your back muscles. The effects of kneeling are similar to those of walking and standing.
- When you can't stand, walk or kneel, *lie on your side*. If you receive pain medication, you will need to lie down. Lie on your left side, then turn to your right.
- Although *lying on your back* is the most common position used for labour, it can decrease the strength and frequency of contractions, which can slow the process. It can also make your blood pressure drop and cause your baby's heart rate to drop. If you lie on your back, elevate the head of the bed and put a pillow under one hip so you are not flat on your back.

Massage for Relief

Massage is a wonderful, gentle way to help you feel better during labour. The touching and caressing of massage helps you to relax. One study showed that women who were massaged for 20 minutes every hour during active labour felt less anxiety and less pain.

Many parts of the body of a labouring woman can be massaged. Massaging the head, neck, back and feet can offer a great deal of comfort and relaxation. The person doing the massage should pay close attention to the woman's responses to determine the correct pressure.

Different types of massage affect a woman in various ways. You and your partner may want to practise the two types of massage described below before labour and for use during labour.

Effleurage is light, gentle fingertip massage over the abdomen and upper thighs; it is used during early labour. Stroking is light but doesn't tickle, and fingertips never leave the skin.

Start with hands on either side of the navel. Move the hands upward and outward, and come back down to the pubic area. Then move the hands back up to the navel. Massage may extend down the thighs. It can also be done as a crosswise motion, around fetal-monitor belts. Move fingers across the abdomen from one side to the other, between the belts.

Counterpressure massage is excellent for relieving backache in labour. Place the heel of the hand or the flat part of the fist (you can also use a tennis ball) against the tailbone. Apply firm pressure in a small, circular motion.

Analgesics and Anaesthetics

There are many different types of pain relief. *Analgesia* is pain relief without total loss of sensation. *Anaesthesia* is pain relief with partial or total loss of sensation.

Analgesia is injected into a muscle or vein to decrease the pain of labour, but you remain conscious. It provides pain relief but can make you drowsy, restless or nauseated. You may find concentrating difficult. Analgesia may slow the baby's reflexes and breathing, so this medication is usually given during the early and middle parts of labour. Examples of analgesia are pethidine and meptazinol (Meptid).

There are two types of anaesthesia – local anaesthesia, sometimes called *regional anaesthesia*, and general anaesthesia. You remain completely unconscious under general anesthaesia, so it is used only for some Caesarean sections and emergency vaginal deliveries. Using a general anaethesia has certain disadvantages. Sometimes the mother vomits or aspirates vomited food or stomach acid into her lungs. The baby is also anaesthetized and needs to be resuscitated after delivery. General anaesthesia is not used very often for childbirth today. Its advantage is that it can be administered quickly in an emergency.

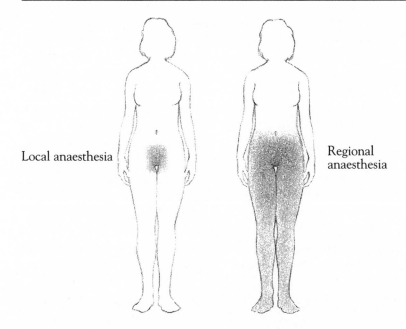

Local anaesthesia

Regional
anaesthesia

Local or regional anaesthesia affects a small area and is useful for an episiotomy repair. It rarely affects the baby and usually has few lingering effects. The three most common types of regional anaesthesia are pudendal block, spinal block and epidural block.

A *pudendal block* is a local anaesthetic injected into the pudendal nerve area in the vagina to relieve pain in the vaginal area, the perineum and the rectum. You remain conscious, and side-effects are rare. Pudendal block is considered one of the safest forms of pain relief, but it does not relieve uterine pain.

Local anaesthetic is injected into spinal fluid in the lower back with a *spinal block*, which numbs the lower part of the body. You remain conscious. This type of block is administered only once during labour, so it is sometimes used just before delivery or for a caesarean section. It works quickly and is an effective pain inhibitor.

A tube is inserted into a space outside your spinal column in the lower back for an *epidural block*. Local anaesthetic is administered through the tube for pain relief, and you remain conscious during delivery. The tube remains in place until after the baby is born so that anaesthetic can be readministered when necessary; sometimes the anaesthetic is delivered continuously by pump. An epidural causes some loss of sensation in the lower part of the body. It helps to relieve painful uterine contractions, pain in the vagina and rectum as the baby passes through the birth canal and the pain of an episiotomy. A woman with an epidural still feels pressure sensations so she is able to push during vaginal delivery. However, an epidural may make it harder to push, so vacuum extraction or forceps may be necessary during delivery.

A spinal block or an epidural block may cause a woman's blood pressure to drop suddenly, which in turn can cause a decrease in the baby's heart rate. These blocks are not used if a woman is bleeding heavily or if the baby has an abnormal heartbeat. One other possible side-effect from these blocks is severe headache if the insertion needle punctures the covering of the spinal cord; this is an unusual complication.

A *walking spinal*, also called *intrathecal anaesthesia*, can be given to women who suffer extreme pain in the early stages of labour (dilated less than 5cm). A small amount of narcotic, such as pethidine or morphine, is injected through a thin needle into the spinal fluid, which eases the pain and causes few side-effects. Because the dose is small, neither mother nor baby becomes overly drowsy. Sensory and motor functions remain intact, so the mother can walk around with help, sit in a chair or go to the toilet.

Caesarean Section

When you have a caesarean section, your baby is delivered through an incision made in your abdominal wall and uterus. Research has shown that women in their 30s and 40s have the highest rate of caesarean sections.

While there are many reasons for doing a caesarean section, the main goal is to deliver a healthy baby and have a healthy mother. Particular reasons for performing the operation include:

- a previous caesarean section
- to avoid rupture of the uterus
- the baby is too big to fit through the birth canal
- fetal distress
- compression of the umbilical cord
- the baby is in the breech position
- placental abruption
- placenta praevia
- multiple pregnancy – twins, triplets or more

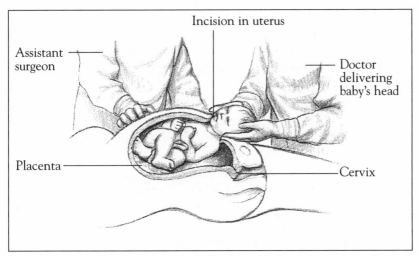

Incision in uterus

Assistant surgeon

Doctor delivering baby's head

Placenta

Cervix

Caesarean section

The rate of caesarean sections has increased. In 1965, only 4 to 5 per cent of all deliveries were by caesarean section. Today, about 15 per cent of all deliveries are caesarean sections. For women over 35, the rate is higher.

We can point to many reasons for the increase. We believe that it is related to better monitoring during labour and safer procedures for caesarean section. Women are also having bigger babies. Another factor influencing this increase may be the growing fear of litigation among doctors.

A woman often wants to know in advance if she will need a caesarean section. A doctor doesn't usually know the answer to this question before labour begins, unless the woman had a previous caesarean section. (Also see caesarean section discussion below of vaginal birth after caesarean section.) We usually have to wait for labour contractions to begin before we can tell if the baby is stressed by them or if the baby fits through the birth canal.

It is a good idea to discuss caesarean section with your doctor several weeks before your due date. Ask why he or she would do the operation. Let your doctor know your wishes and concerns with regard to having this mode of delivery.

How a Caesarean Section Is Performed

When a caesarean section is performed, an incision is made through the skin of the lower abdomen down to the uterus, and the wall of the uterus is cut. Next, the amniotic sac containing the baby and placenta is cut, and the baby is removed through the incisions. After the baby is delivered, the placenta is removed. The uterus is closed in layers with absorbable sutures (they don't have to be removed). Finally, the abdomen is sewn together.

With many caesarean sections an anaesthetist administers an epidural or spinal anaesthetic so you remain awake. You can see and hold your baby immediately after birth, and your partner can be with you.

A caesarean section is major surgery and carries with it certain risks, including infection, bleeding, shock through blood loss, the possibility of blood clots and the possibility of injury to other organs, such as the bladder or rectum.

You will probably have to stay in hospital for a few extra days. Recovery is slower with a caesarean section than with a vaginal delivery. Full recovery normally takes four to six weeks.

Vaginal Birth after Caesarean Section

Today, many women who have had a caesarean section with one pregnancy deliver vaginally with a later pregnancy. A high percentage of these deliveries are successful. About 70 per cent of women who had a caesarean section because of a situation that is not a factor in this pregnancy can expect a successful vaginal delivery.

A number of factors in your situation must be considered. Ask your doctor for information before you make this decision. Certain criteria must be met before you can have a vaginal delivery after a caesarean section, including the following:

- The type of uterine incision from the previous operation is important. (This incision may or may not be similar to the incision made in your abdomen.) With a classical incision, which goes high up on the uterus, labour is *not* permitted in subsequent pregnancies.
- The size of your pelvis is important. If you are small and your baby is large, it may cause problems.
- You have no medical complications, such as diabetes or high blood pressure.
- You are expecting only one baby.
- Your baby is entering the birth canal head first.

If you are considering a vaginal birth with this pregnancy, the

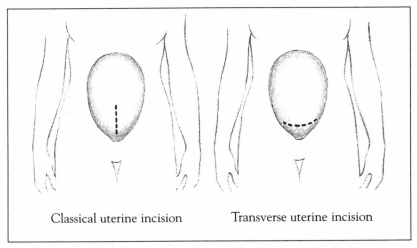

Classical uterine incision   Transverse uterine incision

The incision in the uterus for a caesarean section is not always the same as the one made in the abdomen.

maternity unit should offer the ability to perform an emergency caesarean section within 30 minutes, and have the ability to monitor the fetus continuously and a fully equipped, 24-hour blood bank.

If you are interested in a vaginal birth after a caesarean section, discuss this with your doctor well in advance of labour so that plans can be made. Discuss the benefits and risks, and ask your doctor for his or her opinion as to your chances of a successful vaginal delivery. He or she knows your health and pregnancy history. Include your partner in the decision-making process.

Is an Episiotomy Always Necessary?

An *episiotomy* is a surgical incision in the area behind the vagina, above the rectum; it is made during delivery to avoid tearing or lacerating the vaginal opening or rectum, and to allow room for the baby to fit through the birth canal. Many women do not want an episiotomy for the delivery of their baby; they believe that the procedure is unnecessary.

Whether you must have an episiotomy is something to discuss with your doctor at antenatal visits. Ask if an episiotomy is routine or if it is done only when necessary. Some situations do not require an episiotomy, such as a small or premature baby. However, your doctor may not be able to make this decision until delivery.

An episiotomy is not necessary for every woman. The more children a woman has, the less likely it is that she will need one; it depends on the size of the baby. Factors leading to an episiotomy include the size of the mother's vaginal opening, the size of the baby's head and shoulders, the number of babies previously delivered and whether it is a forceps or vacuum delivery.

Types of Episiotomies

Episiotomies are described according to the relative depth of the incision:

- *1st degree* – cuts only the skin.
- *2nd degree* – cuts the skin and underlying tissue, called *fascia*, and occasionally some muscles.

If You Have an Episiotomy

Apart from delivery of your baby, the most painful part of the entire birth process might be your episiotomy. Don't be afraid to ask for pain medication. Ice, salt baths and laxatives can also help to relieve episiotomy pain.

The Baby's Birth Position

Most babies enter the birth canal head first, which is the best position for labour and delivery. However, some babies enter the birth canal in other positions.

A *breech position* means that the baby is not in a head-down position; its legs or buttocks come into the birth canal first. If your baby is breech when it is time to deliver, your doctor may try to turn the baby or you may need a caesarean section.

One of the main causes of a breech presentation is prematurity of the baby. Near the end of the second trimester, the baby is commonly in the breech presentation. As you progress through the third trimester, the baby usually turns into the head-down presentation for birth.

For a long time, breech deliveries were performed vaginally. Then it was believed that the safest delivery method was a caesarean section; many doctors will prefer to do a caesarean section for a breech presentation. However, some doctors believe that a woman can deliver a breech baby without difficulty if the situation is right.

Abnormal Birth Presentations

There are three different breech presentations and three other atypical presentations:

- *Frank breech* – occurs when the lower legs are flexed at the hips and extended at the knees. The feet are up by the face or head.
- *Complete breech presentation* – one or both knees are flexed (not extended).
- *Incomplete breech presentation* – a foot or knee enters the birth canal ahead of the rest of the baby.
- *Face presentation* – the baby's head is hyperextended so that the face enters the birth canal first.
- *Transverse lie* – the baby is lying almost as if it is in a cradle in the pelvis. The head is on one side of the mother's abdomen and the bottom is on the other side.
- *Shoulder presentation* – the baby's shoulder enters the birth canal first.

Can My Baby Be Turned?

Some doctors try to turn a baby in the breech position. If your baby is in a breech position, your physician may attempt to change its position by using external cephalic version.

The doctor places his or her hands on your abdomen. Using gentle movements, he or she manually tries to shift the baby into the head-down position. An ultrasound is usually done first, enabling the doctor to see the position of the baby, and again during the procedure to guide the doctor in changing the baby's position.

A physician usually uses this method before labour begins or in the early stages of labour. It is successful in about half of the cases in which it is used. Not every doctor is trained in the procedure.

Delivery of Your Baby

After you have laboured through the first stage, you are ready to deliver your baby. You will finally meet your child whom you have carried for so long.

The delivery of the baby and placenta (not including the labouring process) in stage 2 takes from a few minutes to an hour or more. However, the part that takes the longest is not the actual delivery of the baby. Stitching closed the various skin and muscle layers after the baby is born may take a greater amount of time.

In a forceps delivery, the doctor uses an instrument to help remove the baby from the birth canal. Forceps look like two metal hands. They are not used as frequently as they were in the past; today, doctors often use a vacuum extractor.

A *vacuum extractor* is a plastic cup that fits on the baby's head by suction. When you push during labour, your doctor is able to pull gently and deliver the baby's head and body more easily.

After Your Baby Is Born

Things happen quickly when your baby emerges into the world. First, the baby's mouth and throat are suctioned. Then the doctor clamps and cuts the umbilical cord (or your partner may cut the cord).

The baby is wrapped in clean blankets and may be placed on your abdomen. Apgar scores are recorded at one minute and five minutes after birth. An identification band is placed on the baby's wrist or ankle. Usually a brief physical examination or an assessment is done immediately after delivery. The baby is given a vitamin K injection to prevent bleeding.

You may be asked if you want your baby to receive the hepatitis vaccine. Discuss this with your doctor before the birth; the vaccine protects your baby against hepatitis in the future.

Once the initial evaluation is complete, the baby is returned to you. Later, the baby is placed in a heated cot for a period of time.

If your partner wants to cut the umbilical cord after the baby is delivered, discuss it with your doctor or midwife before you go into labour. What your partner may be allowed to do varies from place to place.

Bleeding after Delivery

After you deliver your baby, the uterus shrinks from the size of a watermelon to the size of a volleyball so that it won't bleed. It is not unusual to lose blood during labour and delivery; however, heavy bleeding after the baby is born can be serious. A loss of more than 18oz (500ml) in the first 24 hours after your baby's birth, called *postpartum haemorrhage*, is significant. Bleeding is controlled by massaging the uterus and drugs by injection. Bleeding lessens gradually over time, then stops.

Heavy bleeding after the birth may be caused by a number of factors, including a uterus that won't contract, lacerations or tearing of the vagina or cervix during birth, a large or bleeding episiotomy, a tear or rupture in the uterus, retained placental tissue or clotting or coagulation problems.

If you experience a significant change in bleeding after you go home, contact your doctor. Some bleeding is normal, but it is best to talk to your doctor about it. He or she may want to see you, prescribe treatment or determine if the amount of bleeding is normal.

Kay had delivered two days earlier, and she called me because she was concerned. She thought that she should be feeling a lot better, and she was afraid that something was wrong because she didn't feel well. She said that her breasts were sore and ached, it felt as though her uterus were still contracting (especially when she breast fed) and sitting down was an ordeal because her episiotomy was sore. I told her that all these things were normal, and we talked about what she could do help make things better.

In the hospital, she had taken some pain relief but didn't want to take any more because she was nursing. I told her that the prescription she had been given was safe and would probably help a lot. Breast-feeding had stimulated her uterus to contract to help it to get smaller so that it wouldn't bleed. We talked about salt baths for her episiotomy, and I reminded her that the pain relief would also help with that discomfort. When I saw her a few weeks later, she said that my suggestions had made her life a lot easier.

Inducing Labour

Labour may be induced for a number of reasons, including postdates (overdue) babies chronic high blood pressure in the mother, pre-eclampsia, gestational diabetes, intra-uterine growth retardation and Rhesus-isoimmunization.

Postdates Pregnancies

The most common reason for inducing labour is an overdue baby. Babies born two weeks or more past their due date are called *postdates births*. Nearly 10 per cent of all babies are born more than two weeks late. The majority of these babies are delivered safely. However, carrying a baby longer than 42 weeks can cause some problems for the fetus and the mother, so doctors conduct tests on these babies and induce labour if necessary.

A doctor can determine if a baby is moving around in the womb and if the amount of amniotic fluid is healthy and normal. If the baby is healthy and active, the mother is usually monitored until labour begins on its own. Tests may be done as a reassurance that an overdue baby is healthy and can remain in the womb. These tests include a cardiotocogram and a biophysical profile. If signs of fetal stress are found, labour is often induced.

Emergency Childbirth

Emergency childbirth can happen to anyone, so it is a good idea to be prepared. Read and study the information in the boxes on the following pages. Be sure you have the names and telephone numbers of your doctor and those of friends or family near the phone. And if it happens to you, relax and follow the instructions provided.

Emergency Delivery at Home

1 Call 999 for help.

2 Call a neighbour, family member or friend (have telephone numbers available).

3 Encourage the woman *not* to push or to bear down.

4 Use blankets and towels to make the woman as comfortable as possible.

5 If there is time, wash the woman's vaginal and rectal areas with soap and water.

6 When the baby's head delivers, encourage the woman to pant or blow, and to concentrate on *not* pushing.

7 Try to ease the baby's head out with gentle pressure. Do not pull on the head.

8 After the head is delivered, gently push down on the head and push a little to deliver the shoulders.

9 As one shoulder delivers, lift the head up, delivering the other shoulder. The rest of the baby will quickly follow.

10 Wrap the baby in a clean blanket or towel.

11 Use a clean cloth or tissue to remove mucus from the baby's mouth.

12 Do not pull on the umbilical cord to deliver the placenta – it is not necessary.

13 If the placenta delivers on its own, wrap it in a towel or clean newspapers, and save it.

14 You don't need to cut the cord.

15 Keep the placenta at the level of the baby or above the baby.

16 Keep both mother and baby warm with towels or blankets until medical help arrives.

Emergency Delivery Alone

1   Call 999 for help.

2   Call a neighbour, family member or close friend (have telephone numbers available).

3   Try not to push or to bear down.

4   Find a comfortable place and spread out towels or blankets.

5   If the baby comes before help arrives, try to use your hands to ease the baby out while you gently push.

6   Wrap the baby in a clean blanket or clean towels; hold it close to your body to keep it warm.

7   Use a clean cloth or tissue to remove mucus from the baby's mouth.

8   Do not pull on the umbilical cord to deliver the placenta – it is not necessary.

9   If the placenta delivers on its own, save it.

10 You don't need to cut the cord.

11 Keep the placenta at the level of the baby or above the baby.

12 Try to keep yourself and your baby warm until medical help arrives.

Emergency Delivery on the Way to Hospital

1   Stop the car.

2   Try to get help if you have a cellular phone or a CB radio.

3   Put on your flashing warning lights.

4   Place the woman in the back seat with a towel or blanket under her.

5   Encourage the woman not to push or to bear down.

6   When the baby's head delivers, encourage the woman to pant or blow, and to concentrate on *not* pushing.

7   Try to ease the baby's head out with gentle pressure. Do not pull on the head.

8   After the head is delivered, gently push down on the head and push a little to deliver the shoulders.

9   As one shoulder delivers, lift the head up, delivering the other shoulder. The rest of the baby will quickly follow.

10   Wrap the baby in a clean blanket or clean towels. Clean newspapers can be used if nothing else is available.

11   Use a clean cloth or tissue to remove the mucus from the baby's mouth.

12   Do not pull on the umbilical cord to deliver the placenta – it is not necessary.

13   If the placenta delivers on its own, wrap it in a towel or clean newspapers and save it.

14   You don't need to cut the cord.

15   Keep the placenta at the level of the baby or above the baby.

16   Keep both mother and baby warm until you can get them to hospital or medical help arrives.

PART SIX

Living with Your Baby

CHAPTER 19

After the Birth

Your baby has been delivered, and you have a new person in your life who needs care and attention. But you need care and attention, too – and time to pay attention to your own needs. Soon after the birth, you may start to think about how to get back in shape and feel your best again. Just keep in mind that your body can't recover overnight from nine months of pregnancy, so don't expect it to. Relax and take your time!

The recovery period following your baby's birth (the first six weeks) is called the *postpartum period* or *puerperium*. Your body rapidly downsizes as it begins to return to its pre-pregnancy size. During this time, you go through great physical and emotional adjustments.

You can help yourself during the puerperium in many ways. Eat nutritiously, allow others to help you and accept the fact that you will have to take it easy for a while. You can help yourself also by learning as much as you can about what to expect after delivery.

After the Baby Is Born

You will probably be discharged from the hospital a day or two after your baby is born, if labour and delivery were normal and the baby is doing well. Some women choose to go home 24 hours after the birth of their baby or even sooner. If you have had a caesarean section, you will need to stay a few days longer.

Your blood pressure and bleeding are checked regularly in the first hours after the birth. You will be offered medication for pain relief and be encouraged to nurse your baby.

Changes in the Uterus

Your uterus goes through great changes after your baby is born and takes several weeks to return to its original size. The size of your uterus at birth is quite large to accommodate the baby. Immediately after delivery, you can feel the uterus around your navel; it should feel very hard. You are checked frequently to make sure that it remains hard after delivery. If it feels soft, you or a nurse can massage it so that it becomes firm.

The uterus shrinks about a finger's width every day; this is called *involution*. In hospital, someone will check you every day; the examination can be a little uncomfortable.

You will probably feel after-pains for several days after the birth as your uterus contracts to prevent heavy bleeding and to return to its normal size. Cramps are eased by lying on your stomach and taking mild pain relievers. An empty bladder enables the uterus to work more efficiently, with less pain, so drink lots of fluids and urinate often.

If you breast-feed, you may find that after-pains intensify. When your baby sucks, the pituitary gland is stimulated to release oxytocin, which makes the uterus contract. These extra contractions are good for you, but they may be painful. Mild pain medication can offer relief.

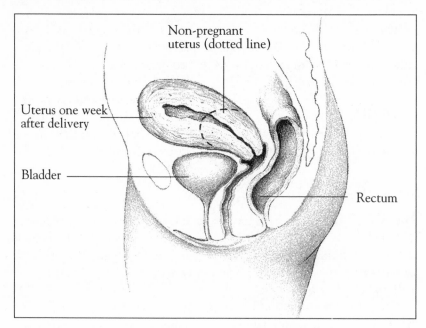

Your uterus shrinks a great deal after delivery. This illustration compares a non-pregnant uterus with a uterus one week after birth

Pain in the Perineum

You may feel pain in the perineum. (The perineum is the area between the vagina and anus.) The area may have been stretched, cut or torn during delivery. Most of the soreness should be gone in three to six weeks.

If this pain is a problem, ice-packs offer some relief in the first 24 hours after delivery. Ice numbs the area and helps to reduce swelling. After 24 hours, a warm bath or a soak in a salt bath can offer relief. Do this several times a day. Other remedies for perineal pain include numbing sprays, walking (to stimulate circulation), witch-hazel compresses and Kegel exercises. *See* page 168 for Kegel exercises.

Urination may be painful; acidic urine can sting the cut area. You may want to urinate standing up or in the shower with running water washing the area.

Bowel Movements

It is not unusual to have sluggish bowels for a few days after your baby's birth. The digestive system slows down during labour, and pregnancy and delivery stress abdominal muscles. You may have had an enema or emptied your bowel during the pushing phase of labour. Pain medication can cause constipation. These all contribute to bowel habits that are different from normal. I tell my patients not to worry about having a bowel movement for the first four or five days. Constipation at this time is acceptable.

To help your system work more efficiently, eat a diet that is high in fibre, and drink lots of fluid. Laxatives are commonly used and available. Prune juice and prunes are natural laxatives. Over-the-counter stool softeners also help. If you don't have a bowel movement within a week after delivery or you become uncomfortable, call your doctor.

An episiotomy or haemorrhoids can make a bowel movement more difficult or make you more apprehensive about having one. If you are left with haemorrhoids after delivery, be assured that they eventually shrink on their own. If you have problems with them, a compress of witch hazel or commercial compresses can offer relief. Ice-packs may also help them to shrink.

Your Breasts

After delivery, your breasts may be sore, whether you breast-feed or bottle-feed. If you bottle-feed, your milk still comes in; doctors don't give drugs to stop it as they did in the past. Your breasts fill with milk, called *engorgement*. Engorgement lasts a few days and can be very uncomfortable. You can ease discomfort by wearing a support bra or binding your breasts with a towel. Ice-packs also help your milk to dry up.

Don't empty your breasts unless you really have to because of pain – your body will replace the milk with more milk! Avoid nipple stimulation and running warm water over the breasts. These practices stimulate breasts to produce milk.

You may find that you have a mild fever with engorgement. Paracetamol can help to reduce the fever and discomfort.

Vaginal Discharge

After delivering your baby, you will experience a vaginal discharge similar to a heavy menstrual flow. This discharge, called *lochia*, lasts from two to four weeks. The discharge is red for the first three or four days, then turns pink, then brown and finally white or colourless at around ten days. You will also have lochia if you have a caesarean section, although it may be less than appears with a vaginal birth.

If the discharge is foul-smelling, remains heavy or is extremely light the first few days, tell your doctor. He or she may want to examine you.

Research indicates that toxic shock syndrome occurs more often in the puerperium. Because tampons are associated with the syndrome, don't use them to deal with lochia. Use sanitary pads.

If you do not breast-feed, your first menstrual period occurs within six to eight weeks after giving birth. If you breast-feed, you may not have a regular menstrual period until you wean your baby.

Postpartum Warning Signs

If you take care of yourself after delivery, you should not feel ill after the birth. Occasionally problems do occur. Refer to the list of symptoms and warning signs below. Call your doctor immediately if you experience:

- unusually heavy or sudden increase in vaginal bleeding (more than your normal menstrual flow or soaking more than two sanitary pads in 30 minutes)
- vaginal discharge with a strong, unpleasant odour
- a temperature of 101°F (38.3°C) or more, except in the first 24 hours after birth
- chills
- breasts that are painful or red
- loss of appetite for an extended period
- pain, tenderness, redness or swelling in the legs
- pain in the lower abdomen or in the back
- painful urination or feeling an intense need to urinate
- severe pain in the vagina or perineum

Your Emotions

Temporary emotional changes are not uncommon during the postpartum period. You may have mood swings, mild distress or bouts of crying. (*See* the discussion of postpartum distress that begins on page 266.) Mood changes are often a result of birth-associated hormonal changes in your body.

Lack of sleep may play a part in how you feel. Many women are surprised at how tired they are emotionally and physically in the first few months after the birth of the baby. Be sure to take time for yourself, and allow yourself a period of adjustment.

Sleep and rest are essential after your baby is born. To get the rest you need, go to bed early when possible. Take a nap or rest when your baby sleeps.

Exercise after Pregnancy

Many women are eager to begin exercising soon after their baby is born. Exercise helps you to feel better, and it can lift your spirits. Start by doing simple isometric exercises the day after delivery. Practise holding in your stomach muscles, or start with mild Kegel exercises. *See* page 168.

When you are up and about again, you can do other forms of exercise. Do something you enjoy, and do it on a regular basis. Walking and swimming are excellent exercises to help you to get back in shape. However, before you start any postpartum exercise programme, check with your doctor. He or she may have particular advice for you.

Be careful about beginning an exercise programme too soon. Don't overtire yourself by choosing a programme that is too ambitious. Always get adequate rest.

After a caesarean section, light activity is very important. In hospital, you will probably have to practise coughing or deep breathing to keep your lungs clear. Wiggle your toes to aid circulation. Walking may not be easy, but it helps to minimize the chances of developing a blood clot in your lower extremities. Check with your doctor before you start an exercise routine or programme of any kind.

Recovering from a Caesarean Section

Recovery from a caesarean section is different from recovery from a vaginal birth. You have undergone major abdominal surgery, so be prepared to take it easy for a while. While you have experienced many of the same situations as someone who has had a vaginal birth, you face some additional restrictions.

You are encouraged to get out of bed as soon as possible after your baby is born. Moving helps to prevent blood clots in the legs, lung collapse and pneumonia. Walking helps to restore body functions, such as relieving constipation and abdominal wind.

Be careful not to strain your stomach muscles. Avoid lifting anything heavy. Once you are at home, keep your incision clean and dry, and watch for any sign of infection.

Infection of a caesarean section incision can occur four to six days after surgery. If any of the following signs appear, contact your doctor immediately. Signs of infection include:

- redness that spreads from the edges of the incision
- fever
- hardness around the incision
- discharge from the incision site

Although you did not deliver vaginally, you will probably experience painful uterine contractions for several days after the operation. This is a sign that your uterus is returning to its pre-pregnancy size. If you breast-feed, you may notice the pains when your baby nurses.

You will have lochia after a caesarean section (*see* page 260). However, your discharge may be lighter than lochia that follows a vaginal birth.

If you are interested in exercising after a caesarean section, you can usually begin light exercise about three weeks after birth. You can probably resume full activity between four and six weeks postpartum.

Resuming Sexual Relations

One concern you and your partner may share after delivery is postpartum sex. Getting back into the swing after the baby is born can be difficult. Your sex drives can be affected by stress, hormone changes, emotions and fatigue.

We used to advise women to wait at least six weeks before having intercourse. If you feel no pain or discomfort and your episiotomy has healed, you can resume sexual relations. Be sure that bleeding has ceased. For most women, this will be at least a few weeks after delivery.

If you decide to have intercourse, you need to take precautions if you don't want to become pregnant again. *You can become pregnant before you have a menstrual period.* Discuss birth control options with your doctor.

Birth Control after Pregnancy

Some women choose to have a tubal ligation done while they are in hospital after the birth of their baby. Immediately after the birth is probably *not* the time to make a decision about a tubal ligation if you haven't thought seriously about it before. Tubal ligation is permanent and irreversible. If you have your tubes tied within a few hours or a day after having your baby, then change your mind, you may regret it.

Most women do not choose permanent birth control after delivery; however, contraception is something you should think about. You will probably begin ovulating six to eight weeks after birth, and you could get pregnant again. If you do not want to have another baby very soon, it is important to discuss birth control options with your doctor in the hospital or at your postpartum check-up.

Breast-feeding protects you against pregnancy to some degree, but breast-feeding is *not* an effective method of birth control. If you breast-feed, it is important to consider birth control methods if you want to postpone pregnancy.

If you used a diaphragm or cervical cap for birth control in the past, you need to be refitted after delivery. The size of your cervix or vagina may have changed.

You may consider condoms or spermicides if you breast-feed.

If you bottle-feed, you may decide on a method that can be started immediately after delivery. These methods include: norethisterone implants (Norplant), depot medroxyprogesterone injections (Depo-Provera), a progestagen-only pill or an intra-uterine contraceptive device (coil). If you want to use a combination birth-control pill which contains oestrogen and progestagen, wait at least two weeks after delivery before you begin taking it.

Common Breast-feeding Problems

Your breasts may become temporarily engorged when your regular milk comes in, which can be painful. To relieve engorgement, continue breast-feeding, wear a supportive bra and apply cold compresses to your breasts for short periods. Take paracetamol if pain is severe, but consult your doctor if you need something stronger.

When you breast-feed your baby, you may get sore nipples, which occur for various reasons. If your baby doesn't take your nipple fully into his or her mouth during breast-feeding, their jaws can compress the nipple and make it sore. Your clothing can also irritate tender nipples. Nipple shields, worn inside your bra between the nipple and fabric, provide some relief. A mild cream can also provide soothing relief. Ask your pharmacist or doctor for the names of products that are approved for use during nursing. Take heart – sore nipples rarely last longer than a couple of days. Continue breast-feeding while your breasts are sore.

Plugged Milk Ducts

Sometimes milk ducts in the breast become plugged. A plugged duct prevents milk from flowing freely and makes some parts of the breast feel tender or firm. These become more painful after breast-feeding.

A plugged duct usually takes care of itself, if you continue to nurse frequently. If it doesn't resolve on its own, apply a warm compress to the affected area or soak the breast in warm water. Then express milk or breast-feed while massaging the tender area. You may take paracetamol. If problems continue, contact your doctor.

Breast Infections

Large red streaks that extend up the breast towards the armpit or a breast that becomes firm or hard usually indicates a breast infection. Call your doctor immediately. A fever may develop within four to eight hours of the appearance of the red streaks. Your doctor will want to start antibiotic treatment quickly because antibiotics work best in the first 12 to 16 hours of infection.

To help prevent an infection, eat healthily and get enough rest to reduce stress and keep your immune system in top fighting form. Don't wear tight-fitting bras, especially underwire bras, because they block the milk flow, which may cause an infection. Empty your breasts on a regular schedule to avoid engorgement. After each feeding or pumping, let your nipples air dry for a few minutes. Don't stop nursing if you have a breast infection or think you have one; continue breast-feeding. If you stop, the infection may get worse. Don't be concerned about passing the infection to the baby.

If you have a cold or any other virus, it is all right to breast-feed. It is all right to breast-feed if you are taking most antibiotics, as long as you know that the drug is compatible with nursing. Ask your doctor or pharmacist if any medicine that has been prescribed for you should not be taken while you are breast-feeding. Ask *before* you begin taking it; some antibiotics should be avoided.

After-pregnancy Changes

After the birth of your baby, you may notice changes in your abdominal shape and skin. Breasts are often affected too.

Abdominal skin Changes

After they give birth, some women find that their abdomen returns to normal naturally. For others, it never quite returns to its pre-pregnancy state. Abdominal skin is not like muscle, so it cannot be strengthened by exercise. Perhaps the most important element affecting your skin's ability to return to its pre-pregnancy tightness is connective tissue, which provides suppleness and elasticity. As you get older, your skin loses connective tissue and elasticity. Other factors include your fitness level before pregnancy, heredity and how much your skin stretched during pregnancy.

Breast Changes

After birth, most women's breasts return to their pre-pregnancy size or decrease a little in size. If you breast-feed, it takes longer for your breasts to return to normal. This is a result of the change in the connective tissue that forms the support system of your breasts. Exercise cannot make breasts firmer, but it can improve the chest area underneath so that breasts have a better support.

Weight Changes

It is normal to lose 10 to 15lb (4.5 to 6.8kg) immediately after your baby is born. You may find that you retain 5lb (2.2kg) of fluid, but it washes out of your system within a few days.

Extra weight may be harder to lose. Your body stored about 7 to 10lb (3 to 4.5kg) of fat as energy for the first few months after birth. If you eat properly and get enough exercise, these pounds will slowly come off.

If you breast-feed, all the nutrients your baby receives depend on the quality of the food you eat. Breast-feeding places more demands on your body than pregnancy. Your body burns up to 1,000 calories a day just to produce milk. When breast-feeding, you need to eat an extra 500 calories a day. Be sure they are nutritious, not empty, calories (eat fruits, vegetables and breads – stay away from junk food). Keep up fluid levels, too.

Postpartum Distress

After your baby is born, you may feel sad or moody. You may wonder if having your baby was a good idea. Many women experience some degree of postpartum distress (puerperal depression); in fact up to 80 per cent of all women get the 'baby blues'. It usually appears between two days and two weeks after the baby is born. The good news is that the situation is temporary and tends to leave as quickly as it comes.

Today, many experts consider some degree of postpartum distress as a normal occurrence. Symptoms include:

- anxiety
- crying for no reason
- exhaustion
- impatience
- irritability
- lack of confidence
- lack of feeling for the baby
- low self-esteem
- oversensitivity
- restlessness

If you believe that you may be suffering from some form of postpartum distress, contact your doctor. Every postpartum reaction, mild or severe, is usually temporary.

Forms of Postpartum Distress

The mildest form of postpartum distress is called the *baby blues*. The baby blues last only a couple of weeks and the symptoms do not worsen.

A more serious version of postpartum distress is called *postpartum depression*; it affects about 10 per cent of all new mothers. The difference between the baby blues and postpartum depression lies in the frequency, intensity and duration of the symptoms. Sleep problems are one way to distinguish between the two. If the mother can sleep while someone else tends the baby, it is probably the baby blues. If she cannot sleep because of anxiety, it is probably postpartum depression.

Depression can occur from two weeks to one year after birth. A mother may have feelings of anger, confusion, panic and hopelessness. She may experience changes in her eating and sleeping patterns. She may fear that she will hurt her baby or feel as if she is going mad. Anxiety is one of the major symptoms of postpartum depression.

The most serious form of postpartum distress, known as *puerperal psychosis*, is rare. The woman may have hallucinations, think about suicide or try to harm the baby.

Causes of Postpartum Distress

At this time, no one is sure what causes postpartum distress; not all women experience it. We believe that a woman's individual sensitivity to hormone changes may be the cause, but hormones are only a part of it.

A new mother must make many adjustments, and many demands are placed on her. Either or both of these situations may cause distress. Other possible factors include a family history of depression, lack of familial support after the birth, isolation and chronic fatigue.

Dealing with the Problem

One of the most important ways to help yourself is to set up a support system before the birth. Ask family members and friends to help. Have your mother or mother-in-law to stay for a while. Ask your husband to take some leave, or employ someone to come in and help each day.

There is no particular treatment for baby blues, but there are ways you can help yourself to relieve the symptoms. Ask for help. Rest when the baby sleeps. Find other mothers who are in the same situation; it helps to share your feelings and experiences. Don't try to be perfect; let some things slide. Pamper yourself. Do some form of moderate exercise every day. Eat nutritiously and drink plenty of fluids. Go out every day.

With postpartum depression, medication may be necessary in addition to the suggestions made above. About 85 per cent of all women who suffer from postpartum depression require medication. Medications of choice include antidepressants, tranquillizers and hormones; often they are used together.

If you breast-feed, medication selection may be more limited. Certain medicines can be used by a women while breast-feeding, if the baby's doctor is aware of it and the baby is monitored for side-effects.

Postpartum Distress Can also Affect the Father

Your partner can be affected if you suffer from the baby blues or postpartum depression. It is important to prepare your partner for this situation. Explain to him that if it happens to you, it is only temporary. You might also suggest some things he can do to help himself:

• Advise him not to take it personally.
• Suggest that he gets support for himself. He can talk to friends, family members, other fathers or a professional.
• He needs to take care of himself by eating well, getting enough rest and exercising.
• Ask him to be patient with you.
• Ask for his love and support during this difficult time.

Your Postpartum Check-up

Your postpartum check-up is the last part of your complete care programme. This appointment is as important as any during your pregnancy. A postpartum check-up is scheduled between two and six weeks after delivery, depending on the circumstances of the birth.

At your visit, your doctor will want to hear how you feel. If you have had headaches or experienced increased irritability or fatigue, he or she may prescribe an iron supplement. You will have a physical examination, similar to the one at your first antenatal visit.

Your doctor will do an internal examination. If you had any birth tears or incisions, he or she will examine them to check that they are healing. An internal examination is also done to determine if your uterus is returning to its pre-pregnant size and position.

This is a good time to discuss birth control, if you haven't already made plans. *See* the discussion of birth control options on page 263.

CHAPTER 20

Back to Work?

Your baby is born, a little person who already brings you great delight. It seems as if the hard work is done, and most of it is. But if you are like many women, you must still address issues related to your work – from the kind of child-care arrangement you choose to whether you will work full time.

Whether to continue working outside the home after the baby's birth is a decision that some mothers wish they did not have to make. Others look forward to returning to jobs and careers they enjoy, even if that day comes sooner than they would prefer. Whatever the reason, returning to work after you have had a baby is as typical these days as staying at home used to be. More than half of all mothers with pre-school-age children work outside the home. For almost all of them, finding adequate child care is a big issue.

Arranging a child care situation for your new baby can be one of the most important tasks you face before returning to work. The best way to choose the right setting and best care provider is to know your options.

You do have choices. Any of a number of situations could be right for you; examine your needs and those of your child before you decide which to pursue. Let us look closely at some of the most common child care arrangements.

Child Care Decisions

'In-home' Care

'In-home' care is the easiest option for you and your baby. You don't have to get the baby ready before you leave in the morning or take your child out in bad weather. You save travelling time in the morning and evening.

In-home care is an excellent choice for a baby or small child because the environment is familiar. It provides her with a great deal of attention. A relative or non-relative may provide this care. A potential drawback to in-home care in the toddler years may be that the child will not have the chance to play with others of the same age.

> Lucy had been thrilled to find Irene to care for Harry at home while she worked. Now that Harry was two, Lucy wanted him to spend some time with other children his age. She decided to ask around about play groups. Maybe Irene and Harry could walk to a nearby group a couple of mornings each week.

When the child-minder is a relative, such as a grandparent or an aunt, you may find the situation somewhat challenging. Can you maintain your relationship with the 'relative child-minder' while asking or telling him or her to do things the way you want them to be done?

If the child-minder is not a relative, the arrangement may be expensive. In addition, you are bringing someone you do not know into your home to tend your child. Ask for references and check them thoroughly. Don't rush into an arrangement with a child-minder in whom you aren't completely confident.

Care in a Child-minder's Home

Many parents take their children to someone else's home for care. Often these homes offer small group sizes and scheduling flexibility (for example, you may be allowed to leave your child a little longer if you have an occasional late meeting). They offer a homelike atmosphere, and your child may receive lots of attention.

Child-minders are required to be registered in Great Britain; check the situation carefully. Contact your Department of Social Services, and ask about its requirements. Sometimes local agencies oversee child-minders. Child-minders must abide by certain standards or rules, such as the maximum number of children allowed in the home (including their own). They may also have to obtain certification in first aid and CPR (cardiopulmonary resuscitation).

Employing a Child-minder

Whether someone comes into your home or you take your child to another's home, these steps can help you to find the best child-minder.

- *Advertise in local newspapers and church bulletins* to find interview candidates. State how many children are to be cared for and their ages. Give information about the days and hours that care is needed, the experience you are seeking and other particulars.
- *Talk to people over the phone first* to determine whether you want to interview them. Ask about their experience, qualifications, child care philosophy and what they seek in a position. Then decide if you want to pursue the contact with an 'in-person' interview. Make a list of what to discuss, including the days and hours the person is needed, the duties to be performed, the need for a driver's licence and a benefits policy.
- *Check all references.* Have the potential child-minder provide you with the names and phone numbers of people he or she has worked for in the past. Call each of the families, let them know that you are considering this person as a child-minder and discuss their experience with the candidate.
- *Keep checking.* After you employ a child-minder, check the situation occasionally by dropping in unannounced. Pay attention to how your child reacts each time you leave or arrive; this can give you a clue as to how he or she feels about the child-minder.
- *To hire a nanny,* contact a referral agency; they are listed in Yellow Pages.

Your responsibilities to your child-minder. Just as your child-minder has certain responsibilities to you, you have responsibilities to him or her. Be on time when you drop off or pick up your child. Telephone if you are going to be late, even when the care is provided in your own home. Pay the child-minder on time. Provide nappies, formula or expressed breast milk, extra clothes and personal items for the baby when they are needed.

Day-care Nurseries

A day-care nursery is a larger setting in which children receive care. These vary widely in the facilities and activities they provide, the amount of attention they give each child, group sizes and child care philosophy.

Ask about the training that is required for each child care provider or teacher. Some facilities expect more from a care provider than others. Look for relevant certificates in day care and education – that is, pre-school Learning Alliance Certificate, Nursery Nurse Education Board (NNEB).

You may find that some day-care nurseries that you are interested in do not accept infants. Other nurseries focus on older children because infants take more time and attention. If the nursery accepts infants, the ratio of care-givers should be about one adult to every three children (up to age 2). One adult for every four 2 to 3-year-olds, and one adult for every eight 3 to 5-year-olds is considered acceptable.

Don't be fooled by facilities alone in a state-of-the-art nursery. Even the cheapest, brightest place is useless without the right kind of care provider. Visit it by appointment, then stop by unannounced a few times. Meet the person in charge and the people who will care for your child. Ask for references of parents whose children are cared for there currently. Talk to these parents before you make a final decision.

Infant Care

Babies have special needs that a pre-school cannot meet; be sure that the place you choose for your infant meets those needs. Babies must be changed and fed, but they also have other needs. Babies need to be held and interacted with and comforted when they are afraid. They need to rest at regular times each day. When searching for child care, keep in mind what is required for your child. Evaluate every situation in terms of how it responds to your baby's needs.

Finding Day Care

Where do you start the search for the right day care for your child? Start with the following ideas:

- Enquire at your local Social Services Department or county under-eights' officer for lists of registered pre-school nurseries, crèches and registered child-minders.
- Ask friends, family and co-workers for recommendations of people or places they know about.
- Talk to people in your neighbourhood.

Whoever you choose to provide care for your child, check references thoroughly before you make a final decision. Ask direct, probing questions as you check references. Share your concerns with the person you are checking with. Beware of references that only tell you wonderful things about the care-giver. They could be close friends who have never really used the care-giver you are checking on.

The Cost of Day Care

Paying for child care can be a big budget item in your household expenses. The cost of infant and toddler care (ages 0–3) typically ranges from £75 to £200 a week, depending on the type of care you choose and your geographic location. Home care (typically nannies) can be the most costly, with placement fees and additional charges you negotiate based on extra tasks you want the care provider to perform.

> 'We were surprised by the costs,' Julie said, as her partner, Bill, nodded vigorously. 'The monetary benefit we expected from my going back to work became negligible, although personally, that's not the reason I want to go back – I like my career. I'd tell anybody to calculate the actual costs involved with day care and then think about why both parents are working.'

Some employers provide day-care facilities at the workplace, while others make a contribution towards the cost of day care.

When to Start Looking for Child Care

Finding the best situation for your baby takes time. Start the process several weeks before you need it. For special situations, such as finding child care for twins, you might want to start the process several months in advance.

You may notice a shortage of quality child care for children under age 2. You may have to get on a waiting list for some arrangements. If you find a care provider you are comfortable with before care is to start, it is usual for them to request a retainer fee and to set a date on which child care is due to begin. Keep in touch with the care provider. Plan to meet again – perhaps arranging to leave your child for a few hours to help him or her to adjust – before you place your child in daily care.

Special-Care Needs

If your baby has special needs and requires one-to-one care, expect to spend extra time finding qualified child care. A child with special needs may be best cared for by someone who comes to your home or with a registered child-minder who has the necessary experience. Ask for references from your paediatrician, at the hospital where your child has received care, or at your local Social Services Department.

Caring for a Sick Child

All children suffer from colds, flu or diarrhoea at some time. If you cannot take time off from your work to stay at home with a sick child, you will have to make other arrangements, perhaps utilizing the services of relatives or close friends, as the majority of all day-care providers in the UK are advised not to accept sick children into their care.

Going Back to Work

If you are like many women today, you may be concerned about returning to work even after you have dealt with child-care issues satisfactorily. It is important to find ways to ease the transition from home to work. Some co-workers will be supportive; others may not be.

You may find that some of your greatest challenges come after work, when you get home. Your baby and partner need your time and attention. Even when you feel tired, you may have household chores to do. Arrange with your partner before you return to work to share these responsibilities. That way, each of you can give your baby undivided attention for some part of the evening. Set aside time just for you and your partner, too!

Managing Your Time

Time is a limited resource; learning to manage your time well is the secret to relishing this busy time in your life. Make a daily plan and stick to it. Do what you can and delegate some responsibilities to others. Change your expectations, if you need to. After that, concentrate on the baby, your partner and other important people in your life. Let less important things go. Enjoy the moment!

'Look at the time!' I said that *all* the time the first month after I went back to work. Finally my friend Mary Beth – she has two kids – told me to get a grip before I burned up and disappeared. She was right. I slowed down, let go of the stuff I couldn't control, and did the best I could with everything else. If it didn't get done that day, it got done the next – or thereabouts!

Can You Modify Your Work Situation?

After having a baby, some women decide to continue working outside the home but not full time or not at their old schedule. You may be happier if you can find a way to work part time or if you can adapt your schedule in some other way. There may be ways to modify your current work situation so that everyone is happy – you, your boss, your partner and your baby.

If you want to work part time, you may be able to share a job with someone else in the company who would also like to work part time. Ask your employer.

Find out if flexible time programmes are available at your workplace. You may be allowed to modify your work schedule (for example, to work four ten-hour days instead of five eight-hour days). Or you may come in early and leave early, or arrive and leave later. You may be able to set your own schedule, as long as you get your work done.

You might be able to work at home part time or full time. Some companies allow employees who work on computers to work at home, connected to the office.

Be aware that if you do work part time or on flexible time, child care may be harder to find. With some day nurseries, you pay by the week, whether your child is there or not. A child-minder may need the money that only full-time work offers. But some day nurseries are more flexible than others, and some child-minders may be delighted at the prospect of a lighter schedule.

Breast-feeding and Work

You don't have to stop breast-feeding when you return to work, but you may need to make adjustments. If you breast-feed exclusively, you will need to pump your breasts or arrange to see your baby during the day. Or you may nurse your baby at home and provide expressed breast milk or formula for your child-minder to give baby when you are away.

One way to smooth the 'back-to-work' transition for you and your baby is to begin storing breast milk a couple of weeks before you return to work. Use an electric breast pump to express milk between feedings for about two weeks before you return to work. Don't start sooner – you may produce too much milk. A breast pump with a double-pumping feature empties both breasts at once.

Freeze expressed milk in quantities of 1 to 4 ounces (28–112ml). This gives the child-minder options as to how much to thaw for a particular feeding.

You can pump and store breast milk while you are at work. You may be uncomfortable if you don't pump your breasts because your milk continues to come in. Take a breast pump with you, and refrigerate or discard breast milk after it is pumped.

If you remain at home until your baby is between four and six months old, your baby may be able to miss the bottle and start drinking from a cup. Earlier than four months, your baby will need to learn to drink from a bottle. After four weeks of nursing exclusively, your baby will be ready to try a bottle without compromising your milk supply or his or her nursing technique. With the first bottle feedings, let someone else feed the baby when he or she is not very hungry. Bottle-feed the baby at the time he or she will get a bottle once you return to work.

If You Stay Home

You may decide to stay home with your baby. If you do, the change from leaving the house each day to staying at home can be dramatic. You may find that being at home isn't as easy as you thought it would be. It is true that you don't have to worry about getting to work or coming home to fix meals and do housework. However, you may find that staying at home means less companionship, less money and the loss of routine.

Try to anticipate some of these changes and meet them half way. Don't bury yourself in motherhood and exclude all other activities. Make an effort to get out, meet people and get involved in new experiences with your baby. Consider joining an exercise class designed specifically for new mothers and babies.

If you have worked full time, you may not have met many people in your neighbourhood. Once you are home full time, you will have an opportunity to make friends. If other new mothers are in the neighbourhood, you might start an infant play group that meets once a week for an hour or so. Take turns being the host. Babies play and mothers talk!

It may be a good idea to stay in touch with your colleagues at work. Drop in to see them or go out to lunch with a group. See what they are up to and stay on top of what is happening in your field.

Going back to work takes some planning. Not everything may go smoothly at first, but what adventure does? With the number of child-care options available today and perhaps some creative approach to your workplace schedule, you will be able to find a truly happy medium – one that works for you, your partner, your employer and your baby.

CHAPTER 21

Looking Ahead

More couples choose to delay childbearing today, and predictions are that more women over 30 will become pregnant and deliver babies in the years to come. I believe there is reason for optimism for these pregnancies. Pregnancy at any age is an adventure full of risk, physical and emotional challenges, and highs and lows. Any pregnancy can end in miscarriage or birth defects; fortunately most babies are born healthy.

People today have become more aware of the importance of taking care of their health. Fewer people smoke. They drink less alcohol and they are more aware of the dangers of drug use. Regular exercise and better eating habits are more often the rule, not the exception. All of these activities help everyone involved to prepare for a pregnancy, and the result is healthier pregnancies resulting in healthier babies and mothers.

Medical advances are made every year. Two of the greatest areas of growth have been in technology for pregnancy and in the care of the premature baby. As a medical resident in training 15 years ago, I remember that babies born before 32 weeks seldom survived; if they did, they had major problems. Today, babies born as early as 25 weeks survive, and there are even cases of babies born earlier than this surviving and doing well.

In this book I have discussed many technologies – ultrasound, amniocentesis, chorionic villus sampling, fetoscopy – genetic counselling and other advances in obstetrics. All promise more advances in the goal of a healthy baby and a healthy mother.

Each individual (or couple) is different. This is an important fact. A healthy 38-year-old woman who eats healthily, exercises and takes good care of herself will probably do better during pregnancy than a 23-year-old who eats poorly, doesn't exercise and doesn't take care of herself. Every pregnancy is different.

There is much reason for optimism and encouragement in pregnancy for the woman over 30. We have come a long way in our care of the pregnant woman and her developing baby. In the past, many doctors frowned on pregnancy after the age of 35, but women decided that they were going to have babies anyway. If predictions are correct, this trend will continue.

Despite the risks and possible problems that can occur during a pregnancy, I hope the message has come through that it is much more likely that you and your baby will do well. The best things you can do are to plan ahead for pregnancy, exercise regularly, eat healthily, take care of medical problems before getting pregnant and seek antenatal care early.

Glossary

Abortion – Termination or end of a pregnancy; giving birth to an embryo or fetus before it can live outside the womb, usually defined as before 20 weeks of pregnancy. Abortion may be spontaneous, often called a *miscarriage*, or induced, as in a legal abortion performed to terminate a pregnancy.

Acquired immune deficiency syndrome (Aids) – Debilitating and frequently fatal illness that affects the body's ability to respond to infection. Caused by the human immune deficiency virus (HIV).

Aerobic exercise – Exercise that increases your heart rate and causes you to increase your oxygen intake.

After-birth – Placenta and membranes expelled after the baby is delivered. See *placenta*.

Alpha-fetoprotein (AFP) – Substance produced by the unborn baby as it grows inside the uterus. Large amounts of AFP are found in amniotic fluid. Larger than normal amounts are found in the maternal bloodstream if neural-tube defects are present in the fetus.

Amino acids – Substances that act as building blocks in the developing embryo and fetus.

Amniocentesis – Removal of amniotic fluid from the amniotic sac; fluid is tested for some genetic defects or fetal lung maturity.

Amniotic fluid – Fluid surrounding the baby inside the amniotic sac.

Amniotic sac – Membrane that surrounds the baby inside the uterus. It contains the baby, umbilical cord and amniotic fluid.

Anaemia – Any condition in which the number of red blood cells is less than normal. The term usually applies to the concentration of the oxygen-transporting material in the blood, haemoglobin.

Anencephaly – Defective brain development combined with the absence of the bones that normally surround the brain.

Angioma – Tumour, usually benign, or swelling composed of lymph and blood vessels.

Antenatal care – Programme of care for a pregnant woman before the birth of her baby.

Anti-D immunoglobulin – Given during pregnancy and following pregnancy to prevent isoimmunization. See *isoimmunization*.

Antigen – Substance formed in the body or introduced into the body that causes the formation of antibodies, which interact specifically with the substance.

Anti-inflammatory medicines – Drugs to relieve pain or inflammation.

Apgar score – Measurement of a baby's response to birth and life on its own. Taken one and five minutes after birth.

Areola – Pigmented or coloured ring surrounding the nipple of the breast.

Arrhythmia – Irregular or missed heart beat.

Aspiration – Swallowing or sucking a foreign body or fluid, such as vomit, into an airway.

Asthma – Disease marked by recurrent attacks of shortness of breath and difficulty breathing. Often caused by an allergic reaction.

Atonic uterus – Uterus that is flaccid or relaxed; lacks tone.

Baby blues – Mild depression in woman after delivery.

Bilirubin – Breakdown product of pigment formed in the liver from haemoglobin during the destruction of red blood cells.

Biophysical profile – Method of evaluating a fetus before birth.

Biopsy – Removal of a small piece of tissue for microscopic study.

Birthing centre – Facility in which a woman labours, delivers and recovers in the same room. It may be part of a hospital or a maternity unit.

Blood pressure – Push of the blood against the walls of the arteries, which carry blood away from the heart.

Bloody show – Small amount of vaginal bleeding late in pregnancy; often precedes labour.

Braxton-Hicks contractions – Irregular, painless tightening of the uterus during pregnancy.

Breech presentation – Abnormal position of the fetus. Buttocks or legs come into the birth canal before the head.

Caesarean section (delivery) – Delivery of a baby through an abdominal incision rather than through the vagina.

Candida infection – Thrush. Infection caused by a yeast. Usually affects the vulva or vagina.

Carcinogen – Any cancer-producing substance.

Cardiotocogram – A test in which the movements of the baby felt by the mother or observed by the doctor or midwife are recorded, along with changes in the fetal heart rate.

Cervical smear – Routine screening test that evaluates the presence of pre-malignant or cancerous conditions of the cervix.

Cervix – Opening of the uterus into the vagina.

Chadwick's sign – Dark blue or purple discoloration of the mucosa of the vagina and cervix during pregnancy.

Chemotherapy – Treatment of disease by chemical substances or drugs.

Chlamydia – Sexually transmitted venereal infection.

Chloasma – Extensive brown patches of irregular shape and size on the face or other parts of the body.

Chorionic villus sampling (CVS) – Diagnostic test done early in pregnancy. A biopsy of tissue is taken from inside the uterus through the abdomen or the cervical opening to determine abnormalities of pregnancy.

Chromosome abnormality – Abnormal number or abnormal make-up of chromosomes.

Chromosomes – Thread in a cell's nucleus that contains DNA, which transmits genetic information.

Clomiphene challenge test – Way of testing for ovulation using a drug that stimulates the ovaries.

Colostrum – Thin yellow fluid that is the first milk to come from the breast. Most often seen towards the end of pregnancy. It is different in content from milk produced later during nursing.

Condyloma acuminatum – Skin tags or warts that are sexually transmitted, caused by HPV, human papilloma virus. Also called *venereal warts*.

Congenital problem – Problem present at birth.

Consanguinity – Being related by blood to the person you are pregnant by.

Constipation – Bowel movements are infrequent or incomplete.

Contractions – Squeezing or tightening of the uterus, which pushes the baby out of the uterus during birth.

Corpus luteum cyst – Normal cyst on an ovary after ovulation.

Cystitis – Inflammation of the bladder.

Cytomegalovirus (CMV) infection – Group of viruses from the herpes-virus family.

D&C (dilatation and curettage) – Surgical procedure in which the cervix is dilated and the lining of the uterus is scraped.

Developmental delay – Condition in which the development of the baby or child is slower than normal.

Diastasis recti – Separation of abdominal muscles.

Differentiating – Changing, especially because of growth.

Dilatation – Opening or stretching of the cervix during a baby's birth.

Dizygotic twins – Twins derived from two different eggs. Often called *fraternal twins*.

Due date – The date your baby is expected to be born. Most babies are born near this date, but only 1 of 20 are born on the actual date.

Dysplasia – Abnormal, pre-cancerous changes in the cells of the cervix.

Dysuria – Difficulty or pain urinating.

Eclampsia – Convulsions and coma in a woman with pre-eclampsia. Not related to epilepsy.

Ectopic pregnancy – Pregnancy that occurs outside the uterine cavity.

EDC (estimated date of confinement) – The baby's anticipated due date. Calculated from the first day of the last menstrual period, counting forward 280 days.

Edwards' syndrome – See *trisomy 18*.

Effacement – Thinning of the cervix.

Electronic fetal monitoring – The use of electronic instruments to record the fetal heartbeat.

Embryo – Organism in the early stages of development.

Endometrium – Membrane that lines the inside of the uterine wall.

Enema – Fluid injected into the rectum for the purpose of clearing the bowel.

Engorgement – Congestion, as filled with fluid.

Epidural block – Type of anaesthesia injected around the spinal cord during labour or some types of surgery.

Episiotomy – Surgical incision of the perineum (area behind the vagina, above the rectum). Used during delivery to avoid tearing of the vaginal opening and rectum.

Estimated date of confinement – See *EDC*.

Expressing breast milk – Manually forcing milk out of the breast.

External cephalic version (ECV) – Procedure done late in the pregnancy, in which the doctor manually attempts to move a baby in the breech position into the normal head-down position.

Face presentation – The baby comes into the birth canal face first.

Fallopian tube – Tube that leads from the cavity of the uterus to the area of the ovary. Also called *uterine tube*.

False labour – Tightening of the uterus without dilation of the cervix.

False-negative test result – Result indicates negatitve outcome, but it is actually positive.

False-positive test result – Result indicates positive outcome, but it is actually negative.

Fasting blood sugar test – Blood test to evaluate the amount of sugar in the blood following a period of fasting.

Ferrous gluconate – Iron supplement.

Ferrous sulphate – Iron supplement.

Fertilization – Joining of the sperm and egg.

Fertilization age – Dating a pregnancy from the time of fertilization; two weeks earlier than the gestational age.

Fetal anomaly – Fetal malformation or abnormal development.

Fetal arrhythmia – See *arrhythmia*.

Fetal distress – Problems with the baby that occur before birth or during labour, requiring immediate delivery.

Fetal monitor – Device used before or during labour to listen to and record the fetal heartbeat. Monitoring of the baby inside the uterus can be external (through the maternal abdomen) or internal (through the maternal vagina).

Fetal growth retardation (IUGR) – Inadequate growth of the fetus during pregnancy.

Fetus – Refers to the unborn baby until birth.

Forceps – Special instrument placed around the baby's head, inside the birth canal, to help guide the baby out of the birth canal during delivery.

Fragile-X syndrome – Abnormal X chromosome.

Frank breech – The baby presents its buttocks first. The legs are flexed and the knees extended.

Fraternal twins – See *dizygotic twins*.

Full-term baby – Baby born between 38 and 42 weeks of pregnancy.

Gene regulation – A gene regulates the operation of another gene.

Genetic counselling – Consultation between a couple and specialists about genetic defects and the possibility of the presence or recurrence of genetic problems in a pregnancy.

Genital herpes simplex – Herpes simplex infection involving the genital area. It can be significant during pregnancy because of the danger to a newborn infected with herpes simplex.

Gestational age – Dating a pregnancy from the first day of the last menstrual period; two weeks longer than fertilization age. See *fertilization age*.

Gestational diabetes – Occurrence or worsening of diabetes during pregnancy (gestation).

Globulin – Family of proteins from plasma or serum of the blood.

Glucose tolerance test – Blood test done to evaluate the body's response to sugar. Blood is drawn at intervals following ingestion of a sugary substance.

Glycosuria – Sugar in the urine.

Gonorrhoea – Contagious venereal infection, transmitted primarily by intercourse. Caused by the bacteria Neisseria gonorrhoeae.

Group-B streptococcal infection – Serious infection occurring in the mother's vagina and throat.

Habitual miscarriage – Occurrence of three or more spontaneous miscarriages.

Haematocrit – Determines the proportion of blood cells to plasma. Important in diagnosing anaemia.

Haemoglobin – Pigment in red blood cells that carries oxygen to the body tissues.

Haemolytic disease – Destruction of the red blood cells. See *anaemia*.

Haemorrhoids – Dilated blood vessels in the rectum or anal canal.

Heartburn – Discomfort or pain that occurs in the chest, often after eating.

Heparin – Medication used to prevent excessive clotting of the blood.

High risk pregnancy – Pregnancy with complications that require special medical attention, often from a specialist. See *perinatologist*.

Human chorionic gonadotropin – Hormone produced in early pregnancy. Measured in a pregnancy test.

Hydramnios – Increased amniotic fluid.

Hydrocephalus – Excessive accumulation of fluid around the baby's brain. Sometimes called *water on the brain*.

Hyperbilirubinaemia – Extremely high level of bilirubin in the blood.

Hyperemesis gravidarum – Severe nausea, dehydration and vomiting during pregnancy. Occurs most frequently during the first trimester.

Hyperglycaemia – High blood sugar levels.

Hyperkeratosis – Increase in the size of the horny layer of the skin.

Hypertension, pregnancy-induced – High blood pressure that occurs during pregnancy. Defined by an increase in the diastolic or systolic blood pressure.

Hyperthyroidism – Elevation of the thyroid hormone in the bloodstream.

Hypoglycaemia – Low blood-sugar levels.

Hypoplasia – Defective or incomplete development or formation of tissue.

Hypotension – Low blood pressure.

Hypothyroidism – Low or inadequate levels of thyroid hormone in the bloodstream.

Identical twins – See *monozygotic twins*.

Immune globulin preparation – Substance used to protect against infection with certain diseases, such as hepatitis or measles.

In utero – Within the uterus.

In vitro – Outside the body.

Incompetent cervix – Cervix that dilates painlessly, without contractions.

Incomplete miscarriage – Miscarriage in which part, but not all, of the uterine contents are expelled.

Induced labour – Labour started or speeded up by the doctor, usually by using a drug.

Inevitable miscarriage – Pregnancy complicated by bleeding and cramping. Usually results in miscarriage.

Insulin – Peptide hormone made by the pancreas It promotes the body's use of glucose.

Intra-uterine growth retardation (IUGR) – See *fetal growth retardation*.

Iron-deficiency anaemia – Anaemia produced by the lack of iron in the diet; often seen in pregnancy. See *anaemia*.

Isoimmunization – Development of specific antibody directed at the red blood cells of another individual, such as a baby in utero. Occurs when a Rhesus-negative woman carries a Rhesus-positive baby or when she is given Rhesus-positive blood.

Jaundice – Yellow staining of the skin, sclera (eyes) and deeper tissues of the body. Caused by excessive amounts of bilirubin.

Ketones – Breakdown product of metabolism found in the blood, particularly in conditions of starvation or uncontrolled diabetes.

Kidney stones – Small mass or lesion found in the kidney or urinary tract that can block the flow of urine.

Klinefelter's syndrome – Abnormal number of chromosomes, XXY.

Labour – Process of expelling a fetus from the uterus.

Laparoscopy – Surgical procedure performed for tubal ligation, diagnosis of pelvic pain, diagnosis of ectopic pregnancy or for making other diagnoses.

Leucorrhoea – Vaginal discharge characterized by a white or yellowish colour. Primarily composed of mucus.

Lightening – Change in the shape of the pregnant uterus a few weeks before labour. Often described as the baby 'dropping'.

Linea nigra – Line of increased pigmentation running down the abdomen from the belly-button to the pubic area during pregnancy.

Lochia – Vaginal discharge that occurs after delivery of the baby and placenta.

Mammogram – X-ray study of the breasts to identify normal and abnormal breast tissue.

Mask of pregnancy – Increased pigmentation over the area of the face under each eye. Commonly has the appearance of a butterfly.

Meconium – First intestinal discharge of the newborn; green or yellow in colour. It consists of epithelial or surface cells, mucus and bile. Discharge may occur before or during labour or soon after birth.

Melanoma – Pigmented mole or tumour that may or may not be cancerous.

Meningomyelocoele – Congenital defect of the central nervous system of the baby. Membranes and the spinal cord protrude through an opening or defect in the vertebral column. See *spina bifida*.

Menstrual age – See *gestational age*.

Menstruation – Regular or periodic discharge of a bloody fluid from the uterus.

Microcephaly – Abnormally small development of the head in the developing fetus.

Midwife – Nurse who has received extra training in the care of pregnant patients and the delivery of babies.

Miscarriage – See *abortion*.

Missed miscarriage – Failed pregnancy, without bleeding or cramping. Sometimes diagnosed by ultrasound weeks or months after a pregnancy fails.

Monozygotic twins – Twins conceived from one egg. Often called *identical twins*.

Morning sickness – Nausea and vomiting, with ill health, found primarily during the first trimester of pregnancy. Also see *hyperemesis gravidarum*.

Mucus plug – Secretions in the cervix; often released just before labour.

Natural childbirth – Labour and delivery in which no medication is used, and the mother remains awake to help deliver the baby. The woman may or may not have taken classes to prepare her for labour and delivery.

Neural tube defects – Abnormalities in the development of the spinal cord and brain in a fetus. See *anencephaly; hydrocephalus; spina bifida*.

Obstetrician – Doctor who specializes in the care of pregnant women and the delivery of babies.

Oligohydramnios – Lack or deficiency of amniotic fluid.

Omphalocoele – Congenital hernia at the belly-button.

Osteopathic physician – Doctor who has trained in osteopathic medicine, a system of treating medical ailments based on the belief that they generally result from the pressure of displaced bones on nerves and are curable with manipulation. Osteopaths rely on physical, medicinal and surgical methods, much as their medical doctor counterparts.

Ovarian cycle – Regular production of hormones from the ovary in response to hormonal messages from the brain. The ovarian cycle governs the endometrial cycle.

Ovulation – Cyclic production of an egg from the ovary.

Ovulatory age – See *fertilization age*.

Oxytocin – Substance that causes uterine contractions; used to induce labour. Also, the hormone produced by pituitary glands.

Paediatrician – Physician who specializes in the care of babies and children.

Palmar erythema – Redness of the palms of the hands.

Paracerival block – Local anaesthetic for cervical dilatation.

Patau's syndrome – See *trisomy 13*.

Percutaneous umbilical blood sampling – Removal of blood from the umbilical cord while a baby is still inside the uterus.

Perinatal death – Death of a baby around the time of delivery.

Perinatologist – Physician who specializes in the care of high risk pregnancies.

Perineum – Area between the rectum and the vagina.

Phenylketonuria – Hereditary disease that prevents oxidation of phenylananine (an amino acid) into tyrosine. Left untreated, brain damage may occur.

Phospholipids – Fat-containing phosphorous. The most important are lecithins and sphingomyelin, which are important in the maturation of fetal lungs before birth.

Phsyiological anaemia of pregnancy – Anaemia during pregnancy caused by an increase in the amount of plasma (fluid) in the blood compared to the number of cells in the blood. See *anaemia*.

PKU – See **phenylketonuria**.

Placenta – Organ inside the uterus that is attached to the baby by the umbilical cord. It is essential during pregnancy for the growth and development of the embryo and fetus.

Placenta praevia – Low attachment of the placenta, very close to or covering the cervix.

Placental abruption – Premature separation of the placenta from the uterus.

Pneumonitis – Inflammation of the lungs.

Polyhydramnios – See *hydramnios*.

Postdates birth – Baby born two weeks or more past its due date.

Postmature baby – Pregnancy of 42+ weeks' duration.

Postpartum blues – See baby blues.

Postpartum depression – Depression after delivery.

Postpartum haemorrhage – Bleeding more than 18oz (500ml) at delivery.

Post-term baby – See postdates-birth.

Pre-eclampsia – Combination of symptoms significant to pregnancy, including high blood pressure, oedema, swelling and changes in reflexes.

Pregnancy diabetes – See *gestational diabetes*.

Premature delivery – Delivery before 37 weeks of pregnancy.

Prepared childbirth – The woman has taken classes to know what to expect during labour and delivery. She may request pain medication if she feels she needs it.

Presentation – Describes which part of the baby comes into the birth canal first.

Preterm birth – Baby born before 37 weeks of pregnancy.

Products of conception – Tissue passed with a miscarriage.

Proteinuria – Protein in urine.

Pruritis gravidarum – Itching during pregnancy.

Pubic symphysis – Bony prominence in the pelvic bone found in the midline. Landmark from which the doctor often measures during pregnancy to follow the growth of the uterus.

Pudendal block – Local anaesthesia during labour.

Pulmonary embolism – Blood clot from another part of the body that travels to the lungs. Can cause closed passages in the lungs and decrease oxygen exchange.

Pyelonephritis – Serious kidney infection.

Quickening – Feeling the baby move inside the uterus.

RDA – Recommended dietary allowance.

Rhesus-negative – Absence of rhesus antibody in the blood.

Rhesus-sensitivity – See *isoimmunization*.

Round-ligament pain – Pain caused by stretching the ligaments on the sides of the uterus during pregnancy.

Rupture of membranes – Loss of fluid from the amniotic sac. Also called *breaking of waters*.

Seizure – Sudden onset of a convulsion.

Sexually transmitted disease (STD) – Infection transmitted through sexual intercourse or other sexual activity.

Sickle crisis – Painful episode caused by sickle-cell disease.

Sickle-cell anaemia – Anaemia caused by abnormal red blood cells shaped like a sickle or a cylinder.

Sickle-cell trait – Presence of the trait for sickle-cell anaemia. Not sickle-cell disease itself.

Skin tag – Flap or extra build-up of skin.

Sodium – Element found in many foods, particularly salt. Ingestion of too much sodium may cause fluid retention.

Spina bifida – Congenital abnormality characterized by a defect in the vertebral column. The spinal cord and membranes of the spinal cord protrude outside the protective bony canal of the spine. See *meningomyelocoele*.

Spinal anaesthesia – Anaesthesia given in the spinal canal.

Spontaneous miscarriage – Loss of pregnancy during the first 20 weeks of pregnancy.

Stasis – Decreased flow.

Station – Estimation of the baby's descent in the uterus in preparation for birth.

Steroids – Group of hormone-based medications. Often used to treat diseases. Includes oestrogen, testosterone, progesterone, prednisone.

Stillborn – When the baby is born, it is dead.

Stretch marks – Areas of the skin that are torn or stretched. Often found on the abdomen, breasts, buttocks and legs.

Surfactant – Phospholipid present in the lungs that controls the surface tension of the lungs. Premature babies often lack sufficient amounts of surfactant to breathe without assistance.

Syphilis – Sexually transmitted venereal infection caused by treponema pallidum.

Systemic lupus erythematosus (SLE) – Connective-tissue disorder likely to manifest in women in the reproductive ages. Antibodies made by the person act against the person's own tissues.

Tay-Sachs disease – Inherited disease characterized by mental and physical retardation, convulsions, enlargement of the head and eventually death. Trait is usually carried by Ashkenazi Jews.

Telangiectasias – Dilatation or swelling of a small blood vessel; sometimes called an *angioma*. During pregnancy, another common name is *spider angioma* or *spider raevi*.

Teratogenic – Causes abnormal development.

Teratology – Branch of science that deals with teratogens.

Term – Baby is considered 'term' when it is born after 40 weeks. Also called *full term*.

Thalassaemia – Group of inherited disorders of haemoglobin metabolism, which results in a decrease in the amount of haemoglobin formed. Most commonly found in people of Mediterranean descent.

Threatened miscarriage – Bleeding during the first trimester of pregnancy without cramping or contractions.

Thrombosis – Formation of a blood clot (thrombus).

Thrush – Candida or yeast infection occurring in the mother's vagina or in the mouth or mucous membranes of a newborn baby.

Thyroid disease – Abnormality of the thyroid gland and its production of thyroid hormone. See *hyperthyroidism; hypothyroidism*.

Tocolytic agents – Drugs to stop labour.

Toxaemia – See *pre-eclampsia*.

Toxic shock syndrome – Overwhelming reaction to poisons made by bacteria.

Toxic strep A – Bacterial infection that can cause severe damage to the mother; usually starts in a cut on the skin, not as a sore throat, and spreads very quickly. It can involve the entire body.

Toxoplasmosis – Infection caused by toxoplasma gondii.

Transverse lie – Fetus is turned sideways in the uterus.

Trichomonal vaginitis – Venereal infection caused by trichomonas.

Trimester – Method of dividing pregnancy into three equal periods of about 13 weeks each.

Triple screen – Measurement of three blood tests to determine fetal well-being.

Trisomy – Extra chromosome.

Trisomy 13 – Extra chromosome at site 13; also known as *Patau's syndrome*.

Trisomy 18 – Extra chromosome at site 18; also known as *Edwards' syndrome*.

Turner's syndrome – Missing one chromosome, 45X instead of 46XX or 46XY.

Umbilical cord – Cord that connects the placenta to the developing baby. It removes waste products and carbon dioxide from the baby and brings oxygenated blood and nutrients from the mother through the placenta to the baby.

Ureters – Tubes from the kidneys to the bladder that drain urine.

Urine analysis – Test of the urine. Doctor tests urine during pregnancy to check for signs of disease or infection.

Uterus – Organ a fetus grows in. Also called a *womb*.

Vaccine – Mild infection given to cause production of antibodies to protect against subsequent infections of the same type.

Vacuum extractor – Device used to provide traction on fetal head during delivery; used to help deliver a baby.

Vagina – Birth canal.

Varicose veins – Blood vessels (veins) that are dilated or enlarged.

Vascular spiders – See *telangiectasias*.

Vena cava – Major vein in the body that empties into the right atrium of the heart. It returns unoxygenated blood to the heart for transport to the lungs.

Venereal warts – See *condyloma acuminatum*.

Womb – See *uterus*.

Yeast infection – See *Candida infection; thrush*.

Useful Organizations

Some of these organizations are large. Many are small. Some offer advice or information face to face or over the telephone. Others concentrate on providing useful leaflets or books. Many have local branches or can put you in touch with local groups or a local contact.

Where there are separate addresses for the same or similar organizations in Scotland, Wales and Northern Ireland, these are given. If the UK is not covered by one or more organizations the area covered is indicated by 'E' – England, 'W' – Wales, 'NI' – Northern Ireland, 'S' – Scotland. If you live in Wales you can contact Health Information Wales 0800 665544 for information on local groups. If you live in Scotland and can't find the information you need in this section, contact the NHS Helpline in Scotland 0800 224488 where trained staff will answer your enquiries.

Organizations marked* produce publications. When you write for information it is important to remember to enclose a large stamped addressed envelope for a reply. Many organizations are run by volunteers and nearly all have a very tight budget.

SUPPORT AND INFORMATION

ACAS (Advisory, Conciliation and Arbitration Service) (E, S & W)
Clifton House
83 Euston Road
London NW1 2RB
(0171) 396 5100
Advice on time off for antenatal care and on matters like unfair dismissal. For your nearest office, look in the phone book or ask at your local library or citizens advice bureau. *

Association of Breastfeeding Mothers
26 Holmshaw Close
London SE26 4TH
(0181) 778 4769
Telephone advice service for breast-feeding mothers and those wanting to breast-feed. Runs support groups (babies welcome).

Help given to those wishing to set up a group in their area. *

Associaion for Improvements in the Maternity Services (AIMS)
40 Kingswood Avenue
London NW6 6LS
(0181) 960 5585
In Scotland:
40 Leamington Terrace
Edinburgh EH10 4JL
(0131) 229 6259
Voluntary pressure group which aims for improvements in maternity services. Support and advice about parents' rights, complaints procedures and choices within maternity care, including home birth. *

British Diabetic Association
10 Queen Anne Street
London W1M 0BD

(0171) 323 1531
In Northern Ireland:
31 Grange Park
Belfast BT17 0AN
(01232) 610630/381213
*National charity offering information and support through a network of local groups to people with diabetes and their families.**

Caesarean Support Network
c/o Sheila Tunstall
2 Hurst Park Drive
Liverpool L36 1TF
(0151) 480 1184
*Offers emotional support and practical advice to mothers who have had or may need a caesarean delivery. Can put you in touch with a local mother who has undergone a caesarean and understands the problems.**

Child
Charter House
43 St Leonards Road
Bexhill-on-Sea
E Sussex TN40 1JA
(01424) 732361
*Self-help organization offering information and support to people coping with problems of infertility and childlessness. Telephone helplines for general problems and special helplines for specific problems like IVF, GIFT, ectopic pregnancies, miscarriages, stillbirths, endometriosis, polycystic ovaries and adoption. May be able to put you in touch with a local contact or group.**

Child Poverty Action Group (CPAG)
4th Floor
1–5 Bath Street
London EC1V 9PY
(0171) 253 3406
In Northern Ireland:
12 Queen Street
Londonderry BT48 7EG
(01504) 267777
Campaigns for children's rights and offers information on welfare benefits.

Citizens Advice Bureaux (CABs)
*Information and advice on topics including benefits, maternity rights, debts, housing, consumer, employment and legal problems as well as family and personal difficulties. Have details of useful national and local organizations. Free and confidential. Opening times vary. Ask for the address at your local library or look in your phone book.**

Community Health Councils (CHCs)
(Local Health Councils in Scotland; Local Health and Social Services Councils in Northern Ireland)
Represent the interests of consumers in the NHS. Can advise you on local NHS services and your entitlements and help you if you are having difficulties or wish to make a complaint. Have information on other local organizations. Look in the phone book under your health authority/health board/local Health and Social Services Board.

Equal Opportunities Commission
Overseas House
Quay Street
Manchester M3 3HN
(0161) 833 9244
*Information and advice on issues of discrimination and equal opportunities.**

Family Health Services Authorities (FHSAs)
These have replaced Family Practitioner Committees. If you are new to an area they can give you a list of local doctors, including those with a special interest in pregnancy and childbirth. If you have difficulty in finding a GP to take you on, contact the FHSA. Look in the phone book under the name of your local health authority/health board.
In Northern Ireland:
Contact your local Health and Social Services Board or the Central Services Agency for Health and Personal Social

Services (CSA)
25 Adelaide Street
Belfast BT2 8FH
(01232) 324431

Family Welfare Association
501–505 Kingsland Road
London E8 4AU
(0171) 254 6251
National charity providing free social work services – eg counselling for relationship difficulties and advice on benefits, housing and other problems. Provides grants for people in need throughout the UK.*

Health Information Wales/Cyswllt lechyd Cymru (W)
Health Promotion Wales
Ffynnon-las
Tŷ las Avenue
Llanishen
Cardiff CF4 5DZ
0800 665544 (Freephone
9 am to 5 pm with Minicom)
A confidential information service on health service matters and self-help groups in Wales.

Independent Midwives Association
Nightingale Cottage
Shamblehurst Lane
Botley
Hampshire SO32 2BY
Free advice to women thinking about a home birth. Offers full care to women who book with them for home births. They also have their own birthing centres. Fees vary. Send an A5 sae for information.

Institute for Complementary Medicine
PO Box 194
London SE16 1QZ
(0171) 237 5175
Charity providing information on complementary medicine and referrals to qualified practitioners or helpful organizations.*

La Leche League (Great Britain)
BM 3424
London WC1N 3XX
(0171) 242 1278 (24-hour answerphone)
Help and information for women wanting to breast-feed their babies and personal counselling to mothers having problems in breast-feeding. Local groups hold friendly, informal discussions on breast-feeding, birth and parenthood.*

Labour Relations Agency (NI)
Windsor House
9–15 Bedford Street
Belfast BT2 7NU
(01232) 321442
Advice on maternity rights in Northern Ireland.*

Life
Life House
Newbold Terrace
Leamington Spa
Warks CV32 4EA
(01926) 421587
Charity offering information and advice on pregnancy, abortion, miscarriage and stillbirth.*

Local advice agencies
There may be a number of helpful local advice agencies in your district offering general advice on a range of topics, like benefits, debts and consumer problems, or specializing in one area such as law or housing. To find out what exists ask at your library or town hall.

Maternity Alliance
45 Beech Street
London EC2P 2LX
(0171) 588 8582
Information on all aspects of maternity services, rights at work and benefits for families.*

National Association for Maternal and Child Welfare
1st Floor
40–42 Osnaburgh Street
London NW1 3ND
(0171) 383 4115
Telephone adbice on child care and family life.*

National Childbirth Trust (NCT)
Alexandra House
Oldham Terrace
London W3 6NH
(0181) 992 8637
National charity with branches throughout the UK. Runs antenatal classes giving information on labour and practice of relaxation, breathing, massage and active positions for labour and birth. Has breast-feeding counsellors who will help with feeding. Also offers postnatal support from other mothers and runs postnatal exercise classes in some areas. Provides information for parents with disabilities or medical conditions and puts them in touch with each other. Local branches.*

National Society for the Prevention of Cruelty to Children (NSPCC)
42 Curtain Road
London EC2A 3NH
(0171) 825 2500
0800 800500 Child Protection Helpline
In Northern Ireland:
16–20 Rosemary Street
Belfast BT1 1QD
(01232) 240311
In Wales:
9 Brindley Street
Cardiff CF1 7TX
(01222) 397148
Aims to prevent all forms of child abuse. If you are in need of help or know of anyone who needs help, look in the phone book for your nearest NSPCC office.*

NHS Helpline in Sctoland
0800 22 44 88

Provides comprehensive information about health services and the NHS in Scotland. Covers health education, patient rights, waiting times, GPs, pharmacists, opticians, community services and hospital services. Free leaflets on a wide range of health topics are also available and calls are free and confidential.*

Northern Ireland Housing Executive
2 Adelaide Street
Belfast BT2 8BP
(01232) 240588
Offers advice and information on all aspects of housing.

Patients' Association
8 Guilford Street
London WC1N 1DT
(0171) 242 3460
Advice service for patients who have difficulties with their doctor.*

Public libraries
Useful starting points for finding out addresses of national and local organizations. Librarians are usually helpful in producing information or in pointing you in the right direction.

Relate: Marriage Guidance
Herbert Gray College
Little Church Street
Rugby
Warks CV21 3AP
(01788) 573241
In Northern Ireland:
Northern Ireland Marriage Guidance Council (Relate)
76 Dublin Road
Belfast BT2 7HP
(01232) 323454
Confidential counselling on relationship problems of any kind. Look in the phone book for your local branch under 'Relate' or 'Marriage guidance' or contact one of the above addresses.*

Shelter, the National Campaign for the Homeless
88 Old Street
London EC1V 9HU
(0171) 253 0202
In Northern Ireland:
165 University Street
Belfast BT7 1HR
(01232) 247752
In Wales:
Shelter Wales/Shelter Cymru
25 Walter Road
Swansea
West Glamorgan SA1 5NN
(01792) 469400
Information and advice on housing matters, including tenants' rights, welfare rights, how to claim improvement grants, etc. If you have housing difficulties, seek advice as soon as possible. Accommodation law is very complex and you could be jeopardizing your chances of finding a suitable home. Contact for details of your local Shelter Housing Aid Centre.*

Social Security: Freeline
For general advice on all social security benefits, pensions and National Insurance including maternity benefits and Income Support, phone Freeline Social Security on 0800 666555 between 9am and 4.30pm on weekdays, and between 9am and 1pm on Saturdays. Calls are free. There is an answerphone service out of hours.
Advice in Urdu or Punjabi:
Phone Freeline 0800 521360 during the same hours.
In Northern Ireland:
Phone Freeline Social Security (Northern Ireland) on 0800 616757 for advice between 9am and 5pm on weekdays.

Social security: local offices
For general advice on all social security benefits, pensions and National Insurance, including maternity benefits and Income Support, telephone, write or call in to your local Social Security office. The address will

be in the phone book under 'Social Security'. Hours are usually 9.30am to 3.30pm. In busy offices there may be a very long wait if you call in.

Social Services
A social worker at your local social services area office will give you information on topics including benefits, housing, financial difficulties, employment, relationship problems, child care and useful organizations. Look up Social Services in the phone book under the name of your local authority/local Health and Social Services Board or ask at your local library. Phone, write or call in. There may also be a social worker based at the hospital whom you could talk to either during your antenatal care or when you or your baby are in hospital. Ask your midwife or other hospital staff to put you in contact.

Society to Support Home Confinements
'Lydgate'
Wolsingham
Co Durham DL13 3HA
(01388) 528044 (preferably after 6 pm)
Voluntary organization helping women who want to give birth at home but are meeting with difficulties. Telephone support.

Twins and Multiple Births Association (TAMBA)
PO Box 30
Little Sutton
S Wirral L66 1TH
(0151) 348 0020
TAMBA Twinline (Helpline)
(01732) 868000 (7pm–11pm weekdays; 10am–11pm weekends)
In Northern Ireland:
PO Box 342
Belfast BT5 5PQ
(01232) 791327
Self-help organization to encourage and support parents of twins, triplets or more. Will put parents in touch with local support

groups, or specialist groups for parents of triplets or more, parents of children with special needs or bereaved parents, if appropriate.*

Women's Aid Federation
PO Box 391
Bristol BS99 7WS
(0117) 963 3542
In Northern Ireland:
Women's Aid Federation
129 University Street
Belfast BT7 1HP
(01232) 249041
In Scotland:
Scottish Women's Aid
12 Torphichen Street
Edinburgh EH3 8JQ
(0131) 221 0401
In Wales:
Welsh Women's Aid
38/48 Crwys Road
Cardiff CF2 4NN
(01222) 390874/390878
Advice, support and refuge to women who have been abused mentally, physically or sexually, and their children. Local groups.*

COPING ALONE

Gingerbread
49 Wellington Street
London WC2E 7BB
(0171) 240 0953
In Northern Ireland:
Gingerbread Northern Ireland
169 University Street
Belfast BT7 1HR
(01232) 231417
In Wales:
Gingerbread Wales
Room 16
Albion Chambers
Cambrian Place
Swansea
West Glamorgan SA1 1RN
(01792) 648728
Self-help associations for one-parent

families. A network of local groups offers mutual support, friendship, information, advice and practical help. Do get in touch if you are pregnant and on your own.*

MAMA (Meet-a-mum Association)
c/o Briony Hallam
14 Willis Road
Croydon
Surrey CR0 2XX
(0181) 665 0357
Support for mothers suffering from postnatal depression or who feel lonely and isolated looking after a child at home. Will try to put you in touch will another mother who has experienced similar problems, or with a group of mothers locally, or help you to find ways of meeting people.*

National Council for One Parent Families (E, W & NI)
255 Kentish Town Road
London NW5 2LX
(0171) 267 1361 (not Wednesdays)
In Scotland:
One Parent Families Scotland
13 Gayfield Square
Edinburgh EH1 3NX
(0131) 556 3899
Information on benefits and employment rights in pregnancy, social security, taxation, housing problems and maintenance.*

Parents Advice Centre (NI)
Room 1, Bryson House
28 Bedford Street
Belfast BT2 7FE
(01232) 238800
A 24-hour confidential service offering support and guidance to parents under stress.

Parents Anonymous
6–9 Manor Gardens
London N7 6LA
(0171) 263 8918
Telephone helpline run by volunteers for

parents under stress who feel they can't cope or might abuse their children.

LOSS AND BEREAVEMENT

(See also 'Child' under 'Support and information'.)

Compassionate Friends
53 North Street
Bristol BS3 1EN
(0117) 953 9639
An organization of and for bereaved parents. Advice and support. Local groups.*

Foundation for the Study of Infant Deaths (Cot Death Research and Support) (E, W & NI)
14 Halkin Street
London SW1X 7DP
(0171) 235 0965
Support and information for parents bereaved by a sudden infant death and support with any subsequent babies. Can put parents in touch with local support groups of other parents who have also suffered bereavement. Produce infant care guidance card including symptoms of serious illness to watch out for in babies.*
In Northern Ireland:
Friends of the Foundation for the Study of Infant Deaths
7 Glenaan Avenue
Belfast BT17 9AT
(01232) 622688

Miscarriage Association
c/o Clayton Hospital
Northgate
Wakefield
W Yorks WF1 3JS
(01924) 200799
Information, advice and support for women who have had, or who are having, a miscarriage. Local contacts and groups.*

SATFA (Support around Termination for Abnormality) (E, W & NI)
73–75 Charlotte Street
London W1P 1LB
(0171) 631 0285
Registered charity offering support and information to parents who are concerned about antenatal testing, or are faced with the decision of whether to terminate a pregnancy following the diagnosis of abnormality in their unborn baby. Ongoing support given to parents who decide to terminate pregnancy. Network of local contacts and groups sharing similar experiences.

Stillbirth and Neonatal Death Society (SANDS)
28 Portland Place
London W1N 4DE
(0171) 436 5881
Information and a national network of support groups for bereaved parents.*

ILLNESS AND DISABILITY

Action for Sick Children (E)
Argyle House
29–31 Euston Road
London NW1 2SD
(0171) 833 2041
In Scotland:
Action for Sick Children (Scotland)
15 Smith's Place
Edinburgh EH6 8HT
(0131) 553 6553
In Wales:
Association for the Welfare of Children in Hospital (AWCH)
4 Chestnut Avenue
West Cross
Swansea SA3 5NL
(01792) 404232
In Northern Ireland:
AWCH
Bryson House
28 Bedford Street
Belfast BT2 7FE
(01232) 799215 (after 6 pm)

Advice and support for families with sick children. Helps them to make use of the health service. Telephone advice. There may be a local group you can join.*

Bliss
17–21 Emerald Street
London WC1N 3QL
(0171) 831 9393
Partent support network providing emotional and practical support to the families of babies who need intensive or special care. Local groups.*

Contact a Family
170 Tottenham Court Road
London W1P 0HA
(0171) 383 3555
National charity offering information, advice and support to parents of children with special needs and disabilities. Links parents to local support groups for general support or to nationally run groups, or, in the case of rare disorders, to individuals in similar circumstances.*

Council for Disabled Children
8 Wakley Street
London EC1V 7QE
(0171) 843 6061
Information for parents and details of organizations offering help with particular disabilities.*

Disabled Living Centre
Musgrave Park Hospital
Stockman's Lane
Belfast BT9 7JB
(01232) 669501 ext 2708
Information and advice on all aspects of disability, especially equipment and dealing with living problems. Referral to other organizations for adults and children with disabilities.

Disability Action
2 Annadale Avenue
Belfast BT7 3JH

(01232) 491011
Provides information and advice on physical disability and local organizations.

Disability Information Trust
Mary Marlborough Lodge
Nuffield Orthopaedic Centre
Windmill Road
Headington
Oxford OX3 7LD
(01865) 227592
Assesses and tests equipment for people with disabilities. Publishes information in series 'Equipment for Disabled People.'*

Genetic Interest Group (GIG)
Farringdon Point
29–35 Farringdon Road
London EC1M 3JB
(0171) 430 0090
Umbrella body for support groups working with those affected by specific genetic disorders. Provides information for individuals at risk and their families about services available within the NHS and elsewhere. Can put you in touch with the relevant support group.

SPECIALIZED ORGANIZATIONS

Association for Spina Bifida and Hydrocephalus (ASBAH) (E & W)
ASBAH House
42 Park Road
Peterborough PE1 2UQ
(01733 555988)
In Scotland:
Scottish Spina Bifida Association
190 Queensferry Road
Edinburgh EH4 2BW
(0131) 332 0743
In Northern Ireland:
Northern Ireland Spina Bifida and Hydrocephalus Association
73 New Row
Coleraine BT52 1EJ
(01265) 515222

*Information, advice, counselling and support for parents. Local support groups.**

Cleft Lip and Palate Association (CLAPA)
1 Eastwood Gardens
Kenton
Newcastle-upon-Tyne
NE3 3DQ
(0191) 285 9396
*Voluntary organization of parents and professionals offering support to families of babies born with cleft lip and/or palate. Feeding equipment available. Local groups.**

Cystic Fibrosis Trust
Alexandra House
5 Blyth Road
Bromley BR1 3RS
(0181) 464 7211
In Northern Ireland:
Cystic Fibrosis Trust in Northern Ireland
20 Bryansburn Road
Bangor
Co Down BT20 3SB
(01247) 272781
In Wales:
Cystic Fibrosis Trust in Wales
18 Pine Tree Close
Radyr
Cardiff CF4 8RQ
(01222) 843394
*Information and support for parents of children with cystic fibrosis and for people worried about the possibility of passing on the illness. Local groups.**

Down's Syndrome Association (E &W)
155 Mitcham Road
Tooting
London SW17 9PG
(0181) 682 4001
In Scotland:
Scottish Down's Syndrome Association
158–160 Balgreen Road

Edinburgh EH11 3AU
(0131) 313 4225
In Northern Ireland:
Down's Syndrome Association
2nd Floor
Bryson House
28 Bedford Street
Belfast BT2 7FE
(01232) 243266
*Information, advice, counselling and support for parents of children with Down's syndrome. Local groups. 24-hour helpline.**

Haemophilia Society
123 Westminister Bridge Road
London SE1 7HR
(0171) 928 2020
*Information, advice and practical help for families affected by haemophilia. Some local groups.**
In Northern Ireland:
67 Woodvale Road
Belfast BT13 3BN
(01232) 740001

Jennifer Trust for Spinal Muscular Atrophy
11 Ash Tree Close
Wellesbourne
Warwickshire CV35 9SA
(01789) 842377
*Self-help group offering information and support to parents of children with the disease. Can put you in touch with other parents. Equipment on loan.**

MENCAP (Royal Society for Mentally Handicapped Children and Adults) (E, W & NW)
MENCAP National Centre
123 Golden Lane
London EC1Y 0RT
(0171) 454 0454
In Scotland:
ENABLE
6th Floor
7 Buchanan Street
Glasgow G1 3HL

(0141) 226 4541
In Northern Ireland:
MENCAP in Northern Ireland
4 Annadale Avenue
Belfast BT7 3JH
(01232) 691351
In Wales:
MENCAP in Wales
169 City Road
Cardiff CF2 3JB
(01222) 494933
*Information, support and advice for parents
of children with mental handicap. Local
groups.**

Meningitis Research Foundation
Old Gloucester Road
Alverston
Bristol BS12 2LQ
(01454) 413344
In Northern Ireland:
29 Springwell Street
Ballymena BT43 6AT
(01266) 652060
*Offers counselling for parents whose
children have died from meningitis and gives
support to people with loved ones in hospital
or at home. A 24-hour national helpline is
available: (01454) 413344.**

**Muscular Dystrophy Group of Great
Britain and Northern Ireland**
7–11 Prescott Place
London SW4 6BS
(0171) 720 8055
*Information, advice and support for families
affected by muscular dystrophy.**

**National Society for Phenylketonuria
and Allied Disorders**
7 Southfield Close
Willen
Milton Keynes MK15 9LL
(01908) 691653
*Self-help organization offering information
and support to families affected by the
disorder. Newsletter.**

**Northern Ireland Council for
Orthopaedic Development (NICOD)**
Malcolm Sinclair House
31 Ulsterville Avenue
Belfast BT9 7AS
(01232) 666188
*Offers advice and support to parents of
children with cerebral palsy.*

**REACH (The Association for
Children with Hand or Arm
Deficiency)**
12 Wilson Way
Earls Barton
Northants NN6 0NZ
(01604) 811041
*Information and support to parents of
children with hand or arm problems. Can
put you in touch with individual families in
a similar situation or local groups.**

SCOPE
12 Park Crescent
London W1N 4EQ
(0171) 636 5020
In Wales:
3 Links Court
Links Business Park
St Mellons
Cardiff CF3 0SP
(01222) 797706
*Offers advice and support to parents of
children with cerebral palsy.**

**SENSE (National Deaf-Blind and
Rubella Association)**
11–13 Clifton Terrace
London N4 3SR
(0171) 272 7774
In Northern Ireland:
Wilton House
5 College Square North
Belfast BT1 6AR
(01232) 705858
*Information and support for families of
deaf-blind and rubella handicapped
children.**

Sickle Cell Society
54 Station Road
Harlesden
London NW10 4UA
(0181) 961 7795/8346
*Information, advice and counselling on sickle cell disesae.**

Society for Mucopolysaccharide Diseases
55 Hill Avenue
Amersham
Buckinghamshire HP6 5BX
(01494) 434156/762789
*Information and support to families of children affected by this and related disorders. Local groups.**

Tay Sachs and Allied Diseases Association
c/o Royal Manchester Children's
Hospital
Pendlebury
Manchester M27 4HA
(0161) 794 4696 ext 2384
(Answerphone)
Screening for carrier status before and during pregnancy. Information, counselling and practical support to families affected by these disorders.

Toxoplasmosis Trust
Room 26
61–71 Collier Street
London N1 9BE
(0171) 713 0599
*Information, advice and counselling for pregnant women with toxoplasmosis, parents of infected children and others with toxoplasmosis.**

UK Thalassaemia Society
107 Nightingale Lane
London N8 7QY
(0181) 348 0437
*Information, advice and support for families affected by thalassaemia and for possible carriers.**

CHILD CARE

Daycare Trust/National Childcare Campaign
Wesley House
4 Wild Court
London WC2B 4AU
(0171) 405 5617
*Information and advice on obtaining suitable forms of child care and on setting up day care.**

National Childminding Association (E &W)
8 Masons Hill
Bromley BR2 9EY
(0181) 464 6164
In Scotland:
Scottish Childminding Association
Room 7
Stirling Business Centre
Stirling FK8 2DZ
(01786) 445377
In Northern Ireland:
Northern Ireland Childminding Association
17A Court Street
Newtonards
Co Down BT23 3NX
(01247) 811015
*Associations for child-minders, child-care workers, parents and others who are interested in day care and wish to improve it.**

Northern Ireland Pre-school Playgroups Association (NIPPA)
Unit 3
Enterprise House
Boucher Crescent
Belfast BT12 6HU
(01232) 662825
A voluntary association of mother and toddler groups, playgroups and families of the under 5s who attend them. Provides help and support through a network covering Northern Ireland.

Working for Childcare
77 Holloway Road
London N7 8JZ
(0171) 700 0281
*Advice and information for employers,
trade unions and parents on developing
child care at work.*

FAMILY PLANNING

Brook Advisory Centres (E, S & NI)
165 Gray's Inn Road
London WC1X 8UD
(0171) 713 9000
*Advice and practical help with
contraception and pregnancy testing, advice
on unplanned pregnancies and sexual
counselling for young men and women.
Free and confidential. For your nearest
centre look in the local phone book or
contact Brook Central Office.*

Family Planning Association
27/35 Mortimer Street
London W1N 7RJ
(0171) 636 7866
In Northern Ireland:
113 University Street
Belfast BT7 1HP
(01232) 325488
In Wales:
4 Museum Place
Cardiff CF1 3BG
(01222) 342766
*Information on all aspects of family
planning and methods of contraception.*

Marie Stopes Clinic
Marie Stopes House
108 Whitfield Street
London W1P 6BE
(0171) 388 0662
*Registered charity providing family planing,
women's health check-ups, male and female
sterilization, pregnancy testing, advice on
unplanned pregnancies and sexual
counselling for men and women. You don't
need to be referred by your doctor, but you*

*do need to book an appointment. A charge
is made to cover costs. For centres in
Manchester and Leeds look in the local
phone book.*

ALCOHOL

Alcohol Concern
Waterbridge House
32–36 Loman Street
London SE1 0EE
(0171) 928 7377
In Scotland:
Scottish Council on Alcohol
137–145 Sauchiehall Street
Glasgow G2 3EW
(0141) 333 9677
*Information on alcohol problems, what
types of services exist and where you can
get help locally.*

**Alcoholics Anonymous (AA) (E, S &
W)**
AA General Service Office
PO Box 1
Stonebow House
Stonebow
York YO1 2NJ
(01904) 644026
*Network of independent, self-help groups
whose members encourage each other to
stop drinking and to stay of drink. First
names only are used to preserve anonymity.
For your nearest group look in the phone
book or contact the AA General Service
Office.*

Drinkline
Alcohol Helpline
(0171) 332 0202 or 0345 320202

**Dunlewey Substance Advice Centre
(NI)**
1A Dunlewey Street
Belfast BT13 2QU
(01232) 324197
*Offers help and personal counselling on
alcohol, drug and solvent abuse.*

Northern Ireland Council on Alcohol (NICA) (NI)
40 Elmwood Avenue
Belfast BT9 6AZ
(01232) 664434
Provides counselling, treatment, education, information and training on dealing with alcohol problems.

Northlands (NI)
13 Pump Street
Londonderry BT48 6JG
(01504) 263356
Gives advice, information and counselling for those with alcohol or other drug-related problems.

SMOKING

Quitline
0800 00 22 00
Quitline in Wales
0345 697500
Advice on stopping smoking and details of local stop smoking support services. Phone between 9.30am and 5.30pm on weekdays. Recorded advice available at other times. If you prefer to write for information:
Quit*
Victory House
170 Tottenham Court Road
London W1P 0HA
(0171) 388 5775

Ulster Cancer Foundation
40 Eglantine Avenue
Belfast BT9 6DX
(01232) 663281/2/3
Carries out cancer research and education programmes in Northern Ireland. Also provides information on the dangers of smoking and provides advice and support to smokers who want to quit.

ADDICTIVE DRUGS

(See also 'Dunlewey Substance Advice Centre' and 'Northlands' under 'Alcohol')

Drugaid Cardiff (W)
1 Neville Street
Cardiff CF1 8LP
Meetings every Wednesday from 6.30pm to 9pm. If you need advice outside of meetings, call freephone 0800 776600 (English) or 0800 371141 (Welsh).

Narcotics Anonymous
PO Box 1980
London N19 3LS
(0171) 730 0009 (Helpline)
*Self-help organizations whose members help each other to stay clear of drugs. Write or phone between 12pm and 8pm for information and the address of your local group. Some groups have a crèche.**

SCODA (The Standing Conference on Drug Abuse) (E, NI & W)
Waterbridge House
32–36 Loman Street
London SE10 0EE
(0171) 928 9500
In Scotland:
Scottish Drug Forum
5 Oswald Street
Glasgow G1 4QR
(0141) 221 1175
*Information on local treatment and services for drug users, family and friends.**

In England you can also ask the operator for Freephone Drug Problems which will give you a contact number for your local area. Or you can call the National Drugs Helpline on freephone 0800 776600. In Wales you can also call freephone 0800 371141 (Welsh).

HIV AND AIDS

Body Positive
51B Philbeach Gardens
London SW5 9EB

(0171) 373 9124 (Helpline 7pm–10pm)
Counselling services and support for women affected by HIV and Aids, their family, partners and friends. For the address and phone number of your local group, phone the National Aids Helpline or the above number.

National Aids Helpline
0800 567123
Calls are confidential, free and available 24 hours a day. There is a Minicom on 0800 521361 for people who are deaf or hard of hearing. Information in other languages: Bengali on Tuesday 6pm to 10pm – 0800 371132. On Wednesday 6pm to 10pm you can call 0800 371134 for Gujerati, 0800 371136 for Hindi, 0800 371133 for Punjabi and 0800 371135 for Urdu. On Thursday 6pm to 10pm there is an Arabic service available on 0800 282447 and on Monday 6pm to 10pm Cantonese on 0800 282446. Leaflets can be ordered in all these languages.*
In Northern Ireland:
Aids Helpline NI
0800 137437 (7pm to 10pm weekdays, 2pm to 5pm Saturday)

Positively Women
5 Sebastian Street
London EC1V 0HE
(0171) 490 5515
Information and practical and emotional support for women with a positive HIV diagnosis for who have ARC or Aids, including women who are pregnant or who have children. Support group.*

SUPPORT FOR STRESS OR DEPRESSION

Association for Post-Natal Illness (APNI)
25 Jerdan Place
London SW6 1BE
(0171) 386 0868
Network of telephone and postal volunteers who have suffered from postnatal illness and offer information, support and encouragement on a one-to-one basis.*

CRY-SIS (E, W & NI)
BM CRY-SIS
London WC1N 3XX
(0171) 404 5011
Help and support for parents whose children cry excessively, have a sleep problem or have temper tantrums and other behaviour difficulties. Local voluntary counsellors who have experienced the same difficulties.*

Parentline (E & NI)
Endway House
The Endway
Hadleigh, Benfleet
Essex SS7 2AN
(01702) 554782
(01702) 559900 (Helpline)
Voluntary self-help organization offering confidential support to parents under stress. A network of local telephone helplines is operated by trained parents. Local support groups.*

AUSTRALIAN ORGANIZATIONS

Australian Natural Therapists Association
PO Box 308
Melrose Park 5039
South Australia
618 297 9533

Australian Traditional Medicine Society Limited
Mailing:
PO Box 1027
Meadowbank
NSW 2114
Office:
12/27 Bank Street
Meadowbank
New South Wales 2114

Childbirth Education Association of Australia (NSW) Limited
Suite 11
127 Forest Road Hurstville 2220
PO Box 413 Hurstville 2220
02 580 0399

The Childbirth Education Association (Brisbane) INC
PO Box 208
Chermside 4032
07 3359 9724

The Compassionate Friends Bereaved Parents Support & Information Centre
300 Camberwell Road
Camberwell
Victoria 3124
03 9882 3355

Diabetes Australia
AVA House
5–7 Phipps Place
Deakin
ACT 2600 Australia
616 285 3277

Oz Child: Children Australia
PO Box 1310
South Melbourne
Victoria 3205
03 9695 2211

Relationships Australia Queensland
159 St Paul's Terrace
Brisbane
Queensland 4000
07 3831 2005

Index